HOW TO BE A
# CRICKET
# FAN

Matthew Appleby

# HOW TO BE A
# CRICKET
# FAN

## A Life in
## 50 Artefacts
from WG to Wisden

Foreword by Paul Nixon

First published by Pitch Publishing, 2023

Pitch Publishing
9 Donnington Park,
85 Birdham Road,
Chichester,
West Sussex,
PO20 7AJ
www.pitchpublishing.co.uk
info@pitchpublishing.co.uk

ISBN 978 1 80150 422 5

Typesetting and origination by Pitch Publishing
Printed and bound in Great Britain by TJ Books, Padstow

# Contents

Foreword . . . . . . . . . . . . . . . . . . . . . . . .7

1. Hawksdale . . . . . . . . . . . . . . . . . . . . . .9
2. WG. . . . . . . . . . . . . . . . . . . . . . . . . 14
3. G Neville Weston . . . . . . . . . . . . . . . . 26
4. 1938 *An Album of Cricketers* issued by John Player
   & Sons. Price One Penny . . . . . . . . . . . . 36
5. Bradman . . . . . . . . . . . . . . . . . . . . . . 47
6. Milburn . . . . . . . . . . . . . . . . . . . . . . 54
7. EK Brown letters. . . . . . . . . . . . . . . . . 63
8. 1930 *Wisden* . . . . . . . . . . . . . . . . . . . 69
9. *Wisden* . . . . . . . . . . . . . . . . . . . . . . 74
10. Mintys . . . . . . . . . . . . . . . . . . . . . . 82
11. England v Australia, Headingley 1977 . . . . . . 87
12. *Defending the Ashes* by Percy Fender . . . . . . . . 92
13. *The Borderer* . . . . . . . . . . . . . . . . . . .103
14. Old Trafford: Lancashire v Yorkshire, 23, 25, 27
    August 1980 . . . . . . . . . . . . . . . . . . . 106
15. Autograph books. . . . . . . . . . . . . . . . . .113
16. Parsons. . . . . . . . . . . . . . . . . . . . . . .117
17. 1981 Ashes scrapbook . . . . . . . . . . . . . . 122
18. YCCC sunhat . . . . . . . . . . . . . . . . . . 126
19. Sportsmen's dinners . . . . . . . . . . . . . . . 129
20. Yorkshire v Sussex 31 July–2 August 1982,
    Scarborough . . . . . . . . . . . . . . . . . . . .140
21. 1983 Panini. . . . . . . . . . . . . . . . . . . . .155
22. Hotspur the otterhound . . . . . . . . . . . . . .166
23. Driff . . . . . . . . . . . . . . . . . . . . . . . .173
24. Autograph album. . . . . . . . . . . . . . . . . 180
25. Lancashire collectors . . . . . . . . . . . . . . . .186

26. NatWest Trophy 1989 . . . . . . . . . . . . . . .192
27. 1995 Cronje cap . . . . . . . . . . . . . . . . . 206
28. Membership cards . . . . . . . . . . . . . . . 208
29. 2001/02 *New Zealand Test Cricket Captains* . . . 212
30. Cricinfo T-shirt . . . . . . . . . . . . . . . . .219
31. 2003 *Durham CCC 100 Greats* . . . . . . . . . 223
32. MCC trolleys. . . . . . . . . . . . . . . . . . 226
33. Ties. . . . . . . . . . . . . . . . . . . . . . . 233
34. 2007 Nixon benefit. . . . . . . . . . . . . . . 240
35. Nixon letter. . . . . . . . . . . . . . . . . . . 250
36. 2008 Lord's invitation . . . . . . . . . . . . . .253
37. *Corridor of Uncertainty* . . . . . . . . . . . . .255
38. Collector wagon wheel. . . . . . . . . . . . . .258
39. Cumbrian cricket grounds . . . . . . . . . . . 264
40. Missing dinners . . . . . . . . . . . . . . . . . 268
41. Funeral booklet. . . . . . . . . . . . . . . . . 272
42. New *Wisdens* . . . . . . . . . . . . . . . . . . 277
43. Funeral . . . . . . . . . . . . . . . . . . . . . 279
44. Chris Cairns . . . . . . . . . . . . . . . . . . 285
45. McCorkell . . . . . . . . . . . . . . . . . . . 288
46. The good stuff . . . . . . . . . . . . . . . . . 292
47. Memorial event. . . . . . . . . . . . . . . . . 294
48. Bodyline . . . . . . . . . . . . . . . . . . . . 305
49. Gardening . . . . . . . . . . . . . . . . . . . .311
50. *Wisden* 2017 Obituary . . . . . . . . . . . . .313

Acknowledgements. . . . . . . . . . . . . . . . . .316
Bibliography . . . . . . . . . . . . . . . . . . . . .317

# Foreword

*By Paul Nixon, former Leicestershire,
Kent and England cricketer*

EDGAR APPLEBY was a wonderful man, a true friend
and a local cricketing legend who spoke brilliantly at my
benefit dinner in Keswick in 2007. He knew way more
about my career than I ever did.

Edgar would have been an outstanding contestant on
*Mastermind* because his knowledge was second to none!
His specialist subject would be 'cricket'. Edgar's passion
for our great game is the lifeblood of cricket in this country
and I know one thing for sure – they don't make them like
him anymore. This book is a wonderful tribute to a true
local legend. I genuinely thought the world of Edgar – he
was a bloody top guy.

Chapter One

# Hawksdale

APPLEBY WAS struggling. His knee was giving way. Lumbering singles were drying up. Appleby was turning them down. 'Git im a runna,' rasped Renyard, his captain. Appleby plodded on. The venue was The Sheepmount in Carlisle, a bleak, council-run collection of cricket pitches and changing rooms, surrounded by tall poplars and flanked by the River Eden, which brought rain from the Lake District fells to the Solway Firth, on to the sea.

I was on the scorebook, sitting on a form bench, under which the grass was worn into a trough at my feet. Among the dust there were cricket bags spilling bats covered in tape and sweaty pads and boxes in the fearsome piles of fag ends.

Appleby called for a runner. He was 50 years old, 17 stones, greying wiry hair, wearing old creamy-yellow whites and bearing a well-oiled Gradidge bat, tiny compared to his bulk. He'd opened the innings batting for Eden Valley Cricket League team Hawksdale, who were a mix of public school masters and ordinary Carlisle men – plus Appleby – against an eleven from nearby village Scotby.

Appleby averaged about 12 runs an innings most seasons – not bad if you looked at the list of averages and runs accumulated on the rough old wickets of the Sheepmount, where teams rarely got much more than 100, and often a lot less. Anyone watching who knew much about cricket could see he hit the ball surprisingly deftly for such as big man. Orthodox, watchful glances through the gully were his most common shots. He didn't get many off his legs, being slow to play across his girth and wincing as he twisted his knees to reach anything on the on side. His highest score ever was 62 not out. I knew this well, as official scorer, aged ten, hunched over the book wearing my peach poodle boucle jumper, stonewash jeans and light blue striped Puma trainers. Dad had only ever scored a couple of half centuries. He'd missed 15 years of prime playing time while in the Royal Navy, and maybe he'd never have been much good anyway. He took it seriously though. At his age and with his knee, he eked out the runs, every one precious.

I marked the singles into the scorebook under the batsmen's names, crossing off the total score and filling in the bowlers' analyses. Because that's what scoring is. I also hung the black metal squares painted with white numbers up on the knee-high scoreboard. There was space for runs, wickets, overs and final score but there was no room for individual scores. I knew them though, pencilling little landmarks in my book. Appleby edged into double figures with a cut slid to the third man boundary, misfielded. Past

12, above his average. Past 20, which would get him a mention in the paper. Past 30 with a second four, a leaden-footed drive, bumping all along the ground just in front of square, for once. Scotby's fielders knew he'd score mostly singles – Appleby had been around a long time. But he had a bit of guile and aimed to miss the fielder, like his hero WG Grace's books had told him to. The outfield was too poor for much hit on the ground (and Appleby always hit on the ground) to get to the boundary. He played each ball on its merits. He was seeing off the decent opening pair of bowlers, so the other batsmen could have a go at the lesser ones. There was a near run-out, as Appleby refused a (not very quick) quick single with a gruff 'no' after the impetuous batsman at the other end had set off. The fielder's throw missed the stumps and no more quick singles were attempted. The younger players waiting to go in murmured a moan.

He was painfully slow. 'Run up,' Renyard shouted, but Appleby couldn't. Batsmen at the other end hit out and got out: 'He can't run; you'll have to twat it.'

Appleby battled on. Renyard, due in next and chain-smoking B&H, asked me: 'How many's y'Dad got?' I knew straight away – 46. Renyard said: 'Why didn't you bloody say!' half joking. 'Fotty-six Edgar!' he shouted. Appleby acknowledged with a raise of his paw. The Scotby bowler lolloped in and bowled a long hop. Appleby stretched outside off stump and wafted it towards the bench. The ball bobbled across the bumpy outfield with a fielder chasing hopefully. The ball beat him and rolled to my feet. I stopped it with my Puma and kicked the ball through the fag ends to Scotby's fielder. Then I marked off the runs, 120/6, added them to the bowler's analysis and then, finally to Appleby's long line of ones, with the odd four – 50 not out made up of 38 singles and three boundaries. That's 38 times 22 yards run, almost exactly half a mile, I worked out (in my head). Plus the runs he limped for the other bloke. No twos or threes, not just for Appleby, but for the fella he was batting with too. Appleby couldn't run them anymore. Definitely no sixes. The players clapped. 'Will done Edgar! D'yu wanna come off?' He didn't. He just looked knackered. 'He's knackered', said Renyard. 'He's killing himself. He can't do it anymore.'

A few minutes later (OK, quite a lot of minutes later), on 55, it was over. Renyard was at the other end by now. He ran over to Appleby, who had put his bat down and rolled up his trouser leg. Renyard spat into his sweaty palm and rubbed Appleby's swollen, purple left knee. It didn't help. The captain put his arm round Appleby and they stumbled off, RETIRED HURT 55 NOT OUT, I wrote in the scorebook.

Appleby couldn't field: 'It'll have to be you, Matthew.' Who has no fielding skills to speak of. And is wearing a peach poodle boucle jumper.

The next season, Appleby was down at the Sheepmount rolling up his trouser leg showing off two long scarlet scars on either side of his left kneecap to anyone who showed a passing interest. But he wasn't playing anymore. He was now just a fan.

Hawksdale, 1978: Martin Shepherd, Ian Henderson, Billy Farren, Kevin Graham, Jimmy Skinner, David

Oliver, Peter Henderson, Duncan McEwan, Neil Cunningham, Don Renyard (captain), Edgar Appleby, Billy Dixon.

Chapter 2

# WG

CRICKET KIND of started with Appleby's hero WG Grace, the first superstar sportsman. Grace set most of the firsts in cricket, and, with his massive beard and belly, remains probably the most recognisable cricketer today, even though he died a century ago.

Grace was a prototype celebrity – just about the most famous man in Britain in the second half of the 19th century. The first to promote products: for instance the iconic Colman's Mustard 'heads the field' advert.

The heroes in my era are Geoffrey Boycott, Ian Botham and Ben Stokes. But none is half the man WG was.

I have no personal connection or reminiscence of Grace, and neither did my Dad, Edgar Lawson Appleby. But we have books and letters and photos that he signed (and therefore touched). And we have scrapbooks collected by an obsessed fan hit by that species-level flaw many men (usually) suffer from. Grace and Appleby had the same John Bull shape that used to be the sign of health and prosperity. They both lived for cricket.

Appleby collected Grace-related stuff. Grace 'mantiques' (or 'fantiques') form the centrepiece of many cricket collections. And because Grace died so long ago, having stuff that belonged to him or is associated with the great man is as close as you're going to get.

Collectors' items are *Wisden Cricketers' Almanack* 1916, which includes Grace's obituary and is the most expensive 20th-century *Wisden*, at up to £6,500. Also essential are 19th-century copies of the cricketers' bible, with Grace's performances described – perhaps the 1896, featuring 47-year-old Grace's Indian summer of 1895, when he scored 1,000 runs in May, at the same time he reached 100 centuries – both firsts. There's an 1895 online for £17,000. Maybe collectors have one of the thousands of letters he sent, no matter how dull it reads. The one I've got is a 'thanks for the match' letter. Many are to do with match arrangements. Even better to have for your collector is a signed book, maybe a limited edition, especially if it's by the greatest of the greats. No one writes letters like this anymore. Autographs are less common too. You'd phone or email and have selfies taken on iPhones instead, to be posted online, ephemeral yet everlasting.

We'd driven to London from Cumbria in his ex-company car, 300 miles in a gold W-reg Ford Cortina estate, which sagged a bit at the bottom because we used it to cart second-hand books up and down Cumbria, to our market stall on Wednesdays in Brampton and Saturdays in Keswick. We were to stay overnight in the car outside Phillips auctioneers in London (you could then), before the (obsessive collector) Tony Winder cricket sale. Conversation was around cricket, even though it was off season. We talked about the auction and what a good investment the books he might buy would be, and how one day they might all be mine. I slept from Spaghetti Junction.

It was November 1985. I was 14 and he was 54 and having a new lease of life, no longer a cricketer but finding a new way into the game, while recovering after the company he ran with his cousin went bust. Two months earlier I'd begun a new school, in Keswick, in the Lake District, where my parents had started a shop as a progression from the market, selling gifts and second-hand books, with an emphasis on cricket. This gave him a great excuse to buy lots of cricket books. Some were for sale, so it was business, not pleasure. No guilt. He'd told my Mum a couple of days off school at a cricket book sale of this importance would be good for me. It might never happen again.

I decided Winder's collection wasn't that big and my Dad's was bigger. Phillips wouldn't give me a catalogue, with its Spy caricature of a blazered goofy Edwardian cricketer on the front, but I did meet some obsessive collectors, including London cricketana nut Tony Baer, dressed in his ill-fitting stained suit, who rang a bell when he pushed a trolley round Portobello Market fruitily warning 'I buy cricket,' which gave market traders just enough time to put their prices up. I met more subdued characters too, including the owner of the world's biggest cricket book collection, the retired Hampstead banker and *Wisden* statistician Geoffrey Copinger, and Yorkshire completist collector Tony Woodhouse (and dealers EK Brown, John McKenzie and Martin Wood).

They were the stars of my Dad's world: cricket stuff. Dad would introduce himself to them. Apart from Brown, they barely knew him. He'd only ever corresponded with them, being stuck in Cumbria, away from where cricket really happened. When they cottoned on that Dad was a buyer, they talked shop, the quality of the lots. This was the big one. Prices were rising. Cricket books were an investment, better than most in the recession-hit 1980s. Then they would feign disinterest in star lots. 'Not a great copy. I won't bid on that. Just looking really. Can't afford the prices these days.'

Winder, the Yorkshire businessman and fanatical collector of cricket books, prints, pictures, ceramics, autographed letters, scrapbooks, postcards and photographs had 'pots of money', said Dad, who couldn't compete. Inherited. Boarding school at Rossall. Winder could have married my Mum. They were from the same time and place, 1950s Bradford. She ended up with my Dad, from a different time and place, the 1930s north-east. Dad and Winder did have one big thing in common. They started collecting seriously at the same time in the late 1960s, soon after marriage. Winder bought a set of *Wisdens*, from John McKenzie. Not cheap. Not hard won. There quickly followed the *Scores and Biographies*, *Lillywhites* and hoard of memorabilia that took my Dad 30-odd years to gather. Winder auctioned his late father's collection of magic books and realised £15,000, a lot in 1974. Winder liked the look of a book on the shelf and loved showing them off.

In 1979, Winder bought much of the cricket collection belonging to the claret-cheeked cricket writer and broadcaster John Arlott, who regretted selling almost immediately. My Dad's main dealer EK Brown took a lot of Arlott's collection too. Winder off-loaded books and binders of sepia county team photos that didn't sit well on his shelves. In 1985, at the height of Thatcherism, Winder's electrical and plant machinery business collapsed, a year after my Dad's much smaller firm went bust.

The A E Winder cricket collection had to be sold.

## 20/11/85:

We wandered round the lots. Appleby wrote the prices he'd pay next to the lot numbers in the catalogue. In pencil, because he knew the catalogue was collectable too – a quick search suggests the slim card-covered record is worth £28 now. There's even a 175-copy limited edition book on Winder, *With The Bookplate of A E Winder*. It's a poignant story, but the book, typically in this genre, mainly lists Winder's books, recording details of each title with its purchase source, purchase date and the cost, all details which Winder had kept on a card index.

Among the lots was a large WG Grace collection. Centrally placed for potential bidders to see was the 'classic' 1891 crown quarto deluxe edition of WG's *Cricket*, estimated £200–£300. Now it's available online from £335. I can find three, with prices up to £600. Before this book, designed for the fan who has everything, the idea of producing a cricket collectors' item hadn't existed.

A good stone in weight, the tome is numbered 481/652 (plus ten presentation copies). The great man had opened the hefty, leather-faced front cover, numbered a thick parchment page and signed in fountain pen 'W.G. Grace' (quite predictably I suppose but pretty exciting for a cricket tragic) with a swish of an underline. On the frontispiece, Grace poses in his batting stance, front foot cocked, striped cap on, high-waisted white trousers with brown belt; his figure the classic well-fed symbol of good living and affluence. He looks very fat for a leading sportsman. But girth was a sign of success back then. And no one was more successful than Grace.

Appleby sat near the front, in the middle, just in case the auctioneer couldn't see him, in his brimmed round hat like Sherlock Holmes' without the ear flaps, with his growing bulk, his (and my) slight hum from a night in the car, and his restless anxiety to 'make the trip worthwhile'.

The number came up. 'Don't move,' my Dad had told me. 'They might think it's a bid.' As a shy 15-year-old with arms locked to his sides because of stinking armpits, I was already rigid.

Appleby held off from bidding too soon. I daren't look round to see where the bids were coming from. Sitting at the front was a bad idea.

At the auction house in Carlisle where I used to go with my Mum to buy stock for the bookstall she set up to supplement income while Dad's firm went down the tubes, the auctioneer knew everyone's names. Lots sold to Mrs Appleby or 'the book lady'. She learnt when viewing pre-auction to hide the good stuff at the bottom of the boxes and re-arrange what was in them so the choice items were together. These should be in higher-numbered lots that went up for sale later, when the other bidders might have gone. The auctioneer laughingly scolded the women who sat at the front, just there to smoke and chat and be entertained: 'Can't see your pretty face, all that puffing.' A few years later, poor auctioneer, a non-smoker, died of a respiratory cancer.

The Winder auction was fully catalogued, so there was no shifting of books around from box to box. Many lots were single items, only on view in glass cases; only to be opened by an auctioneers' flunkey – some snooty trainee Oxbridge graduate, reluctantly, preciously, lifting out the finest quality items, but only if they thought the potential buyer might be serious.

The buzz hushed and the auctioneer began. There was a lot of competition between the dealers and the collectors. Appleby had made a few half-hearted bids early on – and fell well short. It was going to be a long way to come for nothing. I thought he'd given up, bowed by the professionals, realising he was out of his league.

Appleby shuffled around, spreading out so he was overlapping into my seat.

Appleby held off and off. He'd thought about this, all the way from Carlisle, and probably all night too.

Then he raised his number.

And again.

And again.

Up and up and up. He had to have it.

Long way to come for nothing.

'With the man in the hat at the front.'

'Any-more for the Grace? It's a beautiful lot. An-y-mor-e?'

'Going.'

'Go-ing.'

'Gone!'

He became one of the few lucky enough to have one of the 622 copies printed of Grace's *Cricket* tome. 'It was a good price,' he said. 'But don't tell your mother.'

I have the chit from the auction. He'd hidden it away in his files, where my mother, or anyone else, never looked. He'd done a deal with dealer EK Brown not to bid on the Grace book, if Dad didn't bid on some other items. I know that now because he'd noted it on the auctioneer's chit.

Tony Winder died just six years after the sale, aged only 47 years, by his own hand.

Every auction has lots of Grace lots. Graceilia. Gracabilia. Graciana.

In one catalogue I have there's a Grace Stevengraph at £200–£400. Stevengraphs are 5.5 x 2.5 inch pictures woven from silk. In 1860, the Cobden–Chevalier Treaty was signed; this free trade treaty introduced new competition into the silk industry, leading to a collapse in the Coventry silk-weaving economy. Thomas Stevens, a local weaver, responded by adapting the Jacquard looms used in Coventry to weave colourful pictures (from silk), which are now collectible items – there's some sad people out there who don't just collect cricket oddities.

The auction-won Grace *Cricket* autobiography begins: 'I think it is right my readers should know that I have

been much aided in the presentation of this book' ...
it's ghosted by W. Methven Brownlee, so not really an
autobiography at all.

*Wisden* 1903 states: 'MR. W. METHVEN
BROWNLEE, a very great lover and supporter of the
game, who will be best remembered as the author of *W.
G. Grace: a Biography*, died at Clifton on July 3rd, at the
age of 56. He was the father of Mr. L. D. Brownlee,
who has played for Clifton College, Oxford University,
Somersetshire, and Gloucestershire.' Thanks, *Wisden*.

The style of the Winder auction WG Grace *Cricket*
book (and of *Wisden*, which started in 1864, about the
same time as Grace) is formal, crusty, and Victorian.

'I cannot remember when I began to play cricket,'
Grace's book begins, unhelpfully. The history bit of the
book begins in the 13th century with 'club-ball' and
goes on until WG has 'realised the duty resting on every
cricketer who desires to add a page or two to cricket
history'. On and on Grace/Brownlee roll. Nearly 500
pages of history, batting, bowling, fielding, cricketers I
(Grace, not me) have met, Abel to Yardley ('he was not
a good bowler'). Then the stats. Averages from 1891 are
glued in by a previous owner from the newspaper, to make
the book complete. For 1894 and 1895 they are written in
by hand. For 1895 'Grace made nine centuries' the writer
adds, because the average (51) doesn't tell you enough.
Grace is shown to average 49 from 1871–80, 18 more
than the next best, Cotterill. There are other notes, listing
touring teams yet to be picked when W. Arrowsmith of
Bristol published the tome in 1891. They're a bit like the

notes my Dad would correct books with (in pencil) 'No! – 1892!' or 'Kortwright' underlined to show the right spelling. They are what I look out for when I see old books for sale now, to see if they once belonged to him.

In one old catalogue from my Dad's pile, there's *Wisden* 1916 est. £150–£250, which is more alone than a run of ten or more on either side of the WG Grace obituary edition.

The myth is that the Germans had killed Grace. He'd called cricketers to arms in 1914, but grew alarmed and depressed by the Hun bombs. They caused the great old bear's heart to pack up.

*Wisden* didn't care for Grace's individual exploits in the early days, but by his death, the book of records, the cricket almanac, came into its own.

*Wisden* tenets reflected the muscular Christianity ethos of the Victorian age. Team, respect for umpires and fair play, respect for tradition, respect for class (amateurs above professionals), the English superiority over empire, the civilising aspect of cricket as the best game with the most facets and most skills required, the laws (not rules), conservativism personified, all about accuracy, facts not opinion, statistics to tell the story.

A Grace inkwell desk piece in silver plate is estimated £80–£120. All the items have the symbolic figure and face (well, beard) of WG.

There's an iron head of WG. Various ceramic figures from studio clay, bisque, Coalport plates, Doulton china – the Tinworth vase, valued at £3,000–£5,000. George Tinworth was almost an exact Victorian contemporary of WG. He secretly pawned his overcoat to pay for his pottery fees at Lambeth Art College. He took a job at Doulton (Royal Doulton from 1902) to help support his widowed mother. The potter (OK, ceramic Doulton-ware artist) became the foremost ceramicist of the 1867 Paris and 1893 Chicago Exhibitions. He made a 'history of England' centrepiece for the fair but is remembered for his humorous mice and frog groups, including a chess set modelled as mice dressed in medieval costumes.

Who wants a WG inkwell, or a Brian Johnston Toby jug, a Bedser twins salt and pepper set? Or a Colin Milburn beer mat, 19th-century Norfolk CC year books, a signed Graham Monkhouse egg box? Dad did.

Back to the catalogue, there's a banquet menu for Grace's 100th century, WG place mats, prints, photos and more. One problem Grace had was breaking through the class system. The establishment MCC held the impoverished doctor's membership up for four years in the 1870s before Gloucestershire became a first-class cricket-playing county.

This was despite WG being the best in the world. In the 1870s, he made as many centuries as the next 13 best batsmen put together, all on rough old Sheepmount-style pitches. Don Bradman dominated cricket in the 1930s, but by then the sport was established (and scoring was easier – though not as easy as The Don made it look).

Grace has fallen from grace in recent years. Historical revisionism has chipped away at the grandest man of English cricket. Just as the Commonwealth fell apart, and amateurism died, and muscular Christianity became a historical footnote, Grace fell from being a sporting symbol to become a symbol of Victorian hypocrisy.

The physical dominance of WG – the most famous initials in sport – made him a proto celebrity, proto god. No one was more famous in Victorian England. From being an unimpeachable idol, WG is now known as the cricketer who said: 'They haven't come to see you bowl, they've come to see me bat.'

Endless stories say Grace was an amateur who was greedy for under the table cash, who wouldn't walk off the field when he was out. I asked my Dad: 'He said the crowd was there to watch him, so he replaced the bails and batted on. You see, no one dared contradict him. It's what the crowd wanted.'

Appleby hated revisionism. He read the books and studied the *Wisden*s describing the deeds – the facts of a career with 54,896 runs and 2,000-odd wickets, more than anyone else when WG finally retired. Changing stats didn't sit well with Appleby. The 126 centuries lost two when statistical obsessives re-examined the primary sources. But that was too late to change the numbers, which to the cricket buff are as reminiscent of Grace as his beard.

While Appleby was the same build as WG Grace, who had a proper old English Father Christmas shape, with big hands and feet and hair, there's no non-manufactured connection between us and the great man. WG is only known by his initials, but WG is William Gilbert. I called my eldest William Gilbert too. It was kind of my wife to pretend not to notice my reference, designed to amuse Appleby.

## Chapter 3

# G Neville Weston

EDGAR LAWSON Appleby was never going to meet WG, not with WG having died 15 years before Appleby was born. Appleby discovered G Neville Weston too late too.

G Neville Weston was a proper cricket fan. My Dad bought a stack of Weston's research on WG from the cricket book seller EK Brown. What is it with cricket and initials (lbw etc)? Anyway, the story of GNW – the archetypal sports fan obsessive – tells a more general tale.

GNW was the kind of adult who kept scrapbooks like a kid, collecting cuttings and letters in pursuit of a fancy, a whimsy. For instance, who is the last living man who played with WG? Weston doggedly pursued this in one scrapbook my Dad had. GNW was a new FS Ashley Cooper, a generation or two older and also an arch cricket collector, writer, -ophile, child-man addict, fanatic.

Appleby also cherished the WG books, signed pics and letter. Not just the 'cooking' books either. Because sport isn't sport until it is embraced by money and men.

In Simon Rae's 1,000-page 1990s biography of WG (*A Life*), Weston gets one mention for his meticulous collating of minor scores, with the comment that GNW might have missed some! Rae's book is history as anecdote, and opinion, and interpretation – proper popular academic history. G Neville Weston's was all about establishing the facts.

I thought I'd lost the book *Cricket's Historians* by the late cricket stats king Peter Wynne Thomas. Then, turning out stuff to sell at a car boot sale, I found it, in a back layer in the bookshop top shelf. I put it in a special place. 'At least I thought it was there,' as Appleby would have said. The reason I like *Cricket's Historians* is because I'm mentioned in it. I am a cricket historian – the book says so. And my Dad was a collector of cricket history and had cricket's history in his head, even if he didn't write it down. *Cricket's Historians* is a kind of list book of people who wrote list books, including those who wrote bibliographies of people who wrote books of lists of records. My book that's in it, *Durham CCC 100 Greats* was pre-Wikipedia, when writing a books-worth of pen pics was publishable. These books remain collectable.

I'd even asked Wynne Thomas for information about Neville Weston, entering the slightly intimidating territory of the cricket obsessives. GNW was founding secretary of the Cricketana Society, the first non-cricket club cricket society. George Neville Weston was born in Kidderminster in March 1901. That's where my Mum's lot originated before they followed the wool trade to

Bradford. My Dad was Gateshead, then Middlesbrough. Not 'Middlesborough' of course, he'd point out, when he saw it spelt wrong, perhaps on Ceefax as he checked the cricket scores, or in a book, when he'd make his corrections, with an exclamation mark.

GNW studied at King's School, Worcester and Wolverley Grammar School. This was information hard-gained by Wynne Thomas, and typically not necessarily relevant but brilliantly comprehensive. Like the details on a cricket scorecard or the fag end of the cricket book collection, the brochures and old stat books and ephemera, these are the best bits of any book.

Weston qualified as a solicitor in 1923 and had his own practice in Kiddy. He seemed disappointingly normal, apart from the cricket trivia obsession. Many of these collector men's collections overflowed into their bathrooms, made up their entire chat, and caused playground spats with peers played out in their association's publications. Weston even published a book called *My Collection*. He then obsessed about cricketana related to WG Grace and quested to catalogue all the matches in which the great cricketer appeared.

GNW retired to Norfolk in 1970. His great work was the 188-page book published in 1973 – *Minor Matches of WG* – loads of stats unearthed about matches WG 'guested' at and sent thank you letters about. That book is now incomplete.

In August 1984 GNW died. He'd have turned in his grave 38 years later, which was 114 years after Grace's first-class career ended when, in 2022, *Wisden* cut ten matches it decided were no longer first-class, 685 runs, 67 wickets and two centuries from WG's record.

Grace 'forced the hand of cricket writers' (and pre-embryonic cricket stattos), says Wynne Thomas in *Cricket's Historians*, by beating his own run-scoring records from 1868–73. Historians now had a template of records to record. And so they did, with *Wisden* leading the way.

WG was a glutton, hungry for money, runs and food and drink. Appleby gluttoned, banqueted and feasted post-rationing, post-war. WG became a compulsive over-eater. Appleby's about eating it all up, all the skin, all the fat, suck the bones. 'Waste not want not' was one of his many phrases. Grace dominated for decades, but his greed was his downfall and his gluttony eventually slowed him. And gluttons are usually eating for a reason.

I'd imagined G Neville Weston was actually from Norfolk (not the Midlands), a cricket backwater. Appleby loved cricket but lived in Cumbria. No England Test player and precious few first-class players have been born there. Weston lived with his sister and fixated on Grace. After GNW's death, his sister sold GNW's cricket collection to EK Brown, the dealer who mentored my Dad's cricket book collecting.

I could name a couple of hundred books of cricketing 'reference' alone, *Scores and Biographies* (for when you've got all the *Wisdens*), via Padwick's *Bibliography of Cricket* (the complete list of cricket books, listed in a very fat cricket book) to *Barclays World of Cricket*, *Playfair*, county annuals, and beyond.

Books still come out about Grace though. And G Neville Weston would be collecting scraps for his scrapbooks if he was still going. There's always more trivia to find.

Ed Craig, an ex-*Wisden Cricket Monthly* writer and now a colleague at my current job, tells me his family has a copy of the Grace book, and that he wrote about ex-Hampshire CCC captain Desmond Eagar's collection at Christie's auction in 2005 when Neville Weston items came up, as did a unique *Cricketer's Autograph Birthday* book with more than 800 signatures that made about £10,000.

Grace of course hit the ball where the fielder wasn't, which was a sign of his guile. He was the man who the sport's reputation is built on, a kind of Babe Ruth, or Stanley Matthews or Fred Perry of cricket, only earlier, bigger, longer-lasting and the setter of more records. Grace pioneered. He was the epitome of Victorian muscular Christianity and as such was the man to emulate. Pre-radio and TV, writing on his feats told the story. And Appleby collected the writing, 50 years after WG's death. What he achieved far over-rode thoughts of jealous revisionist journalists.

Appleby had four unique G Neville Weston scrapbooks, bought for £5 each from EK Brown. Weston glued his research into A3 check-covered scrapbooks bought from WH Smith's, like I glued my cut-out *Daily Telegraph* reports from the 1981 Ashes series. Only GNW was middle-aged while I was ten, and GNW followed his obsession to as far as it could go, while I just cut some reports out the paper, prompted by my Dad, and glued them in, with wandering captions and wandering scissors lines.

GNW scrapbook one: Cover, in scrawly biro. 'The last surviving cricketer at this date (30 June 1972) to have played both with and against the great cricketer?'

The scrapbook begins on 3 June 1972, recording how cricket writer Irving Rosenwater informed GNW that AL Gracie, the famous Scottish rugby international, was said to be the last person to have played both with and against Dr WG Grace. The word 'with' is underlined twice.

The scrapbook seeks to verify or disprove the Gracie statement and to seek who played last with WG.

On 16 June 1972, Weston attended a meeting at Lord's of the WG Grace Memorial Fund Committee where he found out Lt Col. Gracie's OBE MC lived in Cadogan Square SW1. There's several aspects of fandom at work here: worship of idol, obsession, fixation on the stats, clubbing with liked-minded acolytes, and living vicariously through someone else's achievements.

Weston ventured to write to Col. Gracie from his Wymondham, Norfolk home, on 17 June 1972, explaining his quest to compile all Dr WG Grace's performances in minor matches where he has discovered an unrecorded 10,000 runs including three centuries.

Weston says in 1914 Gracie played for Eltham College against Eltham, on 23 May and 18 July, Grace's birthday, with Grace playing for Eltham, as Gracie did from 1910–14. He includes an SAE.

Gracie was better-known as a rugby player, as demonstrated by a John Player cigarette card showing a caricature of a moustachioed Harlequin-shirted flying centre three-quarter whose 'virile opportunism bewildered his opponents' – this is an example of the theory of the pseudo sexual nature of fandom, all innocent, often heterosexual or asexual men (or very repressed types) interested in other men's achievements they admire and aspire to but couldn't match as their heroes were so skilful and tough.

The then 76-year-old 13-time Scotland rugby international tells Weston the information must have come via the journalist EW Swanton. At a Lord's dinner for the touring Australian 1972 cricketers, Gracie mentioned to Swanton he was probably the only person present who had played against and with WG. Gracie says he was at Eltham College in 1914/15 and then went to Oxford for one term (Michaelmas 1915) before joining the Inns of Court, later winning a commission to the 60th Rifles.

Gracie played against Grace's team in 1914 or 1915 and was photographed standing alongside him. Grace asked him to play for New Eltham the following Saturday but Gracie says he can't remember if he turned out.

Weston has found the statistical record of Gracie's Eltham College career. Gracie bowled WG in 1914, won a Military Cross in September 1917 and was a rugby star. His MC was for conspicuous gallantry and devotion to duty as a Battalion Signalling Officer when commanding tunnellers under intense bombardment. He showed the greatest coolness and gallantry with complete disregard for his own safety during a withdrawal across a river. In February 1923 he won the international against Wales with a last-minute try involving an overhead pass, diagonal scything run, dummy to *Chariots of Fire* Olympic gold medallist Eric Liddell and grounding that saw his boot remove some teeth of a small boy sitting too close to the Cardiff Arms Park pitch. He was Weston and Appleby's kind of guy.

Weston also wrote to the bursar of Eltham College, Mr Ruscoe, in 1952 about the 1914 Eltham v Eltham college match. Ruscoe has found the school magazine which stated Dr RG Bowen Rees bowled WG with an off break. Grace asked him how he did it, but the bowler was too terrified to speak. This does not clear up the vexing mystery of AL Gracie having bowled WG.

Weston keeps writing, Henry Root style (i.e. unwittingly comically persistently), to see if Grace was bowled by Gracie.

To cut a very long story short, there's anti-climactic correspondence with the British Museum Newspaper Library in Colindale. It seems Gracie didn't play against Grace after all. But the dogged GNW found out an old timer born in 1879, so now 93 years old, Major James Gilman, ex-Cambridge University, London County, Middlesex and Northumberland, played with Grace in 1901/02 (against) and 1900 (with). So the Gracie search was a wild goose chase, as Gilman proved to be the oldest living person to play against Grace. I think Weston enjoyed the search though.

Telling of history has changed now. Most of the raw facts have been logged. There's only interpretation left. GNW did facts, as the fan does. But do the facts change the meaning of the man or the game? With Grace, is it more important that he founded the game as it is known now than to debate the trivia?

Appleby's domain in later years was his chair, on the right within reaching distance a Minty sliding door glass bookcase with some choice and new items. Behind him floor-to-ceiling, was a wall-length bespoke-built bookcase.

In front of him three more Mintys, claw-marked in 1983 by Hotspur the otterhound's efforts to reach Easter eggs displayed out of children's reach on top. In the corner is a dining table with a corner glass-doored cupboard, inside of which are china and precious items such as a Brian Johnston Toby jug, gifted by Appleby's sister Aunty Sybil, Hansie Cronje's cap and a Geoffrey Boycott 100 centuries limited edition plate. Through a big bay window beyond the front garden, over the fence and over Crosthwaite Road is the river wall and the not-so-great River Greta coming round the corner from the park where the football and cricket pitches are just out of sight. Over the river is the disused pencil factory with the rooks nesting in its crevices and behind it all, straight ahead, the ridge of Grizedale Pike changing from green to brown to rock as you look up. Behind the big bookcase is little Latrigg and its mother mountain Skiddaw. Between, there's 360 degrees of fells, Causey Pike, Lords Seat, Walla Crag, with lake beyond the town, where the river ends up. Most important for Appleby now though is the telly and the buttons, for Ceefax and Sky and turning the sound up.

In the bookcases, Grace is not far away; on the wall there's a small full-length batting picture of WG, signed.

There are at least three Grace signatures within three steps of his seat. Not that three steps is that easy these days.

He asks me to take him upstairs. I ask him if he wants to, after my mum says he's said he wants to. We're back for the weekend on one of our few trips a year from London where I live with my wife Bethan and sons WG and Ted Dexter Appleby. This is going to be like getting the *Titanic* ready for sea. It might finish him off.

## Chapter 4

# 1938 *An Album of Cricketers* issued by John Player & Sons. Price One Penny

WHEN APPLEBY left home to join 'the Boys' (the Navy apprentices) in 1946 aged 15, his mother threw away the cigarette cards he collected.

He came back from the Navy, first leave, and they'd gone. That pang of loss, that hollow feeling ... like coming back home and your dog's dead and buried? And they hadn't even told you it was ill.

Young Edgar was a big-built boy, son of a tugboat sailor. Edgar's father was born in 1895. Edgar was born in 1931, a late baby and a younger brother for Sybil.

Appleby was given the cricket cards by Uncle Jack (who died young of lung cancer – Appleby never smoked despite being given free cigarettes by the Navy) or whoever he could scrounge them from in 1930s Gateshead. A lot of cricket smells of cigs, in my memory. The cards were his last happy memory before moving to Middlesbrough (aged eight), where his father 'Pa' went to work on a different tugboat. His family had no interest in cricket. Dad was evacuated in 1940, wrapped in brown paper to keep warm, half-starved by rationing.

The cards showed his heroes Hammond, Hutton, Bowes and Verity, and Lancashire's Winston Place ('and chips'). He'd learnt the facts, grown his memory, and become the boy, then the man who can remember dates, facts, anniversaries, who knew the quiz question answers, when this all mattered before you could just Google it. That put know-alls like the *Guinness Book of Records'* walking encyclopaedia Norris McWhirter out of a job. Not to mention fact retentives like *Just A Minute's* Clement Freud, polymath Jonathan Miller, film buff Peter Noble and not forgetting (though most people have) the *Brains' Trust's* CEM Joad.

When Appleby bought his own house (in 1967), newly married, still with black wiry hair, not yet fat but imposing in stature and voice, and opinion, he decorated the walls with frames full of the prettily portrayed little cards. They were art for people who don't like art, like paintings of Spitfires or botanical subjects. I may have one or two framed sets kicking around now, in my house in London. The glass is cracked on a couple. In fact, I actually have dozens.

Nearly 75 years later, I asked him why he liked the cards. Appleby, by now faded and immobile, suggested I write an article on Neil McCorkell, Hampshire's wicketkeeper either side of World War Two. He was one of the 1938 Players cards. 'It was their bright smiling hopeful faces,' Appleby said, losing his gruff northern exterior, forgetting himself in a moment of nostalgia.

The cards were printed from vivid watercolours. By now he had piles of sets, in frames, in books, wrapped in rubber bands. That's what collectors do. And they tend to keep them (and the invoices for them) hidden from their wives.

For the McCorkell piece, I wrote to the archivists at Hampshire, the player's county from 1923–51. Appleby gave me the names of who to talk to. He knew Hampshire chairman Donald Rich, who visited the Lakes and had been identified when he bought a cricket book (or more likely just looked at one or had a cricket tie on) at our second-hand bookstall on Keswick market. Like my Dad, Rich loved to talk. He loved lunches, dinners, clubs, little societies. Dad knew nothing about Rich's private life. He only wanted talk about cricket. What made him tick was bonding over shared experiences and cultural (well, Navy and cricket mostly) references. His strengths were his outward self-belief and unashamed eccentricity. And weaknesses? He wasn't very liberal or understanding of others outside his sphere. But cricket duffers were very much within his comfort zone.

Hampshire CCC archivist David Allen kindly sent me letters McCorkell, now aged 99, had sent him from South Africa, describing playing cricket for the county pre-war. I looked up the *Wisden* references. Twenty years before, my seven-year-old nephew had thought a cigarette card of McCorkell was a picture of me, when he saw it framed as one of the 1938 Players set on the wall at my parents' (his grandparents) house. McCorkell was about to become the best (ever) English cricketer to reach his century (in years). I mined the letters for anecdotes about Tennyson, Alec Kennedy, George Brown and Phil Mead, added the stats, made my thesis (about the century thing), wrote an article and tried to get it into cricket mags. No banana. No reply, in fact. My Dad suggested the Cricket Society. He's been a member for decades. He liked to be a member of a lot of things. I've got the membership cards in a box – Yorkshire CCC from the 1940s, Durham CCC from the 1990s, Cumberland CCC from the 1970s, Association of Cricket Statisticians, Wombwell Cricket Lovers' Society, The Masters Jack Hobbs Appreciation Society, and more. Yet, he lived in Gateshead at first, then when married lived in Carlisle, then Keswick. Not very central, cricket-wise.

The Cricket Society kindly published my article as a letter. I'd said McCorkell was the longest-living England representative ever. Wynne Thomas told me via email McCorkell had never played for an England XI. I'd say the old goat did, in India 1936/37, when Tennyson took the best XI available for unofficial Tests. But who wants to, or even can, win an argument with a GNW, or a PWT?

My boy collects now, Match Attax football cards, like I collected football cards from around 1978. Back then they were cards in paper wraps smelling of plastic pink sweetness from the strip of chewing gum inside. My brother stuck one of mine down the drain once and my mother bought me more.

Looking through Appleby's old cards, as well as the 1938 framed set he has the 1938 booklet, in which there's 14 pages of England cards stuck in, plus five pages of

Australians. The cards are more valuable framed, rather than stuck down. But in the book they're as you would collect them back then. Thin, yellowed tissue paper covers the pictures of the players. They smile back at you. Their descriptions respectfully record how a 'splendid 156 against the New Zealanders attracted the Selection Committee'. Some are signed. That means the player touched them. Obvious – but that's the basis of the appeal of autographs, even if you didn't get them personally. They were there. Selfies don't seem quite the same. How can you collect them?

Les Ames, Charlie Barnett, Denis Compton (I asked for his signature at Lord's during one Gillette Cup Final as we perambulated across the outfield – he said 'no'), Bill Copson, Gover, Emrys Davies signed on the back. I know the first names – they only have an initial or two or three (DCS Compton) on the card. I can recognise them – most of them – without seeing the names. Dad used to cover team line-ups with his hand and test me. ('No that's not bloody Mitchell, it's Barber. No, Kilner was bloody dead!') As if it mattered. Bill Edrich has signed across his description and not the picture, like he wasn't impressed with the blurb, which goes on about his centuries for Norfolk, calls him William and then gets on to the important cricket he's played. Ken Farnes has signed on the Essex badge. Farnes crashed, fatally, in his RAF plane two years later. Appleby had Farnes' autobiography *Tours and Tests*. Perfect copy, he told me, rare dust jacket, now worth £75, or a third of that unclad in its fragile, elusive, detachable outer cover.

Harold Gimblett hasn't signed his card. David Foot's book on Gimblett, *Tormented Genius of Cricket*, was the best I read when I was 13, back in 1984, the year after I collected my album of cricket cards – *Panini '83*, which I've still got. Foot's book was the tragic tale of a local hero depressive who took an overdose. Reading it showed me there was more to cricket writing than just a report of the play. I met Foot, at Guildford, me writing for Cricinfo, Foot for *The Guardian*, Surrey v Northants 2001. The journalists chatted to boundary fielder Ed Giddins from our writers' tent.

I whispered to my fellow hacks that Ally Brown was out injured for the next match. They already knew. At that match I walked round the ground with former *Wisden Cricket Monthly* editor David Frith, one of the greatest collectors and historians, and Clayton Goodwin, who specialised in West Indies cricket. 'Goodwin's not black you know,' my Dad said when I told him who I'd hung out with. This was an observation I found ridiculous. I saw Frith again later that year at the National Film Theatre where he played an annual reel of dug-up cricket films, newly discovered archive footage he'd found, or fans had sent him. I watched an older Grace, during the golden age of 1900, striding out and practising in a boater, looking not unlike my Dad knocking up (apart from the boater and massive beard, so maybe not that much).

By 1938, the game had been usurped in popularity by football. But the summer sport still dominated men's minds, especially when England beat Australia, scoring a record 903/7 declared at the Oval, with Len Hutton making a record 364. This was the match that my Dad said made him start to love the game.

Hutton had signed his card in the 1938 cigarette card book. Another Oval hero, Joe Hardstaff, signed in red ink. Forty-odd years later, my Dad got me to write to the Nottinghamshire batsman, who scored 169 not out at The Oval. I had already written to Yorkshire's Bill Bowes, who took 7-74 in the 903/7 match, which Australia lost by an innings. 'Write "my father remembers your fine batting at … "' They both replied with autographs and notes praising the enthusiasm of an eight-year-old, who they must have thought was quite precocious, if not even a little odd.

McCorkell had signed his cigarette card. The friendly smile of McCorkell, signed neatly across the shirt. More names: George Pope, 'Baldilocks' as my thick-haired Dad called him or 'Eggshell blonde'. Jim Sims and three Smiths, Jim, Denis and Peter. And Hedley Verity, who, like Farnes, didn't last the war and whose card must be worth a few quid. Alphabetically, on to Cyril Washbrook and Tom Worthington, ending at Norman Yardley, who I did meet, at Headingley, when the former England captain was Yorkshire CCC president, if you count getting his autograph as meeting. Yardley resigned in 1984 after pressure from supporters of Geoffrey Boycott. Appleby: 'Say excuse me, Mr Yardley, may I have your autograph please? Make sure you say please.' The old gent obliged, as he mingled among the crowd, being greeted by misty-eyed older members.

None of the Aussies had signed the 1938 cigarette card book. That doesn't matter. This book is still unique.

Unsigned, a full album is available from £3. Signed and you could name a price.

Being a fan of your son is a classic to be a fan. 'Do your best' he used to say – not bad advice. He used to watch me from behind the bowler's arm willing me to do well. That made me worse. More simple advice is to become a fan and then decide what you want to become a fan of.

If you want to be a fan of a sporting team or athlete: try picking a team or athlete who is from or near your birthplace, if possible. This gives you a connection between you and the athlete. Or you can pick randomly, or go with the crowd, e.g. Manchester United. Or go with who you think plays best, or wins most, which may be the same. Do they represent what you believe and want to tell other people about you? Sports academics in the field of fandom suggests they should.

Maybe try and look like your hero. Do you wear a tweed flat cap or waxed jacket to the rugby? Or dress in the dark for the cricket in pastels, too-short slacks, boaters, bow ties, bucket hats, brogues, blazers, blousons, boat shoes, braces, hankies on heads? My Dad wore his trademark earless deerstalker, 'sports jacket' (don't know why they're called that – just a suit jacket and they're definitely no good for sport), and trousers (obviously). Trousers rather than jeans I mean, or shorts or lederhosen. Maybe braces or a strong belt; a tie with so much food in it you could boil it into a broth; a string vest; a watch (not digital); lace-up, brick-like, shiny brown leather shoes, thick Mum-knit hosiery (sometimes made at the cricket) and trolleys (underpants) the size of a house. Trolleys were his string pants – he wore full string underwear. Cricketers did not wear these clothes. My 1980s hero Geoffrey Boycott is 'Man at (1980s Leeds) C&A', modelling light grey Farah slacks with sharp creases, lemon pilot polos, a Panama, weave, tasselled shoes, powder pink pullover, and man-tan. This is what the aspirant fan aimed for. Even cricket fans didn't really dress like my Dad. His look was a mix of expediency, comfort, carelessness and artifice.

How else to be a fan? Join the fan club – e.g. the Cricket Society. Read their stuff, for instance their biographies, *Wisden*, the mags. Attend the live event – i.e. the match. Make friends at the event and meet the protagonists of the event. Keep it up for years to show dedication. Keep in touch with fellow fans. You are now a fan.

I asked Appleby why he liked cricket. He had a stock answer: 'There's batting, bowling AND fielding – three skills. In football you just kick it. There's always something happening.'

To give me a hobby, my parents got me collecting cricket postcards when I was about 12. Collecting is a cheap way into being a fan. You can say you are looking after a memory and keeping it safe for the future generation. There was an old postcard shop near the cathedral in Carlisle, opposite the castle, which is the best bit of the city, although a dual carriageway goes between the two. I'd recently won 10p at school for drawing the East window of the cathedral.

Postcards were cheap, but not cheap enough for a pre-teen. I was being led by the nose into this one. My Mum took me to the shop, but my Dad was behind it. I can imagine their discussion: 'Let's get him interested in something.'

'One day these will all be yours,' he'd repeat portentously. Turned out it wasn't as simple as that, but the postcards are mine. For my Dad, he had acquired another collection, by proxy, and something to talk to me about.

'Cricket Surrey £3.50' pencilled on the back of one. Ducat, Geary, WJ Abel, Shepherd, Sandham, Peach, Bottom, Hitch, Hobbs, JGH Fender, A Jeacocke, Strudwick. 1920s. Initials for amateurs. Fender was of course PGH, not JGH. I knew because *Kissing the Rod* (later the title of a Germaine Greer anthology of 17th-century women's verse) was in the glass bookcase in the living room in our house in Carlisle where I lived until I was 15. Appleby got the house extended when I was about seven, adding the living room, which had a study tacked on, where he fiddled with his collections and where his thunderous wind-breaks echoed from the pleather-covered new but-looked-old chair. This was where I wrote to Bowes and Hardstaff, under his supervision. There were no windows so I wrote fast and got outta there.

I looked up the postcard. It came up on an online list from Boundary Books, owned by Christopher Saunders, who I once sold a signed Peter May book to for £15 at Olympia Professional Book Fairs Association book fair. The postcard is worth about the same.

(SURREY COUNTY CRICKET CLUB). Postcard by C. Smith, Oval. Printed title in white at bottom 'Surrey' with players' names beneath: Back row (l-r): Ducat, Geary,

W.J. Abel, Shepherd, Sandham, Peach; Front row (l-r): Hitch, Hobbs, J.G.H. Fender [sic], A. Jeacocke, Strudwick. A good copy. Postally unused. [ref: 80047] £15.00

Now I'm feeling the thrill of *Wisden* collecting. It's all eBay rather than bricks and mortar shops. I already had one *Wisden* by accident – 1992. Maybe from the schoolbook sale, to make up a 3 for £1 deal. Then a borrowed 1973 from my parents' house and another from Oxfam. Then, 29 for £40 from a guy who delivered. Now I'm watching loads on eBay. I've got some tatty 1970s ones coming. I keep looking them up. Filling gaps.

## Chapter 5

# Bradman

IN 1948, Bradman needed four runs to average 100 runs per innings in Tests. He'd scored 6,996 runs in 69 completed innings. The Don was the best batsman (ever) – about twice as good as the next best statistically, just as Grace had been a half century before. Stats do matter.

My Dad was there, at The Oval, 14 August. Eric Hollies bowled: 'Yardley lined everyone up to applaud. Everyone sang "For he's a jolly good fellow." Then there was silence. It must have made Bradman a bit nervous. It took ages for him to get his first ball. On the second one he just leaned forward and missed it.'

'Then what happened?'

'He turned round and stuck his bat under his arm and walked off. Fast. But no faster than usual. No one made a sound.'

Arthur Morris was at the other end to Bradman. What my Dad said about Bradman's duck was similar to Morris, and leg-spinner Hollies, wicketkeeper Godfrey

Evans and classy amateur Yorkshire captain Norman Yardley. And Bradman.

Another England player, their best bowler Alec Bedser, said: 'If we had known, he could have had a four. We'd lost completely, it didn't matter two hoots!'

And opener John Dewes turned to Hollies: 'My goodness Eric, what have you done?'

So I watched the 1948 match on YouTube. The fans were packed in, smoking Woodbines and Capstans, brimmed hats on, in washed-pale shirts and darker jackets, faces thin and lined by sucking their cigs and years of food rationing. They had crooked English teeth hidden by tight lips, in anticipation of a smile. No one celebrated.

And I listened to the broadcast from voice of cricket John Arlott: 'What do you say in such circumstances? I wonder if you see a ball very clearly in your last Test in England on a ground where you've played out some of the biggest cricket in your life, and where the opposing team have just stood around you and given you three cheers? I wonder if you really see the ball at all?'

Bradman said on the radio in 1949: 'In a war-torn, cricket-starved England, my outstanding memory of 1948 was the part I tried to play in reviving the game, particularly the fourth Test at Leeds. We were set 404 and got them with 15 minutes to spare and the wonderful crowd absorbed in the cricket at least temporarily forgot their worries. More nostalgic for me was being bowled for nought by Hollies at The Oval, but that was an anti-climax to the purpose of the tour and the memory of Leeds.'

'He didn't bike there, you know,' said my Mum. 'He stayed at his cousin Dennis's in Pinner.'

'Really? I thought he'd biked from Middlesbrough.'

'Well, he stayed at Dennis's for that Bradman match. I've heard him talk about Bradman's duck hundreds of times.'

Later: 'He was interesting, but he wasn't that interesting.'

But Appleby had a knack of being there. He was there for Boycott's hundredth century at Headingley in 1977, for instance.

Many years later, after we had both been (separately) to Bowral, Bradman's birthplace in the sticks in New South Wales, we were in Keswick when he told me he'd told the staff there the 1948 tale.

He then asked me to get a Bradman book out of the sliding glass bookcase. 'That one, no that one,' he gasped, ill with some sort of Parkinson's, half a lung gone with asbestosis, facial expressions gone with skin cancer slicing, mobility gone after three new knees ('I've had five knees in my life.')

'Bloody hell, it's signed,' I said. 'I'll look it up … [taps on phone] … 120 quid it says here.'

'Look after it; one day they will all be yours,' he replied.

Appleby was big on dates. And the older he got, the more dates he had to play with. Or so you would think. He liked to talk about anniversaries: 'Do you know what anniversary it is today? I'll give you a clue. 1948.'

Me: 'Bradman's last Test innings.'

Him: 'Good. I remember it well.'

I was talking about the book to 'the dreaded' (as Appleby called him) James, a cricket fan my age who I knew then and still know now: 'You see, sport is about nostalgia I reckon. It's basically for kids, or overgrown kids, who relive it through buying back mementoes of it when they get rich and sentimental enough.' My mate, 'the dreaded' James, had a run of *Wisdens* from his birth in 1973. I had the lot (well Appleby did).

Dad's formative years were spent as a wartime evacuee, from Middlesbrough to Bishop Auckland. Once, after a Durham match at Chester-le-Street was rained off, with James in tow, we detoured to 'Bishvegas' on the way back to Keswick. 'That was it. There,' he pointed at a terraced house. 'Aunty Sybil was meant to look after me but as soon as we set off she wouldn't have anything to do with me, her own brother. And there wasn't enough bloody food. Let's get some fish and chips. Don't tell your mother.' Not that he was miserable, or particularly vengeful. But the vision of a brown paper insulated covered nine-year-old, on his own, lingered, contrasting with the 18-stone, outspoken, eccentric, known-by-all old squire trencherman he'd turned into. 'Don't tell your mother,' became a catchphrase between me and James, when talking about how ELA's gluttony and buffery amused and sometimes appalled us.

After that, he ate, he talked and he made the most of it. And he strung it all together with hundreds of sayings, from 1940s and 50s radio (*It's That Man Again*, *The Goons*), his born-in-the-1890s father's generation ('deliver the French, stone the crows') and most of all the Navy ('your dhobi's in the drying room, chop chop, hubba

hubba, you could get the *Ark Royal* through there') – all in lieu of normal patterns of speech. He served 14 years from the age of 15. I used to wear his Navy uniform to fancy dress parties, until I started going as Morrissey from The Smiths, flowers in back pocket.

Appleby knew a bit about Bradman's conqueror Hollies through Aubrey Hill, an old Warwickshire cricketer team-mate of Hollies, whose sister lived in Carlisle, where we lived from 1967–86. What remained of my Dad's meetings with Hill, who had retired to Blackpool, are several signatures in Warwickshire cricket books, and one recollection. One of my Dad's sayings was 'wild horses wouldn't drag me ashore tonight', as he collapsed to read the *Daily Telegraph* after a hard day's work at what I knew to be 'R Lawson Engineers, Kingstown Industrial Estate, Carlisle', where they made winches and pulleys. I didn't know what they were or what he did really, although he took me there most Saturdays, and often on a Sunday too. He went into an office while I messed about with the R Lawson labelled stationery or pressed the buttons that moved the overhead crane things, if he wasn't close enough to shout at me.

So, to meet Hill, or go to a rare sportsman's dinner, or embark on a big trip to see a day's professional play at Old Trafford or Headingley, was a relief from work, and he'd rouse himself.

'Hill used to say that when you were in and out of the team it was bloody hard to get going again. You'd been playing in the seconds on bad pitches and suddenly you were back in against the best bowlers because someone was injured and you had to perform or you were straight out again. You'd not get proper time in the nets because the first-team players got that and you knew it could be your last chance. You never got the chance to establish yourself.'

WA Hill was in a different world from the popular and successful Hollies and finished in 1948, unfulfilled as a first-class player, just as dressing room character Hollies became briefly famous. *Wisden* 1949 describes Hollies as the best leg-break bowler in the country. Hill doesn't get a mention after averaging 16 in the eight matches he was picked to play in during 1948.

That duck at The Oval showed Bradman was fallible because he couldn't do what he'd programmed himself to do. Stats could mean everything, and that the game and the numbers were bound up so much so that the data could make the players perform worse, or better. The fans who knew the numbers brought them to the fore and the players reacted. So, Bradman failed, and in 1977, Boycott succeeded. It's funny the Poms thwarted the 1948 Aussies in a statistical way, even if not in a 'coming-anywhere-near-beating-them' way.

And you could witness history. And maybe England and ELA had a future, post-war, post-colonialism, post-power.

The cricket statistician, fan, stickler, martyr Irving Rosenwater wrote a Bradman biography in 1978. Rosenwater described himself as a 'writer, essayist, collector, editor, bibliographer, researcher, reviewer, obituarist, spectator, crossword-compiler, publisher's reader, indexer, speaker (and minor player)'.

*Sir Donald Bradman – The Biography* dissects every minute of The Don's life. Rosenwater always was single-minded and apt to be vociferous. His mania for veracity and accuracy with content and copy was legendary. Rosenwater was married to the game and his home was buried in cricketing papers, said the writer Christopher Martin-Jenkins, who believed Rosenwater thought of nothing else.

Appleby wasn't as bad as that, though he liked things to be correct; he felt the experience and empathised with the players as well as recounting the facts and records. Bradman's last innings is a good example. 'Did I ever tell you the time ... I was there ... I remember the hush ... I just sat at the boundary's edge and there was silence ... maybe the occasion put him off ... who bowled the ball, Matthew? What was his average?'

Matches are disposable but they live on in the *Wisdens* and with the eyewitnesses. The fan replays matches again and again trying to relive that feeling.

How do you know it was an important match, one worth remembering? The notable scoring, the special result, remarkable performance or something more personal, an unusual experience, funny moment, or anecdote to tell.

Chapter 6

# Milburn

A CRICKET theatrical play sounds like an unattractive proposition. Only the most dedicated would go. Yet I was desperate to go to see *When the Eye Has Gone*.

In June 1969, in a jacket and tie, grinning in dark glasses and an eyepatch, with a nurse on each arm, Colin Milburn emerged from hospital, England's most exciting cricketer, 'cruelly cut down' by a car crash that had his left eye out. Driving an Austin 1300, like my Dad did, back from a Northants country club piss-up (he was sober says Mark Peel's biography *Cricketing Falstaff* – a book that Appleby provided facts and stats for), Milburn overtook, like a character in the 60s ballad, *Leader of the Pack*. A 10-ton truck crashed into him, and it was over.

But, like Bob Cratchitt, the Dickens *Christmas Carol* optimist who found hope even in the grimmest poverty, Milburn stayed upbeat through his ordeal. 'His infectious good humour and indomitable spirit raised morale throughout the hospital,' said the reports.

The play was co-presented by the Professional Cricketers' Association and toured the 18 main first-class grounds. The Oval, home of the PCA, had no spare tickets. Lord's clashed with the school quiz. There was a chance to see it at Teddington in south-west London. I didn't know why it was playing there, but it was near work. I emailed some committeeman. He said I was booked in. I'd get to meet some true fans, and hopefully get some insight, if I didn't act too weird.

The train was late but I'd taken my bike and set off to where I thought Teddington CC was, somewhere in Bushy Park. Having biked across the wet outfield dodging deer who were eyeing me sideways, I locked up and entered the squat pavilion.

At the bar were a few middle-aged blokes. One other was sat at a pub table on a laptop. I said: 'Is this where you pick up tickets?' 'Not here. Ask him,' he said, pointing, without looking up. I didn't. I went to the bar instead.

'Here's a man who looks like he needs a drink,' said the barman, after I'd dodged away from a fat bar hog, who was backing into me. I felt invisible. Not like ELA or Milburn, who would have made their presence felt, and in ELA's case, knowledge known.

'Only a coke?'

'Yeh, not really entering into the swing of things, I know.'

He told me to talk to the organiser and pointed to the same man as the computer guy had. I started wandering.

The pavilion was set up as a 30-seat theatre, with two rows of settees and some pub seats and bar stools at the edge.

I wandered round with my coke looking for famous names on the old team water-damaged framed pics on the walls.

Best I could do was 1980s Middlesex batsman Andrew Miller, hair wearing thinner as the years passed, from photo to photo.

As I reached the end of this time-wasting activity, I saw a vision in dirty brown and faded buff – a pile of old *Wisdens* stacked under the telly in the corner, behind some newer scorebooks. They looked neglected, like the ones at Penrith CC that my Dad wrote to local paper editor and club chair John Hurst (the author of Cumberland CC's history) about many years earlier: 'I would hate to see them lost.'

The organiser and his wife sat next to me. I gave him my tenner and my spiel about how I wanted to see the play at The Oval but it was sold out – 'guess it's full of PCA people!' I asked if the playwright, former Kent and Derbyshire player James Graham-Brown was there. No, but turned out JGB knows Teddington CC's youth coach, so they thought they'd put the play on here. Just the director's here, and the actor. The director turned out to be the computer guy.

Emboldened, I talked to the computer guy/director. 'How's it been going?' Very well apparently. 'I was going to The Oval, but it was sold out! Guess there was a lot of PCA there.'

'Not really, they're all on tour at this time of the year.'

'Someone asked me if I was going to bring my wife! Thought I'd let her off.'

'Oh no, this is not aimed at cricketers, it's about his life, she might have been OK even if you don't like cricket – it's about the man.'

Appleby was courting my mother when Milburn was taking off. The letters he sent her, from his bachelor shared house (with my future godfather Sibson, a tall, smooth, sport-loving IBM marketing trainee) show his devotion. 'Went for a few pints last night with Sibdog and talked about rugby, cricket and football. You would have loved it but you could have talked about Sutcliffe, Leyland, Rhodes, Hirst, Jackson and the others.' My mother's maiden name was Jackson. When Dad first met her, through a mutual friend called Brian Smith, he asked her early on if she was related to FS Jackson, the Yorkshire cricketer at the turn of the century. She wasn't. He decided she probably was. He ends the letter: 'I do miss you an awful lot and will be mighty pleased when I see you again. Adios the noo (Spanish Scotsman), Love Edgar.'

The organiser's wife listened to me. 'Someone asked me if I was going to bring my wife! Thought I'd let her off. But apparently according to the director, this is not aimed at cricketers, it's about his life, she might have been OK – it's about the man!'

'Hope so,' smiled the nice woman. 'Think it will be good.' I explained myself to my new mates, how I used to work at Cricinfo, guff about the publisher I now worked for being based in Teddington, knowing the area, etc. They knew someone who worked at my employer. I didn't know her.

'You write about gardening?' she asked.

'I'm a cricket writer really.'

The guy playing Milburn was balding, with padding up his shirt, a 70s leather coat and plenty of success with a Geordie accent.

'Enjoy yourself, life's too short,' were his watchwords.

On the piss with Hodge, Sharpy and Breakwell.

Then 3/5/69, 21 years ago, gin and coke – a 'Milburn'.

There were a few fat gags: 'I was used as a roller.' There was a long 'daddy, mummy, baby balloon' gag with a 'let yourself down' punchline.

Former *Wisden* editor and Northants fan Matthew Engel once wrote: 'He was not big-boned or bulked-up – he was fat.' Milburn was always going to health farms to lose weight after posh cricket hack EW Swanton wrote that Ollie's fielding was not up to it. That cost him his England place.

Time jumped around. Young Ollie (nicknamed after Oliver Hardy) pretended to be Wally Hammond (seemed the wrong era for someone born in 1941). Ollie's Dad coaching him to never give up and don't let them know you're hurt. He did everything possible to please his Dad.

There's jokes about going to London in a red jumper and 30 people tried to board him, going to the zoo, where elephants threw peanuts at him and about not being overweight but rather under-tall.

The 11-year-old Colin scores a fifty in his father's team. Then aged 18, a Durham CCC century against the Indians and he was signed by Northamptonshire.

He wants to be one of the lads, to prove them wrong, the ones who said he was fat.

Appleby knew about all the one-eyed cricketers, off by heart – Nawab of Pataudi, Ranji, EP Nupen, William Clarke. He knew all the north-easterner ones too, Chris Old and Bill Athey from Middlesbrough for Yorkshire, Geoff Holmes of Glamorgan and Paul and KD Smith for Warwickshire, from Newcastle. One of the reasons he liked west countryman stylist (batsman not hairdresser) Tom Graveney was because 'brave and bold Sir Tom', who was just about Appleby's age, was born in Northumberland. Then there were Cumbrians Graham Monkhouse for Surrey and Dean Hodgson for Gloucestershire, and Paul Nixon for Leicestershire and England. And later still, fellow Keswickian Paul Hindmarch, for Durham seconds. This is a fan thing – following your kind, the people you might know, no matter where they go. Following their performances gives the matches meaning, especially when you're not too partisan for a team, coming from Cumbria. He used to complain that Nixon, or whoever, never got enough coverage in the paper. Ignorant reporters. Southerners. Public schoolboys. Always talking up their own.

But why the need to be associated with these players? I met him once, saw him once, have a story about him. I like him, support him, am a fan of him. North-easterner professionals who made it against the odds, like Paul Smith, Cumbrians like Ben Stokes, Jordan and Graham Clark. Did Hodgson play for Hawksdale, my Dad's team, when I was a kid? I definitely saw him there. People talked about him, as a local prospect.

Dad liked Glamorgan because he was a member there when he worked at Barry power station, and also because they were underdogs and outsiders, having been latest allowed in to the County Championship, in 1923. Ultimately, he had a chance to support his local team and became a Durham member when they were allowed in, in 1992. Durham usurped Yorkshire after he'd had 40 years of Yorkshire membership. Giving up membership was hard. It was disloyal. He said he was sad about doing it. But he hadn't been much in the last few years.

Appleby liked Somerset because his friend/cricket-book buying client Eddie Lawrence was chairman, and Leicestershire because fellow Association of Cricket Statisticians member Dennis Lambert was their statistician, and he'd met bowler Brian Boshier in Boshier's cafe in Malham in the Dales. As he got old, lame and ailing, watching live cricket became a Keswick-only thing. 'They don't think of me,' he said, when his old mates took off across the Pennines to Durham matches at Chester-le-Street. Back to where he started, stuck away from the big matches and names, then overseas working even further away, with none of the connections like his cigarette cards and books.

In the pre-internet days Appleby researched for cricket authors Don Mosey, Nico Craven and Mark Peel. They rang for info, stats, bits out of books and from his memory, and just to talk cricket anomalies and anniversaries.

Peel, Milburn's biographer, is an old Harrovian, former Fettes School teacher (where Tony Blair was educated) who spent the long school holidays writing books about

1950s and 1960s cricketers Ken Barrington and Colin Cowdrey; a biography of headmaster Anthony Chenevix-Trench; and portraits of pacifist Methodist Donald Soper and politician Shirley Williams. Milburn had written his own book, the naïve and jovial *Largely Cricket* in 1968 before the accident.

In the 2016 Milburn play, everyone knows and loves Ollie. A big-hitting Geordie, with no side, who remembers everyone, and has a joke for all, typically about a pub being as lively as watching Geoff Boycott bat.

Milburn bats on in his dreams after the eye has gone.

The play ends with Milburn about to die in a pub car park, aged 48, of a booze-related heart attack, on Appleby's 59th birthday, incidentally.

I watched the play so I had a story to tell my Dad. He had a thing for Milburn. He identified with his weight, his opening batting, his origins (from the north-east Burnopfield, a few miles from Appleby's own origins in Low Fell). But Appleby also appreciated the finer batting aesthetics of Hammond and Graveney, and Hutton. And of course Grace, who changed the game and was more than the game.

Appleby gave a talk titled *First-class Cricket 1864–1900* to Rotary clubs, Women's Institutes, Lions clubs, whoever asked, in return for a 'nosebag', usually lamb, green beans and potatoes, or chicken and peas. Note the exact dates, and the first-class definition, and the dinner. Appleby straddled the generations and had loads of knowledge, gleaned from his library and his library alone. To learn his words, he walked the dog, a massive, amiable, slobbering otterhound (like a foxhound but chases otters) called Hotspur. While walking, Dad talked to himself, running through what he'd say, and chiding himself for forgetting bits, as the lump of a dog stretched the lead.

All that knowledge is no use anymore though. Any fool can find it online. Back then you needed to own the books – and have a prodigious memory. Appleby's was photographic, and his collecting was obsessive, two traits that seem to often go together.

Both Milburn and Appleby opened the batting. Fred Trueman once told Geoff Cope to bowl at Milburn's legs because Ollie's bulk meant he couldn't get across his gut to hit leg-side easily. Appleby was the same.

But Milburn wasn't Appleby. The fat boozer from Geordieland, with a good eye, ironically, who fought back after the tragic accident to play again one-eyed, bravely, but sadly, unsuccessfully. His ox-like constitution was blunted by gout and booze and sadness. But first there were great times, a century for England at Lord's, when he was talk of the nation.

Milburn was maybe the player Appleby would like to have been, talented, carefree. Milburn showed there was an opportunity for anyone if they were good enough, even if they were from a backwater. I saw Milburn's autograph on eBay for 99p. I bought it. After all, he won't be signing any more and it'll be the closest I get to meeting him.

Chapter 7

# EK Brown letters

I DIDN'T think I had much of Appleby's writing. I didn't think he wrote much, preferring to read and to speak. He never got round to doing a history of Carlisle CC, though he kept bits of the archive. But in an exercise book in the box of precious archives at the Brown Muffs of Bradford department store – 'the Harrods of the north' is a resignation letter. ' ... I alluded to a small engineering firm situated in Carlisle, run by my cousin, and of his desire for me to join him in this venture. In the past I have been tempted by these overtures but refused them, having been perfectly happy with Foster Wheeler but as you know I became engaged earlier this year and the situation has changed.

'My fiancée is eager to settle down and after more than twenty years moving around I feel that now is the time to accept my cousin's offer, so reluctantly I wish to tender my resignation from Foster Wheeler from 31 July.' He carries on for another page with his gratefulness and thanks and unease.

The letter shows his loyalty, expressed through how formally he felt he need to write and above all, showed his desire to settle down: 'It was him that wanted to settle down, not me,' said his wife, my mother. I was uncovering the real Appleby, away from the old-fashioned eccentric, cricket-loving, book-loving, bluff northern persona his clothes, conversation and manner expressed.

Next I found an even better archive: the EK Brown letters. Now, it's the thrill of the internet auction. Then it was being offered something rare by a gentleman book dealer.

In a September 1990 *Wisden Cricket Monthly* magazine there's an article by cricket bookseller David Smith marking EK Brown's 80th birthday; 'emeritus cricket book dealer since 1948'.

Brown took on the Epworth stock in 1967, and subsequently bought the G Neville Weston and Arlott collections. Some found their way to Cumbria. They're not there now. Epworth was a pioneer cricket book seller, known for its adverts in *Wisden*, before going defunct and Brown's subsequent coup. GNW we know about. Arlott was the best cricket commentator, Appleby said, because he didn't force it down your throat. Dulcet tones, not a show-off, knew the game, more than even if he'd played, rather than had just been a policeman-turned-poet-turned-broadcaster. And he reminded Appleby of 1948 and the halcyon days of Bradman and The Oval.

EK Brown said books were all about condition, condition is everything.

All collections need WG and Bradman items, the article says. So, I took some from Dad's. EKB advised Dad on what to collect. He has loads of Grace and Bradman stuff, all in very good or better condition.

On top of the file of letters, housed in the 1960s shirt box from Brown Muffs (founded in Bradford in 1814, sold to House of Fraser in 1977, rebranded as Rackhams in 1978 and all closed by 2020) is a dated (14.11.73) chit from Sporting Handbooks for the cash sale at £50 of 1864–78 *Wisden* facsimiles. These were the original pink Billing & Sons copies rather than the later Lowe and Brydone or Willows. Maybe they're now worth £600? It's easy to check. He always said, unless talking to fellow collectors, that he had a complete run of *Wisdens*. It was easier than explaining about the facsimiles.

The first letter from EK Brown is dated 26 November 1970. I was three months from being born, which I think might be significant. The letter is addressed to CL Appleby. I assumed EKB typed it himself, but it turned out he had a secretary.

Appleby has enquired regarding *Wisdens* 1935–40. The 1930s period has always been difficult as supply doesn't meet demand, particularly for cloth-bounds. Brown has a cloth copy of 1940, a scarce item costing 40 shillings including post. The only way Brown can help Appleby is to report copies as available, but he has a waiting list for some of the years. In time he will be able to meet some of Appleby's requirements.

*Wisden* collectors often start with their birth year issue and aim to get them all from then. Then they get them all before they were born too. And then they upgrade them for better condition ones. Then they upgrade again. Then they rebind them. And buy books about them. And join societies to talk about them.

In the Muffs box, the Brown chit follows letters to EW Swanton about the selection of (Chris) Old for the England team. Old was educated at Acklam School in Middlesbrough, same as my Dad (and Bill Athey). Appleby also wants Swanton to write a tribute to Tom Graveney. Swanton gives a standard reply on how it's interesting to know readers' views and that he admires Graveney.

Then the invoices begin on 15 January 1971 with cloth-bound *Wisdens* 1901 and 1905 at £4 14/6. I was born that February, the day before my Dad was 40. Then there's a gap in the letters – there was a postal strike. And decimal money came in, which will have thrown Appleby. After all, he used the word 'wireless' for radio all his life.

The 15 March 1971 chit when I was a few weeks old is for *Wisdens* 1912 and 1925 at £2.50 and £2.25, plus 24p post. 19 May 1971's is for a 1906 and 1924 at the same prices.

In the Muffs box, there's a Yorkshire v Leicestershire scorecard, Bradford, 21–24 August 1971 when Geoffrey Boycott hit yet another century, 151, adding 182 for the third wicket with Barrie Leadbeater, who, rather more remarkably, notched 95. Leadbeater rarely made centuries, just one in his career. He still was granted a benefit season, joint with Geoff Cope in 1980 raising £33,840. Boycs raked in nearly £150k in 1984 after being given £20,000 in 1974. I remember reading the tributes in the Leadbeater benefit brochure, laudatories mixed with ruefulness about missed potential. Leadbeater did make a match-winning 76 in the 1969 Gillette Cup Final. My sister was a baby then. Appleby went with Soaky Dickinson, a dentist who lived just down the road. Leadbeater became a typical Yorkshire 1970s player. I was around six months old when Appleby took in the Yorkshire–Leicestershire match. My Mum will have been at her parents' in Bradford. Appleby will have sloped off to the ground. He made a record number of boring notes on the back of this scorecard, in a red Bic pen. He's listed all the fours ('Boycott off McKenzie – pull'). Next to it, 'Sharpe did not get over a ball from McKenzie caught low in gully'. Yorkshire were entering the Boycott captaincy years (1971–78), when the stubborn opener's team lost its status as county cricket's best. Internal warfare among committee men, pro and anti-Boycott went on for another 15 years until the end of Boycott's career.

29 September 1971: *Wisdens* 1929 and 1933 at £2.50 each

2 November 1971: 1931 £2.75 and 1899 for £3.50. Appleby's second son and third child, my brother Daniel, is born the next spring.

In 1972, there's three more *Wisdens* bought: 1900, 1932 and 1914 at £2.75–£3.25.

In 1973 there's four: 1908, 1895 (a record expenditure of £4.65), 1904 and cricket novel *Mike* by PG Wodehouse and Plum Warner's *Fight for the Ashes*.

On 19 June 1974, my Dad's ship came in.

19 June 1974: Appleby has managed to obtain a good run of *Wisdens*. Brown will be pleased to have the 16 duplicates.

Everything accelerates after that. From EKB there's 1927, 1926, 1885, 1937 and others.

Little square parcels he called them, 'don't tell your mother'. Though after the windfall, he could pretend everything that arrived was in lieu of credit as Brown allows £35 plus other *Wisdens* in exchange.

Chapter 8

# 1930 *Wisden*

IN THE precious exercise book, in the Brown Muffs box, is a list. '*Wisdens* received from Peter Ingrams on Wednesday 25 May 1974.'

I never really knew where he'd got his collection from. I don't think he wanted to mention the Ingrams *Wisdens* in case Ingrams wanted them back. Not that he could ask for them back. He disappeared in the Andes in 1975.

Ingrams was ex-*Private Eye* editor Richard Ingrams' brother and was head at Lime House School, near Carlisle, where my Dad played cricket on the school pitch, for Hawksdale.

There's a bit of a story here, I thought.

After a bit of digging, including talking to deputy head (and Lime House cricket team player) Basil Budden, later a Cumbrian racing journalist, and Don Renyard, a slow left armer and later Hawksdale captain and as Carlisle as you could get, especially in comparison to the toff outsiders teaching at the private school, I got a bit of the back story of PJ Ingrams.

Turns out PJ bought Lime House with his inheritance in 1965. Younger brother Richard Ingrams had set up Britain's bestselling satirical magazine *Private Eye* with his loot in 1961. The cash came from banker dad Leonard.

Budden, an old gent of the turf, talked about the foundation of the club and how they moved to Lime House. 'And the head Peter Ingrams was better than people thought. He bowled very slow high flighted leg breaks that deceived some people, and he batted a bit. The captain after Renyard was in the paper. I knew him well – he was a bookseller in Keswick.'

Me: 'He was my Dad.'

'He was a delightful man. My friend Dave Cannon met him on Keswick marketplace each week.'

Me: 'But what about Ingrams? He gave my Dad some *Wisdens* once. He sounded like an interesting character.'

'He ran the school. He bought it. He was something of a controversial character. He did a lot of fell walking. There was an accident where a pupil was killed on the lake that was turned into a reservoir. Then he died in Ecuador. He went with a climbing party from Arundel and never came back.'

Budden, who died in 2022, continued: 'I left in 1973 and at that stage your father was captain of the team.

'I had letters from my grandfather from WG Grace, just saying things like "I'm looking forward to playing" that I gave to him. But I must go I'm afraid … '

I'd already rang Renyard, raspier than ever: 'If we wa' short we roped in Lime 'Ouse staff,' he remembered.

'Ingrams, Mike Mertons, John Budden [the racing hack's real name].'

Me: 'What happened to Ingrams?'

'Ingrams? I don't think he was getting on with his missus and he disappeared in the Andes. I don't think he got lost on purpose.'

But maybe he did? Maybe that's why he gave away the *Wisdens*, I thought. Why else would you?

PJ was an overgrown 1940s/50s schoolboy, fond of derring-do. He took schoolboys climbing when he became a teacher, but there were tragedies ahead.

According to Richard's biographer Harry Thompson (who later wrote cricket travelogue *Penguins Stopped Play*) PJ didn't go to Richard's wedding on 24 November 1962, because the Test match was on telly (probably not true, there was no Test on that day – though the anecdote may fit one of his other brothers' weddings). PJ was a tormented man who liked rescuing poor boys from the Third World. The Paaradeekh brothers were two of them but tragedy hit when one of them died of exposure in a blizzard on the Lake District fells on an Ingrams walk in March 1968.

In October 1972, PJ and 13 children went for a climb above Haweswater (the lake that turned into the reservoir Budden referred to) in the eastern Lakes, maybe 20 miles from Lime House. One 14-year-old died and three were injured in a landslip on a dangerous route. PJ became more reckless, perhaps reckless with guilt. Not long after, he gave my Dad an old leather suitcase. Dad laid the case on our living room floor, on an unfolded *Daily Telegraph* and opened the clasp. Jammed inside were some dusty books. He took them out one by one, knocking off the mouse droppings back into the case, un-netting cobwebs and smelling the neglect.

The bored PJ, stuck in his educational and geographical backwater and perhaps now viewed suspiciously by the locals, had been lightly entertained by my Dad's knowledge of facts, anniversaries, Navy humour and the Great War. He told Shrewsbury School old boy PJ about two old Salopian posthumous VCs: Thomas Price killed making a last-ditch bayonet charge in 1918 and Dr Harold Ackroyd's work tending the wounded at Passchendaele in 1917, which gained him 23 recommendations for the highest medal. PJ was impressed that Appleby knew.

The Ingrams *Wisden* list goes from 1879–1930, 44 in total. Some have asterisks ('already in my possession-16').

Missing are 1882, 1885, 1886, 1887, 1916, 1923-5 ('already had'). He now only needed 1934–39 and 1941– 45. Appleby had bought most post-war *Wisdens* 'at the time of publication'.

Before the 1976 season began, PJ joined a party from Oundle School to Mount Antisana in the Ecuadorian Andes, being no longer trusted to lead his own pupils up mountains. He was showing a pattern of repeated behaviour, very sports fan-esque. With one master and five boys, PJ walked to the snowline in darkness, at 19,000 feet. The weather turned, three boys roped up, the masters and a boy roped up. PJ untied himself and set off to join the all-boys roped group. Then he changed his mind and set off up to see what was over the ridge. PJ disappeared, never to be seen again, despite the efforts of the Ecuadorian Air Force's search team. There's a memorial bridge with a PJ plaque at Wylie Gill on Carrock Fell, a gabbro-rocked hill eight miles north-east of Keswick, 661m high.

Lime House was at Hawksdale, near the village of Dalston, near Carlisle. My uncle Russell, MD of R Lawson Engineers, and Dad's cousin and boss, lived in Dalston. There's a team photo from around that time. Appleby in the middle, arms crossed, captain, flanked by the masters Mertons, Budden and Ingrams. Plus Downie, with Renyard in the back row.

Before Ingrams' 'untimely disappearance on a climbing expedition to the Andes', as Lime House records put it, 'P J Ingrams was responsible for introducing girls to the school and making it a co-educational establishment with pupils following GCE O level and A level courses.' As well as the bedrock of my Dad's *Wisden* collection. I played for Hawksdale in the early 80s. No one gave me any *Wisdens*.

So 1974 was the year Ingrams gave the mouse crap suitcase to Dad. The suitcase that was laid out on our living room floor and out of it came an Aladdin's cave, or perhaps it was a Pandora's box.

## Chapter 9

## *Wisden*

APPLEBY'S LUCK was in. He won a Mini in 1974 in the TV quiz *Sky's the Limit*, with Hughie Greene, but sold it pretty quickly, for £900.

An EK Brown chit from 5 August 1974 is to AJ Appleby offering *Wisden* 1885 at £10.

10 August 1974: *Wisden* 1885 £10.00, credit was £37.13½, now £27.13½.

Appleby has offered Brown a Carlisle United FC history in return for cheaper *Wisdens*.

Carlisle United won promotion to Division One in 1974 for the first time. They were top after three games, before quickly going bottom and staying there. Chris Balderstone was a midfielder, and also a pro cricketer. Full -back Bobby Parker used to walk his basset hound Henry past our house.

Striker Frank Clarke later ran the village shop in Houghton, a village just outside Carlisle where I went to primary school. Brown probably liked football more than cricket.

On 3 March 1975, Brown offered *Wisden* 1936 and 1938 at £3.75. Prices are going higher all the time.

It's 27 May 1975 and Brown offers limp covered *Wisdens* for 1935 and 1943 at £3.75 and £2.75 respectively. Appleby has £6.43½ in credit.

Brown, of NatWest Chambers, Liskeard, Cornwall, has the largest collection of cricket books for sale in the country. He offers *Wisden* 1942 at £5 – scarce *Wisdens* cost a lot to buy and Brown has to pay what is asked, with 1880s fetching £12.50 and more now.

The classic *Wisden* is a boxy brown book, with a daff-yellow dust jacket, fat with statistics and reports of the previous season, published as the next one begins.

I tend to turn to the reports of Yorkshire CC matches first. Durham since admission to the first-class game in 1992. I might look at Cumberland CC in the Minor County section, a much briefer set of reports, reflecting relative importance, then the obits to see who has died I didn't know about, then book reviews, and more county stuff. The almanack was always England-centred. Public schools used to fill endless pages with a pungent overview by a sour old martinet called EM Wellings, from 1954-72. Always amusing: 'Without their ridiculous long hair, today's boys' fielding would be much improved.'

'This year was the worst I can recall for the much-neglected art of' ... fielding/back play/leg spin bowling/cleanliness of whites/pad play/bright cricket, etc – he chose one theme a year and pontificated majestically upon it.

There weren't many features in *Wisden* until recent years. Mostly just Wellings reviewing fee-paying schools matches. The father of every boy who played surely bought a copy of *Wisden* to see the family name inside. Not Appleby's scene.

Wellings did not make himself popular. Only five people went to his funeral, including his widow. 'Once again public schoolboy cricket disappointed, with the worst standard in outfielding since the War a feature of the decline of the standards of the game and the coaching of boys therein,' would be a typical start.

Reporting the Eton versus Harrow match at Lord's, he 'again saw a lack of forcing strokes and some wildly inaccurate throwing from the outfield. Inexcusable fielding of a slovenly nature is surely an infection passed down from the first-class game of recent years, as is the insidious habit of hitting straight balls across the line to leg which so pervaded matches against the Tourists on damp surfaces this summer, much to the detriment of the game.'

He has another brush with hair: 'One sad aspect of this year's play was an outbreak of long hair, which surely can only hinder boys' efforts to play correctly, particularly when reaching forward against slow left-arm spin bowling.

'In a wet season, on slow uncovered wickets there is no explanation why forcing back play was not employed or coached in a more correct manner to combat the turning ball from off.'

Books reviewed by John Arlott were much more Appleby's bag.

'This year, one hundred and thirty four books on the subject of cricket, if loosely described as such, were received.

'Of these, no fewer than 48 were county, club or association histories, all of which are valuable records of the game around the country.

'In particularly S Canynge Caple's *125 Years of Hambledon Down Cricket Club*, is a document that scholars will use in decades to come. The author's descriptions of Beldham's back play against the shooters of Mynn in the 1780s are not to be forgotten.

'In *History of England versus North American representative elevens* (and XVs!) Irving Rosenwater has studiously examined many scorebooks and contemporary accounts to correct statistics given by less diligent writers in previous years.'

*Wisden* had a very set formula.

*Wisden* until the 1980s:

'Xshire

Xshire disappointed again, dropped four places to thirteenth in the County Championship final table, the county's worst position since 1934. Four wins were achieved against five last season, with seventeen draws and six defeats, the most ignominious setback being an innings reverse when facing a weak Derbyshire eleven which ultimately finished the season in bottom place, on a damp wicket at Chesterfield in July.

'While three batsmen reached their one thousand runs, the same number as last year, only one topped his aggregate, and that at a lower batting average.

'Wins against Northamptonshire and Glamorgan were offset by a run of nineteen games without a victory between early May and late June. This was checked when several amateurs were able to play during the summer holidays, enlivening the batting with brighter stroke play and much uplifting of the spirit of the team.

'Former captain X stroked the ball elegantly when available, often adding impetus to the middle order. He finished with a creditable 634 runs from 29 innings, while Y, down from Cambridge in the holidays, made a fine century against Essex at Clacton, which included six boundaries.

'The return of an amateur captain, Z, at the age of 38 years and succeeding A, who joined Somerset in the close season following his non-re-engagement, boosted the men. Z was understandably rather slow to reach his optimum having not played first-class cricket since his appearance for Combined Services against Free Foresters at Marlow in 1947, but often held up an end in a crisis.

'He fielded by example at cover point, won the respect of the professionals as he was expected to do through his wholehearted contributions, and made useful runs in the lower order, with 52 against DH Robins XI at Scarborough, including four boundaries, his best.

'The side sorely lacked a leg break or chinaman bowler with the loss of B in the close season. C only reached his 100 wickets in the last game of the season. D's lobs proved useful on occasion.

'All-rounder E, a West Indian, assisted on occasion, winning the single wicket competition and hitting strongly in the new Gillette Cup competition, in which Xshire reached Lord's. The lithe left-hander hit hard but often failed on damper days.

'Fast bowlers F and G again failed to reach their one hundred wickets despite bowling the lion's share of the overs, more than 2,500 between them. Both were not re-engaged at the end of the season. G was again unfit on occasion.

'Wicketkeeper H kept competently and was chosen for the MCC tour of Ceylon.'

Then the averages, the player, where born (Luton, Khartoum The Sudan, Hammersmith, wherever), games, innings, runs, centuries, fifties, catches. Then the bowlers, overs, maidens, runs, wickets, five-fors, ten – wicket matches. All very reassuring and giving a picture to the educated of how a player has done, without even watching a game. Obituaries are next – a social history and not just a list of recently dead players.

'GILLIWAT, ARTHUR WILLIAM STURGESS, who died at Brightlingsea on December 31, three days before his 82nd birthday, was a fixture in the Malvern XI for three years from 1899. His fine 38 in the match versus Bromsgrove in 1901 almost led to the first victory of his school against the old foes for more than 20 years, before a spell from AEGT Boghe-Brusshe wrought havoc on the home side's lower order.

'Gilliwat subsequently went up to Oxford, where he did not gain his Blue, despite a useful 23 against Free Foresters in the opening game of 1902, on a wet wicket at The Parks.

'Following service in the Malay, where he reached the rank of Brigadier-Colonel and played cricket against

Coolies from Sarawak, as well as winning the Military Cross and spending four years as a Prisoner of War, Gilliwat was called upon by Somerset to aid the stricken county in the post-war years, often contributing cavalier innings that raised the spirits of the professional players, including a fine effort of 48 against the Navy at Sandhurst during the hot Whitsun weekend of 1923.

'Occasionally, Gilliwat was called upon to captain the eleven from 1924–28 and despite having to mould an eleven without any amateur aid, won the respect of the professionals and almost led his side to victory on a number of occasions. Famously, when he asked professional bowler Smalls to contribute another spell following an innings of 143 and first innings figures of 8-21 against Essex at Clacton in 1925, the taciturn north-easterner replied: "Not on your nelly, Gilly, I'm spent." Gilliwat, alive to the needs of his men, sent the rebellious Smalls from the pitch, never to be selected again, but won the respect of his men for his jocular comment as policemen took the unrepentant player away: "Don't you Gilly me, little man. Enjoy the workhouse."

'He later became a fine committee man and treasurer of the club before his death while circumnavigating the Isle of Wight on his catamaran *Dryballs* in a storm this winter.

'BRIGG, THOMAS at Bradford on December 1 aged 37, a professional bowler who served Yorkshire for several seasons, before falling on hard times. Lord Hawke described him as a "capital fellow, unless under drink".

Brigg took 1,534 wickets at 15.04 in first-class matches breaching the one hundred wicket barrier a dozen times. He aided the England eleven on a number of occasions and accompanied Lord Harris' team on their tour of South Africa and Ceylon in 1894/95, contributing usefully with the ball. Subsequently, his form fell away and he was not re-engaged by his county after failing to reach his hundred wickets in 1899 whilst simultaneously asking for a shilling a month extra salary. He later fell into penury before the good Lord's charity allowed Brigg to spend his last days sheltering in the groundsman's privy at Park Avenue.'

To spell it out, *Wisden* reassured about the order of things.

Chapter 10

# Mintys

NOW IN the Muff archive is another list, not of *Wisdens* this time, but of party requisites.

This list is from the old exercise book in the Brown Muffs cardboard box. The bash was scheduled after the long hot summer of 1976, to celebrate the completion of the 'new room' extension at our house in Carlisle, which also included a study for Appleby, and a book room, also for the collector. Both quickly filled with Minty bookcases.

'Party for 20 November 1976 (to celebrate extension)
1 Bottle Grants Whisky (in stock)
1 Whyte & Mackay £3.75
Cossack Vodka £3.49
2 Gordons Gin at £3.79 = £7.58
Gonzalez Byass sherry (dry medium sweet) £4.37
Cinzano sweet (dry red martini) £3.87
Johnny Walker £3.70
Beefeater Gin £3.75

Bitter lemon, lemonade, tonic, soda (about 12p each) £10.13

Barrel beer from Rugby Club 88 Pints

6 pint tins Courage Beer £5.56

'Forty-seven people came. Two bottles of whisky and two of gin would have been sufficient and soft drinks were not much used – six of each would have been sufficient and less than that of tonic.'

The neighbours and work colleagues from Dad's work came round, a bit like a Mike Leigh film. We took the best china plates of pineapple chunks and cheddar cheese on cocktail sticks round until the guests could eat no more. They were certainly drunk, what with that barrel of beer. Chat was around the extension, built by Edwin the builder and Jimmy the joiner. Dad had dug out the garden where the extension was going to go, breaking the corner off a spade. I remember watching them throughout that boiling summer. Edwin had a habit of putting mallets through walls by accident. Jimmy asked if I liked helping people, after I endlessly asked if I could pass him his tools, which were right next to him. A decade later, when we moved out, the estate agent said the big double-glazed window that looked over the back lawn where we played cricket all summer was warped. But it was too late now to do anything about it. Out of guarantee, he said.

Dad was soon to join the Rotary Club, looking for the comradeship he missed from the Navy and didn't find with the neighbours or at work, or even in local cricket. He talked about work, manufacturing (not making) winches and pulleys for the booming North Sea oil fields, which frustrated him, because of the hours and because he worked for his cousin, who was decisive but so often wrong! In the tradition of the day, we furnished and draped the room in brown artificial fibres. There were a couple of big differences from the typical provincial suburban living room. There were framed cigarette cards hanging everywhere and rows and rows of *Wisdens* in Minty bookcases against every available wall.

I remember drinking bitter lemon for months afterwards. And I remember him showing anyone who showed an interest (and plenty that didn't) his cricket books, sliding open the glass on the bookcases and showing off their rarity and value.

In another notebook there's some notes from a New Zealand holiday, many years later.

'4 times in 9 years. Drive 20–30 miles then small town with war memorial.'

His writing's getting smaller. And spindlier.

'Biggest growing holiday destination. Why? Outdoor activities. Safer after 9/11. Lord of the Rings. Far more traffic than nine years ago.'

(I think this is notes for a talk to the Rotary Club.)

He talks about flat whites, diaries, meat pies (rat's coffins), ethnic restaurants, wine at Marlborough, land flowing with milk and honey. A lot of mutton – 'couldn't eat it all'.

It's not all food, there's 'no air force, political correctness!'

11 March 1976 more chits:

*Wisden* 1939 £6.50.

Credit now £6.43½.

22 March 1976 finds credit is now 93½p and a 1945 is available at £5.25 in brown cloth.

All Appleby requires are 1882, 1886, 1887, 1916, 1941 and 1944. Prices for 1880 copies will be from £15–17.50 each.

5 July 1976:

Brown offers a fine copy of *Wisden* 1887 at £15.50 including postage. Appleby has credit of £5.68½.

1977: more chits

Credit £25.10½.

The very rare 1916 is available for £17.50, plus a limp covered 1944 at £5.25.

These are not sent on spec as they aren't cheap.

19 January 1977: *Cumberland and Westmorland Herald* editor John Hurst has mentioned Appleby's concern about the Penrith Cricket Club *Wisdens* to colleagues on the committee and promises to take good care of them. He suggests a newspaper story about Edgar Appleby, cricketer and collector of cricketana?

By March 1977 Appleby has admitted to Brown he is buying from another dealer, John McKenzie, who was a customer of Brown before he started dealing.

Brown cannot offer 1941 but can send an 1886 at £15.58 including recorded delivery.

Appleby has £2.35½ in hand so his credit is £9.35½ and this leaves £6.32½ due.

Brown continues to try and find 1882 and 1941.

1 April 1977: Appleby has sent a cheque for £10 which leaves him with credit of £3.77½. He still cannot help with 1941 or 1882. Appleby offers Brown some rugby programmes.

## Chapter 11

# England v Australia, Headingley 1977

I'M LOOKING at the fourth Test match scorecard, England v Australia, 11–16 August 1977, at Headingley.

I was six. I wasn't there. Appleby was. He'd go and see 'how the lads are shaping up' (usually with Soaky Dickinson or my godfather Sibdog) but the family was too young to go yet. He's filled in the scorecard fully. The bare facts were England scored 436. Australia then made 103 and 248.

The story was that Boycott scored 191. Well not actually that he got 191 but that he reached 100, his 100th century.

Choosing the right events to go to is part of being a fan. You get a vicarious thrill from being in the right place at the right time.

A couple of years earlier, at the Headingley Ashes Test, Appleby was outraged at 1975's 'George Davis is innocent' pitch-dug-up affair. Davis was doing 20 years for armed robbery. His mate Peter Chappell got 18 months for delaying the Test match with his pitch digging, oil pouring and graffiti, committed as a protest against Davis's sentence. 'It had to be done,' he wrote. 'Hang 'em,' said Appleby.

Australia had needed 255 to win with seven wickets in hand when the night-time crime occurred. To Appleby the worst bit was vandals prevented a good finish – the umpires abandoned the match. It rained anyway.

Davis got let out, after mod rockers The Who and punks Sham 69 joined the protests.

Two years later, Appleby was on the way in to Headingley. 'Hello Mr Smith,' he said to the ancient scorecard seller, as he always did, copying Hutton.

England captain Mike Brearley got a duck, caught behind off Thomson. Appleby told this story about how 20 years later he went to see Brearley at Charlotte Mason College in Ambleside speaking on psychoanalyst stuff. Appleby would have been uncomfortable with that. He wanted to hear about cricket, maybe get a book signed. He could have got this Headingley scorecard signed if he'd had it handy. Grandee Lake District writer, Molly Lefebure, spoke up in the questions: 'My father once got caught at short leg' – more of a comment than an enquiry. My Dad was unimpressed. He was the local cricket expert and showed off, talking about the ex-England captain's father Horace's appearance for Yorkshire in 1937 and service in the 'Wavy Navy' RNVR during the war. He wouldn't have asked about Brearley's seminal cricket theory book *The Art of Captaincy*, which gave me a decent steer when I wrote a book called *New Zealand Test Cricket Captains* 25 years later.

Back at Headingley in 1977, Brearley looked on from the pavilion as Boycs added 82 with Woolmer, 23 with Randall and 96 with Greig, who snuffed it aged just 66 between Christmas and New Year in 2012. It was a badge of honour to Appleby, outliving these people.

Appleby had added on the scorecard which over each batsman was out. Greig was in the 64th. Appleby must have had a bit of time on his hands. You do at the cricket. We kids were at Granny's in Bradford. Grandpa had died, shortly after retiring from his GP practice. Granny had moved to a bungalow, opposite where former Yorkshire stalwart Ticker Mitchell lived. Appleby visited. Ticker signed books and reminisced, in his flinty way. Mitchell had died on Christmas Day 1976. Granny told her daughter, my Mum, who told my Dad, who didn't really have anyone to tell.

On the back of the scorecard there's screeds of notes, on top of adverts for Trumans for Steel, Charles Best (Leeds) for V belts and pulleys, G Evans & Sons for HIRE and SALE of scaffolding equipment corrugated sheets. The ads reminded me of *Indian Cricket* annuals' (the 'Indian *Wisden*' that Brown distributed in the UK) homespun ink-drawn adverts for cement and chemicals. On the '77 scorecard, Owen & Robinson 'craftsman quality jeweller' is illustrated with a skilled manual worker in an apron looking through a magnifier, then it says *Wisden* 1977 is for sale at this ground (in case you hadn't bought it by August). Finally, the 8p scorecard had Smallans the Caterers who 'welcome you to Headingley and trust you will be suitably refreshed during your visit'.

Smallens did 'banqueting', illustrated with an 'XL snacks for suppliers of crisps and snacks' logo at the bottom of their advert. It doesn't sound like much of a banquet to me. Or indeed to Appleby, who by that stage of the day would have banqueted on all the sandwiches he'd have had made for him at home, any pies, sandwiches and cakes available at the ground, several pints of bitter, and possibly a Scotch egg (or seven). An angel's kiss, a cackleberry. 'I'll have that old one', 'that was a pleasing snack' – he had a unique food lexicon, just as cricket has its own language.

The Avengers and Peugeots and Minis drove past the gates as the men in flares and long moustaches and shirts and slip-ons watched while Boycott in a 'cast iron shell of concentration' moved slowly on. In the previous Test, on his return after three years of refusing to play for England (he said he'd lost his appetite; Appleby thought this inexcusable), Boycs had scored 107 – his 99th first-class century – and 80 not out, while running out local favourite Randall. But Boycs' run-scoring and record-making overcame most qualms about his selfishness. And his timing to reach the 100th ton, at Headingley, was perfect. Hutton's 364 was at The Oval, for instance. His run-scoring might have meant even more if it had been at Headingley – and if Appleby had gone to the match. He was only seven years old, but Hutton's epic fired his enthusiasm (alongside the musty cig cards of course).

The notes on the Boycott 1977 scorecard are also faded but one stands out, just above the Bedford Trumans truck advert picturing a load of girders. '5.50pm Boycott 100 in

80th [crossed out] 77th over 234/4, a drive off Chappell, Roope 12.' The notes cover the scores at lunch and tea, with landmarks such as half-centuries and centuries although, apart from Boycs obviously, only Alan Knott (57) and opposition keeper Rod Marsh (63) reached 50.

Boycs went on to 191 in more than ten hours. He'd met all expectations for accumulation and beating the odds. He was so loved locally that fans donated more to Boycs' 1984 testimonial than the previous three beneficiaries put together.

The scorecard delighted Appleby, though delight wasn't a word he'd use. Just like when he'd got me to write off for Bill Bowes' autograph, Appleby would write off for signed scorecards. He didn't plan to sell them but must have known they had value. He was a collector and the signed scorecard got him close to the remarkable, to the player who did the feat, the statistical anomaly. Here in the pile of old papers is the scorecard of Middlesex bowler Richard Johnson's 10-45 for Middlesex. He had Surrey's 14 all out scorecard framed on the wall in the hall of 15 Southey Street, Keswick, for years. Beneath the dark wood banisters with the finial balls on the end I drew for art homework. Norbert Philip and Neil Foster sent Surrey to their lowest first-class score in England. The best thing about the 14 was that the Cumbrian Graham Monkhouse scored 2. Things wouldn't have been half as bad if they'd all scored 2.

Monkey reminded me of Jimmy Skinner or Peter Henderson from Hawksdale CC. That was the limit of all-rounders I knew.

## Chapter 12

# *Defending the Ashes* by Percy Fender

THE CHITS carry on.

1 November 1977 and there's a *Wisden* 1941 at £7.50 post free. Credit is £3.77½ and 70p postage on a programme sent and £15 received with thanks.

2 November 1977 and Brown has a run of *Wisdens* arrived with a good copy of 1941 in it. Prices still rise and people with copies always want a lot for them. This leaves him with only 1882 to get but he can't offer that at the moment.

Appleby also buys 1920 tour books, Fender, Sidney Smith, Old Ebor, scorecards. Brown wants to 'close down the everyday side of the business and build up the good stock' – cricket book collecting is prospering.

Percy Fender's books were a cornerstone of the collection. Fender looked old-fashioned to me with his crinkly side-parting and moustache but could have been a modern household name – he was a pundit, wrist spinner and hard hitter (in 1920 he hit the fastest first-class century in 35 minutes, equalled under 'contrived circumstances' by Lancashire's Steve O'Shaughnessy in my peak cricket year of 1983 – the two were pictured together, Fender aged 91). In Fender's 1921 signed book *Defending the Ashes* Appleby has inserted a note, written in 1990 'VERY SCARCE' £125-£150. It's worth that unsigned now.

28 February 1978 (Dad's 47th birthday, the day after my 7th). Appleby has sent a *History of Queen of the South* to Brown, who is just out of hospital after having a pacemaker implanted.

Appleby's cheque of £15 makes his credit £25.22 1/2. There's no 1882 yet.

## 14 April 1978

Appleby pays £31.25 for books including *Scores and Biographies* Vol 2.

In June, Appleby sends a cheque for £15 which gives him credit of £8.97½.

Brown offers a signed scorecard of the Somerset v Surrey game 15–18 August 1925 when Jack Hobbs scored a century in each innings – his 126th and 127th centuries. The cost is £7.50 including postage. Appleby has asked Brown to come and stay in Carlisle.

The Hobbs scorecard was still on Appleby's wall, 40 years on. You need a JB autograph in the collection. The invoice is for £22.50 including *24 Years of Cricket* and two others.

On 16 August 1978 there's a list of books bought from McKenzie, including Fred Root, Eddie Paynter, PR Warner, Lord Harris, FS Ashley Cooper – £43.50's worth. Then another invoice from McKenzie on 27 September 1978, £24.70 for three books including Noble, Hawke.

Appleby asks McKenzie for an 1882 *Wisden*, but his wait continued.

8 December 1978: £35.20 spent with McKenzie including Daft, Giffen included in eight items ordered from the catalogue with five already sold.

15 December 1978 and Brown has had diabetes and thought of retirement.

Dad has £25.68½ credit, the 68½ from last time. He's still on about 1882 which might now cost £50. Prices of *Wisden* have soared and Appleby was lucky to buy his a few years before because a good copy in the 1920s and 30s fetches £12.50 and Brown can no longer buy at reasonable prices.

Appleby offers Brown Sportsman's Book Club items, which he doesn't want. He wants football books. He sells Appleby Fender's *Kissing the Rod* with dust jacket at £8.50, which could be worth £100 now.

9 January 1979: (Dad's writing) bought from GW Keats of Warwick Road (a part-time Carlisle book dealer's home): 'Charles Box [the first comprehensive history of cricket] £17. And for £6, sent to Brown, Coldstream Guards cricket.' The next month Appleby also sent books to Brown and the next, including Kendal's cricket history.

Brown is also contacted regularly about *Wisdens* and some clubs think if a bookseller contacts them he is after *Wisdens* on the cheap. However, another bookseller gives the dealer a better deal than people who are selling their own items.

Appleby is invited to Cornwall.

## 31 March 1979

The 1882 is now quite a problem, £80 or so is what is being asked in some quarters. Two 1916s made £135 at auction this week and Brown will continue to look for a copy at a high but not astronomical price.

Brown mentions his health – diabetes is tiring him.

1 April 1979: Brown is sending Appleby a South African cricket annual. This is significant – given what was to come.

22 June 1979: Appleby has tipped off Brown about Carnforth auctions selling *Wisdens* 1951–79, which Brown buys with a postal bid.

22 June 1979: Appleby spends £37.20 with McKenzie including Farnes at £12.

Dad's writing: 'Bought from EK Brown at his premises in Liskeard 2 August 1979.

*Wisden Cricketers Almanack* 1882 £85-00.'

There were 15 more items including two Graces and another set of 1938 cigarette cards (£1.25). This was on holiday, with the other four of us, in the caravan. His collection was complete. He did the article with John Hurst, the *Lake District Herald* editor who also wrote the *History of Cumberland Cricket*. Dad is pictured with his 1882, in front of the Mintys. He talks about the cigarette cards, Bradman, Grace, EK Brown and Hawksdale. Not Boycott. Mostly about *Wisdens*.

The newspaper piece was on Appleby completing his collection. 'Fame at last,' he said. I remember visiting Brown's place. I was after football annuals, and I think I got a few *Topical Times* annuals.

We'd been to see Gloucestershire (subsequently known as Proctershire) v Yorkshire at Cheltenham that summer on the way to Brown's. Muscular fast inswing bowler/hard-hitting all-rounder, the South African Mike Procter took a hat-trick of lbws. They were lugubrious Richard Lumb, Boro prospect Bill Athey (who has a Union Jack tattoo) and John Hampshire (who almost certainly didn't) – all from round the wicket. Appleby was amazed. My mother looked up from her knitting.

Dad told how it was against Somerset at Bramall Lane in August 1932 that Horace Fisher created cricket history by claiming the first all-lbw hat-trick in first-class cricket when he dismissed Mandy Mitchell-Innes, Bill Andrews and Wally Luckes to finish with 5-12. Yorkshire won by an innings. Fisher was only playing because Verity was playing for England. 'Damn sight better bowler than what we have now.' An old Gloucestershire fan joined in 'never mind Verity, they don't make them like Charlie Parker anymore'. My Dad said Fisher would 'walk into the England team these days', as would Parker, said old Glos. Only played one Test, said Glos. Fisher 'only played one bloody season', said Appleby. 'Bloody good player Procter, though,' Dad added, not wanting to sound like a 'things aren't what they used to be' merchant, like Fred 'I don't know what's going off out there' Trueman. Not that Appleby would ever criticise Freddie. 'Would walk into the Yorkshire side even now, and he's nearly bloody 50.'

Procter only played seven Tests for South Africa before they were banned. Appleby was 'bloody angry' that politics got in the way of sport. To show his admiration, he took several photos of Procter walking back from the middle, after his success. Small boys in beige clothes, like me, swarm around their hero. The camera wasn't much good for shots of actual play. So Appleby took pics of the players warming up or walking on or off the field, like he had done with his slides camera, pre-marriage in the 1960s. I've got piles of them now, but no slide viewer to look at them. Boycott, then the biggest name in cricket, features in a few pics from Cheltenham. He's looking belligerent walking to practice, with a Datsun Sunny in the background.

In EK Brown's biography, published by cricket book dealer David Smith in 2011 (Smith once visited Appleby in Keswick and kindly bought my *New Zealand Test Captains* book) is a Christmas Greetings card, 'Ted and Iris, 12 only, signed limited edition.' There's an out of focus Polaroid photo tucked inside, John Arlott at the head of a table, EKB on his left, two more blokes I should know but don't, all toasting with claret. Maybe his wife Iris took the photo. Turns out the blokes are collector Tony Winder and Winder's driver. Brown also sent Appleby the Christmas card. The *EK Brown Cricket Bookseller* book is also a limited edition, number 26 of 90. There's a note inside, thanking Appleby for his help.

Michael Down has written the foreword. He was another significant Keswick visitor and Brown's successor, taking on some Brown stock and customers and becoming Appleby's favourite, post-EK Brown. Down writes in the foreword about writing to EKB in 1967, asking for a catalogue. At Brown's base at NatWest Chambers, Liskeard, opened by the *Wisden* cricket book reviewer and doyen of cricket broadcasters John Arlott in 1970, Down bought *Scores and Biographies* 1 and 2 for 10/6d each. They were formerly owned by pre-Grace cricketer George King, of Sussex. Down invented holidays to go to Liskeard. Sounds familiar. 'Through Ted you could join the freemasonry of collectors, historians and researchers who shared his passion.' Appleby is mentioned alongside obsessive collectors, the Yorkshiremen Tony Woodhouse and Tony Winder. There's none of that now. Internet buying saw to that. Late in life, EKB introduced Down to G Neville Weston's daughter, who was selling Weston's Grace collection.

Meanwhile, Dad has been sending Brown football programmes from Annan and Queen of the South. Brown won't get another secretary after this one leaves.

But the old book dealer isn't finished yet. He's been engaged in buying John Arlott's cricket collection. He resigned from Rotary last June but will be pleased to see Appleby's article on Lord Mountbatten once it is published in the Rotary magazine.

12 November: Appleby buys, from John Arlott's collection, *71 Not Out* [William Caffyn's 1899 early cricket autobiography now worth £65], which Brown had mentioned as scarce before, at £27.50. Credit is now £3.00.

Brown enjoyed reading about himself in John Hurst's Appleby-based *Wisden* collectors' article in the local Cumbrian paper.

Later, in the book about Brown, the true Brown story comes out. He was from Nuneaton and had moved to Cornwall in 1940. EKB, then a headmaster, began serious bookselling when he took on UK dealership of the *New Zealand Cricket Annual* in 1948. Appleby took it on from Brown almost 40 years later.

Former Warwickshire cricketer Canon JH Parsons was a school governor and mate of Brown's. Parsons is the only player to have appeared in first-class cricket under five different guises: Parsons (pro), JH Parsons (amateur), Lt Parsons, Captain Parsons and Reverend Parsons. A favourite quiz question of Appleby that sent cricket types he knew away to research their collections. EKB knew Aubrey Hill too, back from his Warwickshire days.

Brown followed the tradition of gentleman/fan cricket bookseller begun by AJ Gaston of Brighton in the 1890s. The 'Leather Hunter' advertised in *Wisden* from 1922–28. EF Hudson followed, advertising in *Wisden* from 1934–69. In the late 1950s Epworth Books took over Hudson's second-hand stock. Epworth was the publishing arm of the Methodist Church. In 1967, when Brown took on Epworth's stock, he retired from his headmastership aged 58 and went full-time as a cricket book dealer, moving to the Liskeard Bank Chambers not long after.

In 1976, EW Swanton wrote a report on the trade in *The Cricketer*, including a photo of Brown. *Wisdens* were leading a boom in cricket book collecting. Prices were rising fast. Collectors wanted tangible memories of the glory days. Others were looking to invest. Brown advertised in *Wisden* from 1968–83, and became Appleby's dealer of choice, discreet, kindly, knowledgeable and respected. His early adverts for hardback *Wisdens* from 1920–62 priced them at under £2 each.

Brown knew everyone who had a decent collection. Appleby made sure he was one of them. He was out on a limb at the other end of the country, but his obsession grew as did his delight that people recognised what he was doing. Brown acquiring some of Arlott's collection in 1979 excited Appleby. Winder got most of Arlott's stuff, either because Brown couldn't afford it or because Arlott thought Winder richer. But Brown bought the more esoteric G Neville Weston's collection, in 1985. I know because of the amount of their bookplates that are in Appleby's books. Arlott, a Liberal candidate for Epping in 1955 and 1959 and backer of South African sporting boycotts, believed there were only half a dozen non-Tories in the county game. Appleby ignored Arlott's philosophy – the books were more important.

14 January 1980: EK Brown, born in Nuneaton in 1910 says he knew Aubrey Smith well as an opening batsman when he was playing in the Coventry area.

Dad has sent a long letter about how he knows Smith and about Annan FC programmes.

Brown talks of Mr Hollett, a Cumbrian bookseller who charges 'a bit more' then EKB would but doesn't know his *Wisden* prices though, selling at £35 when they are fetching £75–£100 in London. He reminisces about

Aubrey Hill playing pre-war for Coleshill Albions v Griff and Coton. Former England captain Bob Wyatt calls in sometimes.

*And Then Came Larwood* is offered. It's by Australian cricketer/cartoonist Arthur Mailey, belonged to Arlott, and includes a likeness of Mailey and Arlott, drawn by Mailey. It's £10.75 including post and would be £12.50 to anyone else.

Then there is a letter from Tony Woodhouse, the great Yorkshire collector and superfan. Dad has sent Woodhouse his 500th soccer book, which is about Morton FC. Woodhouse and Appleby chat about how badly the 1980 England tour of the West Indies is going and swaps a Trent Bridge book for the Morton book. Brown never talks about cricket matches. Woodhouse worked in the family advertising business in Leeds and never missed a Yorkshire match home or away for several decades, until he was run over by a car and broke both his legs and was never quite the same again. Woodhouse was a reasonably moderate Yorkshire committee man (i.e., not stubborn about everything) and had a massive collection of cricket books, including shelves in the bathroom of his unremarkable red brick suburban Leeds house. He also wrote very factual histories of Yorkshire. It's fair to say Appleby drew influence from him.

Dad has written out a chit for 13 items bought from Hollett on 31 March 1980. Three, including the classic *71 Not Out* (£10), go to Brown. Dad also bought beagling and otter-hunting books from Hollett. We'd just bought an otterhound for £100. He was named Hotspur, after

Harry Hotspur the king of Northumberland, rather than Spurs. My Dad became the local big dog man, as well as the local cricket man.

27 May 1980: Brown says there's often nothing to buy in the shops he visits now. He also would be delighted to see us again but not until the first week of August, as he's moving. Guess where we went on holiday that year?

Chapter 13

## *The Borderer*

AT ABOUT this time, Appleby started editing the monthly Carlisle Rotary Club newsletter *The Borderer*. He kept the pieces he wrote (and my mother typed, reluctantly) in folders for more than 30 years.

Typical newsletter notices were about:

Visit to Windscale nuclear reprocessing plant – Vocational Service Committee

Salvage paper collection

Talking Books for the Blind

Quiz

Clay pigeon shooting

Burns nights

'Hunger' charity suppers

Golf competitions

Italian-style lunches

A treasure hunt – driving round the Border country looking for clues

Cultural evenings. Carlisle was not a very cultural city, partly caused by its out-on-a-limb northern location, close to nowhere, and partly because of the Government State Management Scheme that nationalised pubs, beer and restaurants during World War One. The beer was all the same, expensive and weak, the opening hours were short and the only food available in town was in the pubs, and that was all the same too.

This was all to stop the thousands of munitions workers (often Irish navvies who the government believed may turn revolutionary while drunk) based nearby at Gretna armament factories where they made cordite explosives, coming to town and drinking. They could also possibly have smashed up the town when drunk and even blown up the factory when hungover, or at the least not produced enough incendiary devices. Carlisle State Licensing lasted until 1973. It seemed the government, and everyone else, had forgotten about Carlisle. If they'd ever heard of it in the first place.

Attendance statistics (in great detail).

Fundraising updates, e.g., caravan of charity supplies to Yugoslavia: 'Talk about service before self,' wrote Appleby when a Rotarian drove a laden self-contained trailer-based recreational vehicle across Europe.

Photographic evening: 'An equal number put their names down and didn't bother to turn up or tell anyone. A disgraceful display of bad manners. "My wife won't let me out" is not an acceptable excuse. This column is sometimes decried for urging more members to attend such functions as Charter Night. "Why can't he be quiet," they say. "We are old enough to make our minds up as to what we wish to do." True enough but we are unabashed. Rotary is dedicated to fellowship and service. The fellowship part is generally fairly easy but service is equally important and we lose a bit of self-respect once it is lost.'

Anniversaries: e.g. Foreign Legion: 'What caused this mixed bunch to be as good as they were? Discipline and esprit de corps i.e., service, is the answer.'

Observations: 'If Robert Browning was to return from abroad now he would most likely find that he couldn't land because of a strike by the wretched air traffic controllers or delayed because of "industrial action" by customs officers. When I was a boy, officers did not go on strike nor should people who claim officer status now. It is surely incumbent upon Rotarians to stand firm against this encroaching evil and do their duty as best they can. If in doubt, apply the Rotary Four Way Test:

1. Is it the truth?
2. Is it fair to all concerned?
3. Will it build goodwill or better friendship?
4. Will it be beneficial to all concerned?

Is there a message for Rotarians here?'

Chapter 14

# Old Trafford: Lancashire v Yorkshire, 23, 25, 27 August 1980

PROBABLY MY classic Yorkshire team. Boycott, Lumb, Athey, Hampshire, Love, Bairstow, Carrick, Old, Sidebottom, Stevenson, Cope.

Boycott, who we probably know enough about. The Boycott who signed his autograph for me when I carried his cricket bag at Bradford Park Avenue. Back then, he'd only sign if you did a job for him. From his mark one Ford Granada up the wooden steps to the dressing room where Simon Dennis and the rest of them looked up as they applied their eye-wateringly pungent liniment and adjusted their jockstraps, with their hairy legs and clip clop boots all in a dour atmosphere in a gloomy, windowless room.

They looked like they were off down the pit for a double shift. I remember my Dad asking for the details about the dirty white walls and wooden benches of the rickety Victorian pavilion, and the clock on the small grandstand. Park Avenue closed in 1985. 'They couldn't afford the improvements,' Yorkies said, in their best Alan Bennett whiny voices.

Phil Carrick had signed up the side of the 10p scorecard below the Schweppes County Championship logo. 'Today's cricket balls donated by Philip Glennon Associates Pension Schemes of Stockport.'

Carrick was the last in the line of the Yorkshire slow left armers, after Wilfred Rhodes (4,104 wickets, which I know off by heart having been tested on the way to the match by my Dad), Verity (who I wrote a school project on the next year featuring a pencil crayon picture of him in his Green Howard uniform shooting a pistol because he died in the war in 1943), the rebel Johnny Wardle (who we once saw adjudicate a Gillette Cup one-day match), Don Wilson (who coached Cumberland's future England wicketkeeper Paul Nixon, who I played against at school when he was with the MCC youngsters at Lord's.)

Carrick was a trier, always frowning, fielding close, waiting to bowl his maidens, always unlucky. He suffered in comparison with his predecessors. All the Yorkshire team did, except Boycott.

Richard Lumb, another glum-looking bloke, told me to 'gum it in, lad', when he pulled a page out of my autograph book (accidently). At least he signed readily, not like Boycs. Opener Lumb and middle-order bat Jim Love used to share Benson and Hedges cigs sitting on the benches in front of the pavilion.

As a kid, Geoffrey Boycott was my hero, simply because he scored most runs, at the best average. Another reason was he was hard to get. His autograph, that is.

He'd sit on the front of the pavilion at Headingley next to John Hampshire and say, loud enough for the autograph hunters to hear: 'I'm not signing today.'

Everyone else signed, including Hampshire. We got most of them as they left the ground smelling of Brut after the day's play on the way to their sponsored saloon cars. They drove off together to the pub. Boycott left on his own, talking to no one.

One day me and my Dad buggered off to Bradford Park Avenue, near my grandmother's house in Baildon, where, of course, he told me yet again that the old Yorkshire batsman Ticker Mitchell had lived across the road.

It was 1980. As we were staying nearby at Granny's, we could get to the ground early to hang around the car park for a few hours. I'd pestered my Dad – he didn't need much persuasion – to get there straight after breakfast, which Granny called 'break-fast', so I could maybe get the one signature I was missing – Sir Geoffrey.

Eventually, the players started to arrive. Hampshire, Chris Old, Arnie Sidebottom, Graham Stevenson, David Bairstow, Neil Hartley, Jim Love, Bill Athey, Howard Cooper, Alan Ramage and 12th man Dennis – they all signed.

Sir Geoffrey drove in piloting a yellow mark one Ford Granada. The rest mostly had more modest cars – maybe Cortinas or Cavaliers. Me and a few boys hung about forlornly, hoping he'd sign for once. I was at the front.

'Carry my bag and I'll sign,' said Boycs. He opened the boot and passed me his cricket coffin, which was about my

size. I heaved it after him towards the rickety, Victorian
pavilion. Back down at the bottom of the steps, I told my
Dad all about it. The old Tykes nearby joined in. 'Boycott's
a miserable bugger.'

Boycott scored 66 that Sunday. *Wisden* said Yorkshire
lost 'handicapped by a slow opening stand of 66 in 23 overs
by Boycott and Hampshire'. Athey and Love 'repaired some
of the damage' but there was 'poor bowling' – Ramage and
Cooper both went for six an over as Younis Ahmed scored
98 not out for Glamorgan, which caused much chuntering
among the disappointed thousands watching.

Bradford Park Avenue's days were already numbered.
The football team had left in 1973, then gone defunct. The
pavilion was demolished six years later in 1986, the year
Boycott retired.

Athey had gone to Gloucestershire by then, but a few
years earlier, he was the one Appleby most wanted to do
well, because he was a trier from the Boro, the 'Athens of
the north', as the old man never failed to call it. My Dad
was on nodding terms with Bill's Dad Colin, Acklam
Park's groundsman. Colin was a Boro face. My Dad left
Boro 40 years before but when we went back he looked
for people he knew and hoped they remembered him.
They never did anymore. People like Mays, another
Colin, who became a High Commissioner to the Bahamas
at one point, and who Appleby rediscovered, and sent
a Christmas card, one of a couple of hundred recipient
names listed in his precious exercise book.

My Dad could always remember everything (that he
was interested in), and he was good with faces. At Old

Trafford in 1980, Brian Statham walked by in the car park. Not that I knew he was Brian Statham, the opening bowling partner of Fred Trueman, the most successful England opening pair of all time (at the time). 'Quick, that's Brian Statham, get his autograph,' my Dad said. Statham, already looking old and worn (he died in 2000 aged 69) signed. I suggested Statham must have got wickets from batsmen avoiding Trueman, because we all know about Trueman, he was the best. My Dad wouldn't have a bad word said about Statham, who got on with the job and didn't boast like Trueman. He reminded Appleby of warm summer days in the 1950s.

Statham was on the Lancashire committee, but he was skint. In 1969, a second benefit year raised only £1,850 compared to over £13,800 for his 1961 benefit. Trueman organised some fundraising dinners for Statham in 1989. My Dad was generous too. He said 'It's alright if Lancashire win it every now and again' after I got a bit enthusiastic about Yorkshire winning (not that Yorkshire won the County Championship between 1968 and 2000).

I changed my attitude. I'd rather be a cricket fan than a fan of Manchester United (rather than football as a whole), who are also, I think, based at Old Trafford. My Dad also got me to stop saying things were 'rubbish'. I hear it from my children now. My Dad shouted at me once, probably after Stuart Hartley or Colin Johnson got a duck: 'He's not bloody rubbish. No one's rubbish. That's a bloody stupid word. Don't use it.'

Close to where I got Statham's autograph a few years later I queued for Derek Randall's. 'Arkle' was a characterful batsman of the 1970s and 1980s. He was near the end and I was too, of my autograph hunting career. I decided Randall was a whacky character and wouldn't mind if I queued again for another signature. He said, a bit like Ringo Starr but not as bad (Ringo would never sign): 'I'll only sign once.' Starr used to go to Chelsea Flower Show and men with piles of Beatles records would stand at the edge of crowds trying to get him to sign stuff so they could sell it. He sounded off once: 'I'm not signing ANYTHING. You might as well go NOW.' His signature was once worth about £80. It's gone up to several hundred pounds since he imposed the ban in 2008.

At the match, the players and the play was what we talked about. Bloody Boycott, bloody Bairstow – Bluey once stomped to the boundary to berate a spectator who shouted 'get a long stop' when the wicketkeeper let through some byes. That was often the way at Headingley, and on Sunday afternoon, when the pubs were shut, you could drink at the ground and get boisterous. Once they chucked the hired seat cushions at Kent's West Indian John Shepherd. A young steward picked them up in despair, as the cushions flew down on him faster than he could gather them.

Then there was Chris Old, who ended up behind the tills at Sainsbury's in Truro, after running a chippy on a Cornish beach not too far away at Praa Sands. At that match in 1980, I played behind the sightscreen with his twin blonde sons. The tennis ball went on to the outfield. The crowd mumbled disapproval as I ran on to get it.

Old's brother Alan once stayed at ours. I mainly remember that he didn't drink milk. He slept under a winceyette blanket in the spare room with its two single beds after a charity match at Edenside, Carlisle. This was when he and younger brother Chris and some more Yorkshire players took on a local team. Boycott was not there I don't think. Appleby told a tale about how, at the bar, after the match, at midnight, one player offered to buy a round for those left standing, which wasn't many.

Sidebottom, ex-Manchester United goalkeeper, father of Ryan, bowled well albeit with a wince on his face, and was one of the lower-order players still left to come in who might save the day.

Umpires were Ron Aspinall and Dave Halfyard. Aspinall was ex-Yorkshire and Durham. Halfyard drove a camper van round the grounds with 360,000 miles on the clock. He lived for the game. This is what we talked about as the match went on.

Being a fan becomes a progression, from watching them, reading about them, writing to them, talking to them, writing about them, autographs, hearing them, having snatched conversations, hearing them speaking at events, then MC-ing those sportsmen's dinners. And these days, following them on Twitter, and taking a selfie with them.

Chapter 15

# Autograph books

BY JUNE 1980 EK Brown is offering Appleby commission on *Wisdens* that Appleby is buying locally.

10 July 1980. Appleby sends 21 *Wisdens* and gets offered £80 plus £4.01 postage.

Appleby has written a list of cricket books 'acquired on holiday 4 August 1980'. We'd gone to Cornwall again, mostly to see Brown.

On the list, there's some *Scores & Biographies*, autographs of 1930 Australians at £15, autographs of 1930/31 tour members of MCC to South Africa at £5 and the England v Australia scorecard at The Oval 1926 at £25. The holiday was with us lot, and the caravan.

We were at Weston-super-Mare for Somerset v Yorkshire on 6 August 1980, stopping off for the day and night on the way south. My mother told me: 'I insisted on a proper holiday or he would not have taken any.'

This was on the way back from Cornwall. Our caravan was a Thomson, an old Scottish manufacturer that went out of business around this time as Britain hit recession.

It was like a tin can on wheels. A bit of its fascia fell off near Wells and I nearly got run over when we all got out of the car to find it.

In Cornwall 'soon after a water tower is seen' – as the instructions to get there from the Caravan Club said – just after the village of London Apprentice, we turned off to the farm where we stayed for two weeks in a field. We went to the beach every day, apart from when we drove to Liskeard to see Brown. I played cricket with my Dad, for the first time really.

I'd bowl a tennis ball and he'd hit it and tell me where it might have got caught: 'Straight to mid-on, that one.'

'Could I have caught it?'

'You would have given that one a good go. Maybe when you are a year or two older.'

He had his mind on other things – Brown's cricket books most likely. I'd inherited his sporting ability, if not his tenacity. Walking the walk is a sensitive area for the sports fan. 'Do you play?' is a common question.

We were both more at home at the match, a special occasion with all the rituals. The autograph books, filling in the scorecard, notes on the back of statistical landmarks, the sandwiches, the ice creams, the looking for tales to take home.

Weston 'super-duper' Mare was a festival ground. Most counties stopped their out-ground fixtures in the 1990s because of the expense, but for people like us who watched most of our matches on holiday they provided an introduction. As did the minor county v first-class Gillette/NatWest first round matches, which are now long gone.

Somerset's openers were the now forgotten Martin Olive and the unforgettable Indian world record Test batsman, Sunil Gavaskar. Sunny was replacing Viv Richards, because the world's most exciting batsman was playing for West Indies. His giant fast bowling mate (6ft 8in) Joel Garner was too. Hallam Moseley, a bespectacled West Indian, plus Hugh Gore, a novice, and Colin Dredge, a local from Frome, led the attack.

On the scorecard is Gavaskar's autograph, scratchily written in a still warming-up biro, in the right place against his name in the batting order. Gore's is against his name, but upside down. Moseley's is correctly positioned. Vic Marks is scrawled across the card. Dredge's is neatly written at the bottom of the line-up.

'Dredge is the best writer,' I said to my Dad after getting the signatures. I'd just wandered into the pavilion, which was as modest as one in a public park. The players were just sitting around at the front, even Gavaskar. I even weed next to him. I don't think I was meant to be in the pavilion toilets, but I was only nine and I needed to go.

'So he should be, I taught him,' said a woman nearby. Turned out she was Dredge's primary school teacher in Frome. Popplewell was a name that we thought was funny. So was Sidebottom. 'Sidebottom did a Popplewell' was a line Appleby used for the rest of his life. Cricket writer and broadcaster Alan Gibson called Dredge 'the demon of Frome'. Appleby liked facts more than Gibson's rambles around the match, and he disapproved, not of Gibson's dangerous drinking, but of his inability to hold it. That's why he liked John Arlott, who stuck to facts, added bits of purple and intellectualism, was big on books and could hold his booze.

There were a couple of unusual signatures. Yorkshire reserves Neil Crawford and Jim Airey and Geoff Cope (twice) signed in the sun in those halcyon self-conscious pre-teen days. I remember being at my Aunty Sybil's with the extended Appleby family one Sunday after we'd all driven over to Sunniside in the north-east from Carlisle. My Dad said: 'Show them your bowling, Matthew.' I did – in front of everyone in the sitting room. No one said anything, It was easier at the cricket. Just talk about that.

Remember that thing about being a fan when you collect favourite players to support through links to them, often self-created? Dredge was now on the list. There was Old and Athey. Milburn was an even better one. Geoff Holmes, a Geordie at Glamorgan. Paul Smith, a Geordie who played for Warwickshire. Boycs. It was more about individuals doing well than a team. Cricket wasn't that partisan then.

Alan Ross's poem *Cricket at Brighton* could have been written about Weston or any another festival, going on about people 'decanting' from trains with 'baskets, litter and opinions' and John Langridge's 'unfussed' singles.

The often-repeated Yorkshire cricket poem is more succinct: Harold Pinter to fellow playwright Simon Gray: 'I saw Len Hutton in his prime. Another time, another time.'

That's the one where Gray asked Pinter if he'd read it. 'I haven't finished it yet,' he replied.

Chapter 16

# Parsons

IT'S 11 February 1981. EK Brown talks of his old mate Jack Parsons' funeral, with only Bob Wyatt, who lived in Cornwall, sprightly at 81, of well-known cricketers attending. Parsons was born in Oxford where his father was a chef at Brasenose College. He worked at Humber Cars in Coventry before becoming a prominent Warwickshire batsman from 1910–36, dates split by his war service, during which he won the Military Cross after being one of the few survivors of a cavalry charge which secured Jerusalem. He probably would have played for England but for his career break post-World War One, when he served in the Indian Army. He became a vicar during his playing days, switching from professional to amateurism and was vicar in Brown's adopted hometown of Liskeard after the war.

I've got the Parsons book Appleby bought from Brown, a signed memento worth maybe £20. But the book is more than that. South Lakes bookbinder Philip Brook's stamp is under the leather and jacquard printed board covers that surround the slim paperback. A coat of arms ex libris Edgar L Appleby bookplate is stuck on the front-end paper. Opposite that in Appleby's wobbly copperplate is written: 'Signed by Aubrey Hill below a photograph of Warwickshire team 1931 and identified by him.' Parsons is captain, in Wyatt's absence. The first day, 15 July, was lost. Alf Freeman and Wally Hardinge bowled 99 overs of spin (taking a joint 6-217) between them on the second. Bill Ashdown, the only man to play first-class cricket before World War One and after World War Two, caught and bowled Parsons for 11.

Brown says he won't bid in a 'blind auction' of the late AH Wagg, with books removed beforehand, including New Zealand annuals Brown had sent Wagg.

18 February 1981: Dad's bought six books including MA Noble's *The Game's The Thing* as presents to himself – he's 50 in ten days.

John Hurst wrote to Appleby about a 1926 Australians picture taken in Carlisle, wanting identifications. Appleby identified them and his caption is underneath the photograph of Whitehaven fan G. Palmer's Cumberland XI, on page 43 of Hurst's 1982 book *Cumberland County Cricket Club: A History*. Lancashire captain Tom Higson helped Palmer attract a strong home team. Although Jack Hobbs pulled out at the last minute, home players included Herbert Sutcliffe, Percy Holmes (who scored 94 not out), George Gunn, 'Dodge' Whysall (who died four years later of septicaemia after slipping on a dance floor), Patsy Hendren (who hit two sixes into what became Edenside's dry ski slope), Roy Kilner (died 18 months later of enteric fever), George Macaulay (died in 1940 of alcoholism-related pneumonia in Shetland) and Charlie Parker – not the American jazz saxophonist but a far more significant character (to my Dad), Gloucestershire spinner Charlie Parker, the third-highest first-class wicket-taker (3,278). Cumberland XI captain Roland Saint, a big-hitting, autocratic Carlisle chartered accountant, hit a boundary off the first ball and was bowled by Arthur Richardson with the second. Charlie Macartney hit a century in return and Hendren bowled a ball with an apple.

15 May 1981. Cumbria-based cricket writer Nico Craven (1925–2010) writes to Appleby how it is most useful to have someone like him to whom he can refer when it comes to facts and figures. He lived at Ponsonby in West Cumbria and wrote books about Gloucestershire CCC, whimsical rambles that were likely to include nostalgic references to the likes of Parker. He sent a copy to Dad, every one inscribed with his sincere thanks.

David Foot wrote an obituary of Craven in *The Guardian*. This was Footy, the West Country cricket writer I admired for his Laurie Lee style, who wrote about Harold Gimblett, sixes and cider, and later Botham-era Somerset. Foot wrote how Craven had been to Cheltenham Festival every year since 1935. Perhaps that's why we went to the Mike Procter hat-trick match, to see Nico. I went again, in 1999, when I was training to be a teacher and playing at Bredon CC. It was not the same without Dad in tow, although I told him the story of how, at Bredon, Tom Graveney once saw me bowl in the nets. 'Good shot,' said the rosy-cheeked epitome of stylish batting as the ball flew out into the car park.

On Nico, Foot said it took him three hours to stroll round the boundary, humming Cole Porter between overs and talking about Mike Procter's wrong-footed pace or Zaheer Abbas's 'graceful choirboy style'.

Old Harrovian bachelor Nico, an MBE, taught at an approved school in West Cumbria from 1950. He wrote more than 30 books in the end, self-published slim volumes of memories of Bomber Wells, Barnett, Parker and Goddard. Appleby could have written books himself, though not like Nico's because Dad's would be all facts and opinions. So it was through his book collection that he achieved recognition within his chosen field, cricket, in Cumbria anyway.

18 June 1981: Brown is interested to hear about my mother's venture. The old bookseller says it's better to specialise in one or two subjects as well as the general stuff, say Cumbria books and possibly cricket, or soccer if it goes better in the area. You then build up a regular clientele. He could let Appleby have some at a cheap rate when he comes down.

My mother had set up a market stall at Brampton market, on our yellow Formica fold-up kitchen table, selling whatever the locals would buy – mainly Mills & Boon romances for 35p each or three for £1.

Then among Appleby's archive there's a list of Carlisle CC scorer Alan Straker's books. Dad's written 'condition is critical' on the list, probably prompted by Brown, who he hoped to sell the swaps to. Dad got Sir Pelham Warner's

*Imperial Cricket* from Straker, the super deluxe, not just the limited edition. Thirty-odd years later I sat that book on his knees on a rare trek upstairs in Keswick to see the 'good stuff', when the weight of the book half sank him.

Chapter 17

# 1981 Ashes scrapbook

I KEPT a scrapbook in 1981, filled with Ashes cricket clippings from the *Daily Telegraph*.

My Dad bought the paper every day during our summer holidays and I cut out the reports, beginning with 'Michael Melford from Headingley', the 'THIRD TEST AT HEADINGLEY' as I underlined my headline. The big picture was of England captain Mike Brearley 'sharing a joke' with bearded England star Ian Botham. It was captioned: 'Mike Brearley, restored to the England captaincy, pictured at Headingley yesterday with Ian Botham, who stood down from the post after the second Test.'

'Thurs July 16th, 1981' I'd written at the top, because that was the date in question.

Melford led the preview to the match with a now forgotten controversy about Australia's best bowler Dennis Lillee changing his shirt.

At the end of the article, Melford writes about '*Wisben Book of Cricket Records*' [sic] mentioning Bradman's 334 in 1930 at Headingley, scored in the month my Dad was conceived (hard to imagine). Melford speculatively points out that England opener Geoffrey Boycott will not reach Wilfred Rhodes' record of 881 appearances for Yorkshire (a figure my Dad knew by heart) until 2017, when he will be 77. 'Even his prodigious patience may be tested.'

By the end of the match, all this would be forgotten, because Headingley '81, the first Test I ever went to, is the best-known match of the era.

17 July: 'Dyson (102) Makes England Pay For Dropped Chances'. The picture was of Dyson edging Botham, with Brearley and England fast bowler Bob Willis looking on in anguish. Dyson scored 102. England bowled 82 overs. Chris Old took 0/46 from 26 overs, mainly aimed – and left – just outside off stump.

18 July: 'Hughes & Yallop Consolidate But Botham Hits Back'. Botham ended with 6-95. Australia declared at 401/9. England were 7/0. All this was still the prelude.

The next morning, at seven o'clock, my Dad and I packed the T-reg metallic duck egg blue Austin Princess with its new smelling, scratchy-Dralon and set off from Carlisle to Leeds, down the M6 to Penrith, over to Scotch Corner on the A66, down to Leeds, parking in 'a place I know' two miles from the ground. All the way, he was anniversary-ing, which of his ancestors lived where-ing, and 'when I was in the Boys-ing'.

'England Bowlers to Blame for Day of Disaster', titled Melford's sub-editors. A German sub-editor would be nicknamed U-Boat, Appleby would have joked. What we saw was England score 174, then 2/1 on a gloomy day at the ugly Leeds ground, which had a brick pavilion that butted on to the boundary, a stand that backed-to-back with Leeds Rugby League, and an unmade car park where I'd stand waiting for autographs.

Mr Smith was at the gate, that old Tyke in a medical orderly's coat, selling scorecards, as he'd done since before the war. 'I remember Len Hutton saying, "Good morning Mr Smith" to him in 1946,' my Dad said, again. The story, part of the folklore we built around the day, would be told many more times until it became like an anecdote ripe for sticking in a cricket book.

Melford's piece talked up Australia's bowlers, but only in comparison to England's Willis (0-72), Old (0-91 off 43) and Graham Dilley (2-78). Botham was excused criticism.

We were laden with sandwiches, salmon paste, cheese and celery with mayonnaise, PEK ham, all in crusty white bread. We'd eaten them all by midday. Boycott was still in. Dennis Lillee was celebrating his 32nd birthday, which seemed pretty old to me, aged 10. He ran in to bowl like a racehorse (if thoroughbreds had moustaches and yellow towelling headbands). But mostly it was Terry Alderman, who struggled in like he had his knees glued together, but still got out Graham Gooch, Mike Brearley (and later Old). Lillee shifted Mike Gatting, grey-haired wicketkeeper Bob Taylor and Graham Dilley (which rhymed, which I liked and mentioned, adding in a fantasy [Peter] Willey just for fun). Geoff Lawson, who bucked in like a pony and had a long face like a nag bowled Boycs for a slow (of course) 12. I wasn't so bothered after that, because of my hero worship of the great opener. Botham smashed 50. England followed on. Gooch was out again, for the second time in a day. After close of play, Lawson had a queue a mile long, signing in the middle of the pitch. 'What a great bloke,' I said to my Dad as we eked the most out of the day.

At the bookies that night as we drove home you could get 500/1 on an England win, so the story goes. At least my story went that way whenever I talked about the Test in later years. The next day Botham hit 145 not out, and the next Bob Willis was fired up and England won.

*The Borderer* August 1981: 'Also on the credit side this month we have Ian Botham; every generation claims that the game is not what it was or has gone to the dogs or that there are no personalities in the game anymore. Botham has certainly scotched that for a while. He bats in the classical manner. He attacked the bowling and hits hard high and often with fearsome power and comparing him with a normal batsman is like comparing a carthorse with a Derby winner. The writer advocates his immediate appointment as Home Secretary instead of the present incumbent in that post, if there is one.' (Local MP Willie Whitelaw was Home Secretary).

Chapter 18

# YCCC sunhat

HAWKSDALE 1981. EDGAR Appleby 55 retired hurt.
This was the beginning of the end for my Dad. He
wasn't a natural player. He was ambidextrous, batted right-
handed and bowled left. Like so many from his generation,
he was changed from being a lefty to orthodox. He threw
left-handed too.

Dad's whites were cotton, baggy and old and creamy-
yellow round the edges. He dubbined his boots and wore
a hand-knitted jumper (by my Mum), plus a faded extra-
large Yorkshire CCC bucket hat. 'Not too tight around
the arms' he liked. The whites were too short. His bag
was a brown canvas ex-Navy type thing. Probably Korean
bunfight-era (where he'd served in the Navy and a bit of
flak hit his locker, making a hole in his dictionary which
opened at the page with 'lead' at the top). About this time,
my brother sent that tale to the comic *Victor*'s letters pages
and won £5. His bat was wrapped in tape and stank of
linseed. He had his own stuff but didn't splash out. 'Waste
not want not.' He did bring plenty of tea. You had to bring

your own. There were loads of sandwiches, mostly tinned meat, which you shared among the team. One player, a fast bowler who was not from Jamaica, always brought two Jamaica ginger cakes. In fact, hardly anyone from Carlisle was from anywhere else and Jamaica ginger cakes were seen as pretty exotic fare.

Dad stood in the gully. 'There's nothing more satisfying than taking a catch,' he used to say. He didn't run much. Gully's a good position for that. He'd be 'pitch it upping' from there to the bowlers. He'd open the batting and when out, often run out, he'd be 'run-upping' from the bench on the boundary.

Hawksdale played at the Sheepmount, that desolate set of poplar-lined fields round the back of the river with jerry-built changing rooms, screwed-down benches and two-foot-high scoreboards.

Captain was Don Renyard: 'You're just like y'Dad,' he said, when I rang him, to find out about Ingrams.

Another senior team member was a 1950s-styled Carlisle bloke. Once, he took off his wicketkeeping gloves to show me how to field (at third man). He ran about sweeping up the ball, while I fielded at fly third man, watching. It was the nerves that made me fumble. A younger pair of players once ribbed me for only being interested in cricket. They'd just been to a Smiths gig at Carlisle Market Hall, in 1984. I actually liked The Smiths. I went next time they came, in 1986, and climbed on stage, using guitarist Johnny Marr's leg as a handhold.

Renyard said on the end of the phone from Carlisle: 'There's only one still playin'. He's in his fifties now. Me and Jimmy Skinner are groundsmen at the new ground; it's our own ground at Garlands on the right-hand side of Creighton rugby club.' The Sheepmount? 'We moved from there 20 year ago.'

Renyard explained how the club ended up there, on the grounds of the old mental hospital south of Carlisle. I wanted to know about my Dad. He talked about the Hawksdale team back in the day: 'We were excellent at the time. We won everything for years. In the Junior Cup, we were winners or runner-up every year. Now we've got a lovely ground, but not a very good team.'

I still wanted to know what happened with Appleby, in that last game. It wasn't what I remembered: 'We were playing Morton at Scotby and he did his knee and then returned for a cup game.'

That was it. Plus this: 'He was a character. I last saw him 18 months ago at Keswick. He was on a mobility scooter. We had a talk.'

*WG Grace batting in the nets at Lord's Cricket Ground, 1895 with a large crowd watching.*

*Star: WG Grace was the first sporting celebrity and a signed limited edition of his 1891 book* Cricket *is a cornerstone of many collections, including Edgar Appleby's.*

This Crown Quarto Edition de Luxe consists of 652 copies (and 10 Presentation copies), of which this is No. 481.

Signed *W. G. Grace*

Postcard: Surrey County Cricket Club from 1923. (top l-r) Andy Ducat, George Geary, William Abel, Thomas Shepherd, Andy Sandham and Alan Peach. (front l-r) Bill Hitch, Jack Hobbs, Percy Fender, Alfred Jeacocke and Bert Herbert. Cricket book collectors value Fender's tour books, such as Kissing the Rod.

Jack Hobbs displays his batting technique to fans in the nets.

*Alan Kippax, the Australian cricketer who wrote the book* Anti Body-Line, *about the 1932/33 Ashes series*

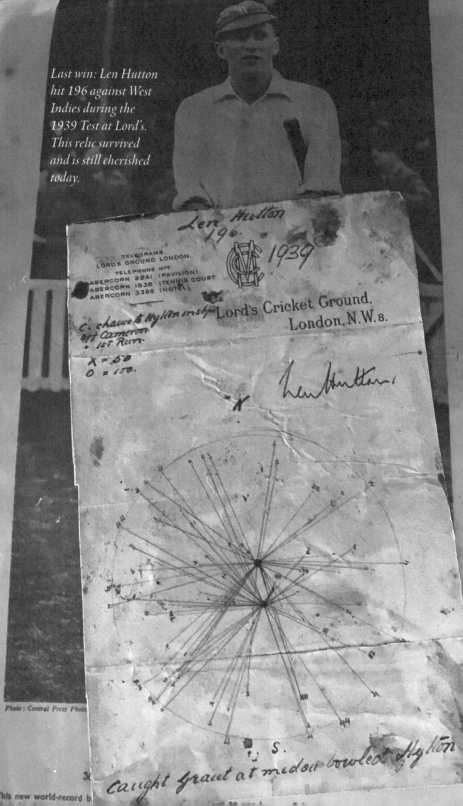

*Last win: Len Hutton hit 196 against West Indies during the 1939 Test at Lord's. This relic survived and is still cherished today.*

Len Hutton
196.
1939

The MCC leave for South Africa for the 1913/14 tour aboard the Saxon. Seated on the windlass (bottom, third right) is JWHT (Johnny) Douglas (captain), to his right is Sydney Barnes, and Frank Woolley. In 1930 Douglas drowned in the sea off Denmark, while trying to save his father.

Autographs: JWHT Douglas collected a remarkable set of signatures including Ranjitsinhji, CB Fry and Malcolm Campbell in this unique, if unprepossessing leather album.

*Youthful autograph hunters surround Don Bradman, Bill Johnston and Ernie Toshack (foreground) as they come in at the end of the day's play at Headingley, 23 July 1948. Appleby saw Bradman's final Test innings three weeks later.*

*Ollie: Enjoying a meal pre-season in April 1967 is 25-year-old Northamptonshire and England cricketer Colin Milburn, who said his 18+ stone weight helped his balance after newspaper talk of having to slim to regain his Test place.*

*Century of centuries: Geoff Boycott hit 191, his 100th century, at home ground Headingley for England against Australia in August 1977 and Appleby was there.*

YORKSHIRE COUNTY CRICKET CLUB | CROWN PAINTS were used to redecorate this ground | HEADINGLEY CRICKET GROUND, LEEDS

**FOURTH TEST MATCH**

8p

# ENGLAND v. AUSTRALIA

8p

THURSDAY, FRIDAY, SATURDAY, MONDAY & TUESDAY, 11th, 12th, 13th, 15th & 16th AUGUST, 1977

**ENGLAND**

First Innings

*1—J. M. Brearley c Marsh b Thomson ... 0
2—G. Boycott c Chappell b Pascoe ......191
3—R. A. Woolmer c Chappell b Thomson 37
4—D. W. Randall lbw b Pascoe .......... 20
5—A. W. Greig b Thomson ............... 43
6—G. R. J. Roope c Walters b Thomson 34
7—I. T. Botham b Bright ................ 0
†8—A. P. E. Knott lbw b Bright ......... 57
9—D. L. Underwood c Bright b Pascoe .. 6
10—M. J. Hendrick c Robinson b Pascoe . 4
11—R. G. D. Willis not out ............. 5

Extras... 39
Total...436

Second Innings

Extras...
Total...

**AUSTRALIA**

First Innings

1—R. B. McCosker run out ............. 27
2—I. C. Davis lbw b Hendrick .......... 0
*3—G. Chappell c Brearley b Hendrick ... 4
4—D. W. Hookes lbw b Botham ........ 24
5—K. D. Walters c Hendrick b Botham .. 4
6—R. D. Robinson
†7—R. W. Marsh
8—R. Bright
9—M. H. N. Walker
10—J. R. Thomson
11—L. S. Pascoe

Extras...
Total...

Second Innings

Extras.
Total.

**FALL OF WICKETS**

England:
First Innings: 1-0  2-82  3-105  4-201  5-275  6-398  7-398  8-412  9-422
Second Innings: 1-  2-  3-  4-  5-  6-  7-  8-  9-

Australia:
First Innings: 1-8  2-26  3-52  4-57  5-60  6-  7-  8-
Second Innings: 1-  2-  3-  4-  5-  6-  7-  8-

**Bowling Analysis**

| | Overs | Mdns. | Runs | Wkts. | | Overs | Mdns. | Runs |
|---|---|---|---|---|---|---|---|---|
| J. R. Thomson | 34 | 7 | 113 | 4 | | | | |
| M. H. N. Walker | 48 | 21 | 97 | 0 | | | | |
| L. S. Pascoe | 34.4 | 10 | 91 | 4 | | | | |
| K. D. Walters | 3 | 1 | 5 | 0 | | | | |
| R. Bright | 26 | 9 | 66 | 2 | | | | |
| G. Chappell | 10 | -2 | 25 | 0 | | | | |

* Denotes Captain

† Denotes Wicket-Keeper

Umpires:
W. E. ALLEY & W. L. BUDD

Scorers
E. I. LESTER & D. SHERWOOD

Hours of Play: First Second Third and Fourth Days, 11-30 a.m. to Fifth Day, 11-00 a.m. to 5-30 p.m. or 6-00 p.m.
Lunch: 1-30 p.m. to 2-10 p.m.     Tea: 4-15 p.m. to

**PREVIOUS RESULTS IN THE SERIES**

First Test — Lords — MATCH DRAWN.
Second Test — Old Trafford — ENGLAND won by 9 wickets.
Third Test — Trent Bridge — ENGLAND won by 7 wickets.

**NEXT MATCH IN YORKSHIRE**
YORKSHIRE v. LANCASHIRE at Bradford
20th, 22nd and 23rd August, 1977

Advertising Contractors: Bermitz Publicity, Ferres Chambers, Whitefriargate, Hull

Completed copies of this Score Card (20p each post free) are available
Norton & Wright Ltd., The Sports Printers, 67-79 Kirkstall Road, Le

# Cornhill Insurance Test Series

| Cornhill Team Awards | |
|---|---|
| Winner of the Series | £3,000 |
| England Match Win | £1,750 |

| Cornhill Player Awards | |
|---|---|
| Player of the Series | £700 |
| Player of each Match | £350 |

15p

# England v. Australia

15p

## Third Test Match

Thursday, Friday, Saturday, Monday & Tuesday, 16th, 17th, 18th, 20th & 21st July 1981

### ENGLAND

| First Innings | | Second Innings | |
|---|---|---|---|
| 1—G. Boycott | b Lawson | c Alderman b Lillee | 0 |
| 2—G. A. Gooch | | | |
| *3—J. M. Brearley | | | |
| 4—D. I. Gower | | | |
| 5—M. W. Gatting | | | |
| 6—P. Willey | | | |
| 7—I. T. Botham | | 50 | |
| †8—R. W. Taylor | c Marsh b Lillee | 5 | |
| 9—R. G. D. Willis | c and b Lillee | 13 | |
| 10—G. R. Dilley | | 0 | |
| 11—C. M. Old | c Border b Alderman | 0 | |
| Extras | | 5 | Extras |
| Total (for 0 wkt) | | 174 | Total |

FALL OF WICKETS—

First Innings: 1-12 2-40 3-42 4-84 5-87 6-112 7-148 8-166 9-167

Second Innings: 1-0 2- 3- 4- 5- 6- 7- 8- 9-

| Bowlers | Overs | Mdns. | Runs | Wkts. | Bowlers | Overs | Mdns. | Runs | Wkts. |
|---|---|---|---|---|---|---|---|---|---|
| Lillee | 1 | 0 | 0 | 1 | | | | | |
| Alderman | 1 | 0 | 1 | | | | | | |

*Denotes Captain  †Denotes Wicket Keeper

Umpires: B. J. Meyer and D. L. Evans
Scorers: E. I. Lester and D. Sherwood

### AUSTRALIA

| First Innings | | | Second Innings |
|---|---|---|---|
| 1—J. Dyson | b Dilley | 102 | |
| 2—G. M. Wood | lbw Botham | 34 | |
| 3—T. M. Chappell | c Taylor b Willey | 27 | |
| *4—K. J. Hughes | c and b Botham | 89 | |
| 5—G. N. Yallop | c Taylor b Botham | 58 | |
| 6—A. R. Border | lbw Botham | 8 | |
| †7—R. W. Marsh | b Botham | 28 | |
| 8—R. J. Bright | b Dilley | 7 | |
| 9—D. K. Lillee | not out | 3 | |
| 10—G. F. Lawson | c Taylor b Botham | 13 | |
| 11—T. M. Alderman | | | |
| Extras | | 32 | Extras |
| Total (for 9 wickets declared) | | 401 | Total |

FALL OF WICKETS—

First Innings: 1-55 2-149 3-196 4-220 5-332 6-354 7-357 8-396 9-401

Second Innings: 1- 2- 3- 4- 5- 6- 7- 8- 9-

| Bowlers | Overs | Mdns. | Runs | Wkts. | Bowlers | Overs | Mdns. | Runs | Wkts. |
|---|---|---|---|---|---|---|---|---|---|
| Willis | 20 | 8 | 72 | 0 | | | | | |
| Old | 43 | 14 | 91 | 0 | | | | | |
| Dilley | 27 | 4 | 78 | 2 | | | | | |
| Botham | 38.2 | 11 | 95 | 6 | | | | | |
| Willey | 13 | 2 | 31 | 1 | | | | | |
| Boycott | 3 | 2 | 2 | 0 | | | | | |

Hours of Play: Thursday to Monday, 11.00 a.m. to 6.00 p.m.

Tuesday, 10.30 a.m. to 5.00 p.m. or 5.30 p.m.   Tea: 3.40 to 4.00 p.m.

Lunch: 1.00 p.m. to 1.40 p.m. (Tuesday 12.30 p.m. to 1.10 p.m.)   (Tuesday 3.10 p.m. to 3.30 p.m.)

The 1982 Headingley Test ENGLAND v. PAKISTAN (26th—31st August)

# Cornhill Insurance Group

Head Office: 32 Cornhill, London, EC3V 3LJ

Cornhill Insurance Test Series

*Famous innings: Appleby and the author attended the day before Ian Botham's legendary Ashes knock at Headingley in 1981.*

## Chapter 19

# Sportsmen's dinners

THERE'S A Cumbria Celebrity sports dinner menu in the folder of Muffs' stuff. My mum had rammed all his papers in folders, annoyed that he didn't look after the letters, scorecards, pictures, memorabilia – the bumf – properly. It was all mixed up. He just liked having it there. Having the memories to hand is part of the fan's life. It's all very well having them upstairs, but you need them on the bookshelf nearby. As long as you know they're there.

This is for Sports Aid Foundation (Northern) Limited, organised by Carlisle United Promotions, at Shepherd's Inn, Carlisle, 3 May 1981. I was in my last year at Houghton primary school.

Dad got the menu signed for me. Jonjo O'Neill, Bob Stokoe, Ivor Broadis, Malcolm Allison, Chris Balderstone. Jockey O'Neill rode, then bred, thoroughbreds not far away at Plumpton, near Penrith. Stokoe lived down the road from us. The current Carlisle United manager was best-known from wearing a trilby and car coat while running about on Wembley's pitch celebrating Sunderland's 1973

FA Cup Final win over Leeds United. A mile the other way lived Broadis, who was an old England cap and Carlisle player-manager who once sold himself to Sunderland (he got a good deal at £18,000). Allison was the talker, the motormouth, sheepskin coat, football manager turn, while Baldy was a local hero who once played for Leicestershire during the day, Doncaster Rovers at night then completed his century the next morning. You can't do that anymore.

The next local sports hero was about to make his name. Future Surrey CC medium-pacer Graham Monkhouse also played football at a good level. He was at his peak from 1983–85 with 40 wickets or more a season at a low average with his leg cutters. Monkey hit a century once too and would have prospered in today's limited-overs-dominated game. Not a bad career for a player who had to make the grade from Cumberland. In the end, he went back to egg farming after starting at Cumberland in 1973 and playing for Surrey from 1980–87. That just shows how hard it is to make it from a backwater and why the fan from the sticks backs his man so much.

John Moyes and Adrian Gray were playing in 1973. I had played against Moyes, edged and was sledged. Turns out he was a socialist, Renault 4-driving teacher, which I wouldn't have guessed while he was calling 14-year-old me 'lucky'. Gray was a Border TV type – you got a few as ITV opened franchises in the sticks. He captained Yorkshire Cricket Federation juniors in 1957 with future first-class players John Hampshire and Duncan Fearnley opening, Barrie Whittingham (who played for Nottinghamshire then Cumberland alongside Gray), Tony Clarkson and

Barry Stead in the team. The next year Gray captained Yorkshire under-18s, with John Hampshire and Geoffrey Boycott playing.

The broadcaster was a mate of David Lamb, another radio type, who died in Paris after a mugging following the Prix de l'Arc de Triomphe. Lamb lived near us, in the same road as Jimmy Little, who opened the bowling for Cumberland, sent a thank you letter about my Dad's speech, and died tragically aged 40. The Carlisle CC pavilion extension was named after him. Stokoe lived in the next road, close to Carlisle United full-back Bobby Parker and his basset hound. They were all at the dinner.

The menu was:

> Prawn Cocktail
> Vegetable Soup
> Roast Beef and Horseradish Sauce, Roast and Creamed Potatoes, French Beans and Cauliflower-au-Gratin
> Fresh Fruit Salad and Fresh Cream or Lemon Mousse
> Cheese and Biscuits
> Coffee

'As long as there was loads,' as my Dad would say. He'd have taken leftovers from neighbours' plates and had seconds. Monkhouse (i.e., Graham's family) Eggs were a sponsor. The draw prizes included a bottle of Harvey's Bristol Cream, a Rudi Krol Vancouver Whitecaps football shirt, 1½lb box of chocolates and a £5 voucher from local food factory Cavray. My Dad did the raffle, and the intros.

What he said was not recorded, but his *Borderer* writings probably give a flavour.

There's another sportsman's dinner card, Rotary Club of Carlisle on 28 October 1980 at Shepherd's Inn, which was a country club-style barn on an industrial estate in Carlisle, near the M6, near the football ground, near where it floods. Appleby worked on an industrial estate at the other end of town called Kingmoor.

Rosehill, where Shepherd's Inn (now The Auctioneer) trades, was an auction mart really, for sheep. Dad was at the engineering end of town, and the sportsmen's dinners were at the rural end. This Rotary event was a fundraiser for Chris McKean's electric wheelchair. Chris had broken his neck playing rugby. He was playing alongside schoolmates Rob Andrew and fellow future England rugby player Rory Underwood in County Durham in 1978 when the tackle left him quadriplegic. He was just 15.

Appleby had joined Rotary in 1978. Rotary's brotherhood, mostly of provincial business owners and bank managers, was just right for him as a former Navy chief petty officer (the equivalent of a staff sergeant in the Army), bashing away as a director of a struggling firm.

Back to *The Borderer*:

A fellow Rotarian 'was duly presented with an illuminated address to commemorate his 40 years in Rotary, a figure that not many of us in Rotary will achieve'. The address was inscribed by a gifted club member, 'who must surely have served his apprenticeship in calligraphy under the

Venerable Bede at Jarrow Monastery. It is good to know that the Club has such artistic talent in its ranks.'

Another: 'There has been a lot of sympathy lately for [Great Train] robber Ronald Biggs and shoplifter Lady Isobel Barnett [a panellist on 1950s BBC radio programme *What's My Line* who was fined in 1980 for stealing a can of tuna and carton of cream worth 87p from the village shop]. Tragically, she took her own life after her exposure. As Rotarians, should we extend sympathy to cases like these? On balance, the answer must be NO! We must keep our feelings under control and if the writer didn't, he would have stolen half the books from the MCC Library at Lord's by now, as well as being apprehended for making lecherous advances to attractive females with plenty of money.'

And: 'It's good to be alive at the beginning of May, with the first-class cricket season and the weather warming up. It is the writer's difficult task to try and persuade his wife that she can now manage with the central heating turned down, or better still, off. There is not much chance of winning that one.'

There's some great signatures on the menu card under the 'Introduction of sporting personalities by Edgar L Appleby' blurb. He kept doing these for 30 years. Roger Uttley, the weather-beaten ex-England rugby player, signed. My Mum didn't know what to say to him at the dinner of Salmon Florida, Minestrone, Roast Beef and Black Forest Gateaux. This was posh food for the Shepherd's Inn. Lunch at Rotary on Wednesday's was £2.20. There was never enough meat (for Appleby). The pudding was heavy going. Even Appleby complained. He joked about the cabbage going on the stove at 2am. But he ate it all and helped other people too.

At the Chris McKean dinner were Jonjo O'Neill again, Balderstone, of Carlisle United, Leicestershire and England cricket fame, John Bell, the lawn green and indoor bowler, Broadis, and fell runner Joss Naylor MBE. And 1970s dinner-jacketed, frilly-shirted Welsh rugby comedian/singer Max Boyce was presenter of the electric chair. Thirty years on, and very lame, my Dad bought his own 'buggy'. 'I feel a fool,' he told my Mum, but he got used to it, and even made it into a motif. Garrulous Welsh rugby maven Cliff Morgan spoke at the McKean event. He's signed the front of the card alongside Uttley and Boyce. Master of ceremonies was Rotarian Edgar L Appleby.

*The Borderer* 4 October 1981: 'Cricket was again in the news in September. If, twenty years ago, you had suggested that Northamptonshire v Derbyshire at Lord's on a Saturday in September would have commanded a full house and at twenty minutes to eight in the evening that crowd (which included the writer) would have been sitting enthralled, you would not have been taken seriously, to say the least. Nevertheless, such did occur, and up in the Elysian Fields the immortal doctor will have stroked his beard and nodded in approval.

'As we get older, we are apt to say "things aren't what they used to be" or "standards are slipping", but here is something which has got better. May it not be so in other spheres? Perhaps, as Rotarians, we should be extolling the good fortune which surrounds us, instead of doing otherwise.'

3 October 1981: Brown and Appleby discuss *Scores & Biographies* as the next statistics-based cricket book series to collect for those who have all the *Wisdens*. Then there's red and green *Lillywhites*, which were *Wisden's* rival almanack. Some were coming over from South Africa at £35 each. Brown talked of the silly prices for editions of *Wisden*. The late cricketer/journalist/Old Etonian Robin Marlar had paid £580 plus 10% commission for *Wisden* 1885–87 at auction. These prices, far above those in Brown's catalogues, became the going rate.

The Appleby's book venture is progressing. Run of the mill books are where they start. Overheads are slight. They'd love to sell rare books, in time.

Brown sent six copies of the book *Alletson's Innings* at just 75p each, from the John Arlott collection, or 'stock' as Brown called it. Arlott wrote the slim monograph, published in a limited edition in 1957. The ones Brown sent were the ordinary issues, published by Epworth in 1958. Edwin Boaler Alletson had an Appleby-like physique, over 6ft and 15 stone, but was a pretty average pro for Nottinghamshire. Until, on 20 May 1911, he scored 189 in 82 minutes against Sussex at Hove, the last 142 in 40 minutes after lunch – fast even by Twenty20 standards.

Sixes broke clocks and smashed glasses on the bar as one over went for a then record 34 runs. In 1991, McKenzie published a third edition, including extra letters from those involved, of 250, shakily signed by Arlott, who died that year. That's the one I've got. Appleby will have had all three editions, worth anywhere between £10 and £120 for one signed by Arlott and given to RP Keigwin, who bowled at Alletson, though not in that match, played Wimbledon tennis champion Tony Wilding at university, translated Hans Christian Andersen fairy tales into English and was present when the German Fleet surrendered in 1918.

Appleby instigates 'Thumbnail Sketches' of Rotary Club members in *The Borderer*. He goes first.

'Edgar Lawson Appleby

'Born in Gateshead 28th February 1931 (a collection on the nearest Wednesday after that date would be appreciated). After being evacuated on the outbreak of war to Bishop Auckland, family moved to Middlesbrough (Second Division next season) in June 1940. Educated at Acklam Hall School, which, as far as it is known, has produced no scholars of note, but several well-known sportsmen.

'Joined Royal Navy as Artificer Apprentice 4th February 1947. After Apprenticeship at Rosyth, served in Korea 1951–53, Mediterranean 1954–55, Home waters, mainly Scotland, 1956–57 Malaya and Borneo 1958–60.

'Left Navy, aged 30, in February 1961, and joined firm of large boiler manufacturers. For the next six and a half years worked on boilers (mainly at Power Stations) at a number of places in England and Wales and also in Denmark, Eire, Finland, Spain and Kuwait.

'Married Susan Jackson from Bradford (no she isn't coloured) on St Swithin's Day (15th July) 1967 and it hasn't stopped raining since.

'Family consists of one daughter, 13 this month, and two sons, one 11 this month and one 10 in March.

'Moved to Carlisle on marriage to work for present engineering firm, now employing about 40 people, of which his cousin is Managing Director. This is what got him the job in the first place, but if you think that working with, or under, a relation is harmonious, you can think again.

'Interests, apart from family:

- Cricket. Playing (badly), watching it, reading about it and collecting cricket books. All additions to the library are welcome.
- Most Maritime matters, apart from Yachting and Pleasure Sailing.
- History, especially World War I and II.
- Travel, although family commitments and shortage of cash means that he now thinks about it but doesn't do it.
- Gardening and exercising large dog.
- The Rotary Club of Carlisle, which he thinks is a grand institution.
- Rugby Union. Football to a lesser extent. Interest decreased in inverse proportion to the players' length of hair, their antics after scoring a goal and the size of the transfer fees.
- Was press ganged on to Stanwix Rural Parish Council because nobody else would take the job on.
- Eating, although trying to cut down.
- Books, generally.
- Doing what his wife tells him to.'

## 4 April 1982 *The Borderer*

'As a self-confessed cricket fanatic, the Editor is often asked his opinion of the recent cricketing tour of South Africa. The unpalatable truth, gentlemen, is that top level sporting is getting to be sport no longer. Top tennis is pure showbiz, with a few contrived tantrums to keep the crowd amused.

'Top level golf exists for television coverage and fees. More third world countries play Test cricket, so it has become a political pawn with those nations. A few years ago, a sporting commission visited South Africa and recommended no further cricketing tours there until cricket was multi-racial. Non-racial cricket has now been achieved and a mixed cricketing tour could do nothing but good for all races in South Africa.

'It will not take place for political reasons, because the politicians now want more, and will want more again. The policy of appeasement never did work and how much appeasement will you have to give? Until they get another Idi Amin in power? Or will it be until the last white man is thrown out of South Africa and the last homestead burnt to the ground? It will be interesting to see how many of these countries will be supporting us in the Falklands crisis.'

On 26 May 1982 Appleby and Brown discuss Appleby's frustration about his unsuccessful knee operation.

A fortnight later, Brown offers £60 for *Wisdens* Appleby has for sale. He doesn't want 1950s but takes 1948, 1961–62 and four from the 1930s.

By July 1982 Brown and Appleby are talking about *Indian Cricket* 1982. Brown wants to hand over his UK dealership of the Indian annual. Dad of course said yes and becomes the UK dealer for *Indian Cricket*, and places his first advert in *Wisden Cricket Monthly*. *Indian Cricket Annual* 1982, now available for £5.50 including P&P from EL Appleby, 29 Millcroft, Carlisle, Cumbria CA3 OHX.

Chapter 20

# Yorkshire v Sussex 31 July–2 August 1982, Scarborough

WE STAYED in the caravan at Filey. My Dad thought the caravan was a good idea because he would be able to go to seaside cricket festivals, like Scarborough. And it would be cheap. 'This won't buy the baby a new hat,' Appleby would say, when we were idling. 'Trying to send me to the poorhouse,' he'd exclaim when we'd left the lights on.

Cementation Construction were hosts, the scorecard said. Catering was by Scarborough Cricket Club. The scorecard was 17p. Last year it was 15p, but 20p would have been a step too far. Scarborough had been the favourite holiday destination for many loyal Yorkshiremen since Victorian times, and particularly since 1896, when Yorkshire started playing at the elegant North Marine Road ground. The golden age of cricket saw marquees, flags and bands for the end of season festival, which included several exhibition matches, often featuring HG Leveson-Gower's XI against the tourists, and later DB

Close's team trying to relive the same spirit in the fret sea air, 90 years on, when Yorkshire were engaged in internal warfare, between Boycott fans and those who thought his selfishness was ruining the team.

In nearby Peasholm Park serious hobbyist men played out toy ship re-enactments of world war naval battles that every Bill Bryson-style travel book now wryly details. We'd watch in delight as they came down zipwires to bomb the model *Graf Spee* in the 'Battle of the River Plate'. This was all right up Appleby's shipping lane.

The scorecard advertisers also included Scarborough Building Society, promoting D.B. Close's XI v Pakistan Touring Team on Sept 1, 2 & 3. Close was born in the same month as my Dad and died at the end of the 2015 season, just as Yorkshire won the championship, which I saw them do at Lord's with Dad's old mate Sibdog. Ryan Sidebottom, mop-haired son of the 1980s flame-haired all-rounder Arnie, took four wickets in his first four overs, including a hat-trick. Luckily Sibson is a stickler for time-keeping and we saw it all from the white benches in front of the pavilion.

Yorkshire had become good again at the turn of the century after 30 years of strife. Boycs had made a success of the role of president. The loyalists still loved his plain-speaking Yorkshireman act, later as a TV commentator.

The programme advertises 'Boyes 18 bargain packed departments … catering for all your holiday requirements … lifts to all floors … smiles and smiles of bargains for all the family.' The advert shows the beach deckchairs and buckets abandoned with a signature saying 'Gone to

Boyes', pictured as a grand Victorian emporium, in a line drawing. Could have said 'Gone to Boycs', I thought.

I expected Boyes to be long gone, like Brown Muffs of Bradford.

But Boyes is now a 50-plus store discounter chain. They changed with the times.

Under the Boyes ad is one for Home Charm paints, from SPL (Holdings) of Batley. A paint pot styled as a cartoon batsman is smashing a six. I'd blacked out a tooth and given the bat a splice, back in 1982.

Other writing on the scorecard is more informative:

'Barclay dropped by Illingworth in gully when
4. 122/2.'
'Wells to 51 with 6 (long on) off Illy 140/3.'
On the back of the scorecard: 'Yorkshire 53/0
in 16 overs.'
'B(oycott) 23 L(umb) 23.'
Just as well we recorded that.
Then by me 'Boycott 52 out of 102-1 in 35 with
a four.'

The bits of scorecard I'd filled in show CM [Colin] Wells was not out 71. I'd see Wells later through the open door of the back of the pavilion.

Barclay, the posh captain (middle name Troutbeck) was 'ct Bairstow b Ramage 8'. So that 'dropped by Illy' was a bit of premature pessimism. My Dad was a bit like that. 'I doubt it' was one saying he'd often use, especially when I asked for a *John Mouse* book on a Saturday afternoon trip to Dring's bookshop in Carlisle, or if I asked if Yorkshire would win, or Boycs would get a century. The actual answer was usually: Yorkshire wouldn't, Boycs would. At Scarborough, my Mum later told me that she'd take us to the pool and he'd go to the match. We'd come along later. 'Remember the ladybirds,' she said. Kids don't forget a plague of ladybirds crunching underfoot, floating in their millions in the pool, coating every surface. I remembered the ladybirds.

And I remembered meeting the players. We were after autographs and Adrian Jones, Garth le Roux and Tony Pigott were warming up. Le Roux was a massive South African fast bowler with a handlebar moustache. My Dad was a fan. Jones was the English version of Le Roux – quick but often injured and not as scary. Pigott used to run up to bowl in a fury but wasn't as rapid as the smoother Le Roux or gangly Jones. Pigott played once for England in New Zealand in a match that showed if you were nearby and half decent and England were short, then you were in.

All three played in the 1986 NatWest Trophy Final win over Lancashire. Only Pigott took a wicket, though it was an important one, bowling Neil Fairbrother for 63. Man of the match, chosen by Len Hutton, was Dermot Reeve, who took 4-20 including West Indies captain Clive Lloyd lbw for a duck. The Sussex players had been taken by captain Ian Gould to The Foresters pub near Slough, later run by my mother's brother Tony, on the night before the final, to calm them down.

At Scarborough, Le Roux shouted: 'Do you want to yield?' as we hung around and the players practised.

'Not with that hard ball,' I thought. 'I'm not as good as I look, and I'm also 11 years old and weigh six stone, so I probably don't look much good either.' My brother is ten and weighs about nine stone. He's worse than me. We put our books and pens down and attempted to help, as the players batted and bowled to each other. They quickly realised we weren't going to save them time by stopping the ball when they hit it. Or maybe they were just spending a few minutes trying to give me a memory that would last the rest of my life. They signed my scorecard. Jones, neatest with a slopey J joining his fore and surnames, Pigott in capitals, which must say something.

The only other signature on the card is Richard Lumb, who was lbw to balding spinner Chris Waller for 46 (LBW in caps, as I wrote on the scorecard). Boycs was LBW PIGOTT for 52, at 102/2, my disappointment apparent in every slowly formed letter. Yorkshire declared at 150/4. Needing quick runs, they'd nevertheless started with Boycs. When he was out, 35 overs had gone, which meant they'd scored at almost three an over, which was going some for Geoffrey B.

Sussex had declared at 213/5. There must have been rain. I'll check *Wisden*. 'There was some elegant stroke play from Wells, Boycott, Lumb and Parker in particular as both teams worked hard to make up for time lost to the weather on the first day.' OK then, there was some precipitation.

Parker had scored 69 not out. Ramage had snared Gehan Mendis. My Dad watched Ramage warm up before the game. 'He's the worst-dressed cricketer I've ever seen. He looks like he's slept down the pit!' It was a bit of a joke, maybe because he knew Ramage also played football for Middlesbrough and Dad rated cricket well above football as a sport. A look round the Boro online message board today shows fans respected him back then for playing dual code. The chat on the boards is like it was at the ground as the men watched the match. People sitting near each other who had never met before chipped in when someone e.g., my Dad, made a loud comment, to no one in particular.

Appleby: 'Stone the crows. His whites are a disgrace, looks like he's been down the pit.'

Fan A turning to Dad: 'Typical footballer.'

Fan B, a row in front turning round: 'He's a better footballer than cricketer.'

Fan A: 'I wouldn't bet on that.'

Appleby: 'Brian Sellers would be turning in his grave, wearing whites like that.'

Yorkshire needed 251 to win without enough time. The Tykes were in a trough. They hadn't won the County Championship since Close left in 1969, because he'd been too cussed a Yorkie. Boycs was blamed by some, unfairly I thought. They said he 'held back the young players', 'played for himself', was 'painfully slow', 'played for his average', was a 'bloody awful captain', was 'too selfish to be a captain, or even a bloody team-mate'.

Athey went for 5. Boycs was nicking the strike to get away from Le Roux, said my Dad. He probably was. Pigott was easier to handle. Stuart Hartley was no. 3. Hartley stood his ground and they put on 93. Boycs scored more than half of them, which was even more unlikely than Hartley being a Yorkshire no. 3.

Boycs was 'in the mood to show 'em', my Dad said. He added 87 with Jim Love, a stroke-playing middle-order batsman, face red in the sun, another who Boycs also held back. Love got 56. David Bairstow came in with his boxer face, red hair, redder face – the angry bugger.

Waller and Barclay were on and getting smacked.

Then it happened.

I gazed at the high Victorian mansions overlooking the ground following a cricket ball's flight. The tall houses were right up against the edge of the ground. They usually dominated the scene. But today the charismatic figure of Boycott, getting ready for the next ball out in the middle, was the be all and end all for most of the 10,000-plus watching.

Boycs had hit a six into the houses. High over long-on, down the wicket, 'one very rare six', as *Wisden* described it. He never hit sixes. It was a beautiful drive, the best shot I'd ever seen, strong forearms in shirtsleeves, straight over the boards and into the crowd.

Boycs ended on 122 not out. Yorkshire won. That Boycs hit a century was not remarkable – he scored 151 tons in his career. But the way he got them was. He'd led the team to victory from the front, taking risks that might have got him out, which was something he hadn't done since the Gillette Cup Final in 1965, when captain Brian Close threatened the then 23-year-old and told him to get on with it. Boycs, of course, denies that Close instigated the change of pace.

I've got the Boycott autobiography limited edition of 151 (the number of first-class centuries he scored), in slipcase. Each book features a century, handwritten and signed by Boycs. Guess which one my Dad, who abhorred Boycs' selfishness, got? Scarborough.

The previous season, 1981, Boycs had been dropped from the end-of-season Scarborough match, and its holiday atmosphere, big crowds arranged intimately close to the pitch and chance to boost your average thanks to small boundaries and tired-out bowlers. Boycs was omitted by manager Ray Illingworth as punishment for slow scoring. Martyn Moxon, later Durham and Yorkshire coach, stepped in. A year on, Boycs proved a point that he could score fast when he wanted, which is always the thing that frustrates coaches most – they have seen evidence the player can do it but 'they just don't want to'. Fans don't care if they are fans of the player anyway. Because that's the difference between cricket, particularly Appleby's cricket, and the average fan. It's being partisan. Boycs fans loved his runs no matter how he scored them. A cricket fan like Appleby loved to see a good game.

Later I read John Barclay's *Life Beyond the Airing Cupboard*. He'd been locked up in a Sydney mental hospital the winter before. On lithium, he said he may have declared the Sussex innings closed at 197/6 'too generously'. Yorkshire only needed 251. But Boycs showed 'he could do it if he tried'.

The stats interested me as a way of gauging if players were good or not, more so than the results. I'd read a Test cricket records book when I was supposed to be practising the piano, ten minutes before school. Every four-wicket haul, every fifty, all the records. Then I'd read the averages in the *Daily Telegraph*, by Brian Croudy, of the Association of Cricket Statisticians. I'd be told every time: 'Good bloke, Croudy.' Appleby sent him books.

On Sundays at 1.55pm, Peter West would ponderously introduce the John Player League on BBC2. I'd have the *Playfair Cricket Annual* open at the JPL records so I'd know when Underwood set his career best at 28, for that frisson of extra interest.

I got my kicks keeping score for Hawksdale in 40-over matches on Saturdays. Dad had pushed me into it, but one day he said: 'Best you let someone older do it today. It's a big match.'

In the week, I'd be writing averages on the desk at primary school. I memorised the bowlers' analyses and batters' scores. I knew the team as well as Yorkshire's or England's, or the Panini 1983 cricket stickers, or 1938 John Player cigarette cards.

The Hawksdale players were odd shapes and sizes and wearing old cricket clothes, unless they were dead keen and had saved up and cut back so they could buy new stuff. Then it was, 'Why is he batting with my bat?' Or worse: 'Why's he using my box?'

Hidden at third man, I had plenty of time to think about why people played cricket. To set records? For fitness? For aesthetic expression? For camaraderie? To test yourself? To win? I couldn't do any.

So why watch? To see quality, see records, see aesthetic expression, to see winners. To relax. Something to do, nostalgia, be part of a tribe you didn't have to talk to, or you could if you wanted.

Appleby would say: 'Would make a good cricket field that,' out of the car window, passing a farmer's field with a barn at the side. 'Make a good fast bowler out of him,' about a gorilla on the telly.

'Here at Lord's,' he'd exclaim, as he relaxed at home, one of hundreds of stock phrases that stood in for normal chat.

'You'll know today's anniversary,' every day. We groaned. Hobbs's birthday or the Battle of Waterloo.

'Name those players,' mock exasperation. As you look at the black and white team line-up photo in the book he holds, you don't know Wilf Barber or someone. 'No, not bloody Paul Gibb. Ticker Mitchell? Not a bad guess.' Then he'd go into the stock anecdote about how Mitchell lived near Granny's in Baildon, and he was proud to add that he was a 'miserable old bugger just like they said'.

## *The Borderer* 3 August 1982

'Wandering along the front at Scarborough, with a little plastic tray of whelks, the Editor can observe thousands of families – mums, dads, children, babies, grandparents – all together and enjoying their summer holidays. This brings home again the fundamental principle and importance of family life. As our children grow up and leave home we sometimes tend to lose sight of this a little, and all the time there are outside influences deriding its value.

'"Do Gooders", 'Free Thinkers', "Reform Groups", the "Civilised Society", pornography now freely available to all ages, just about every play you see on television, every left-wing idiot on television and radio (and they get too much time allowed to them) try to knock family life and parental control.

'Anything to do with Rotary all this?'

Later: '4 August is the 68th anniversary of Germany's refusal to stop Von Kluck's 1st Army marching in long, grey dusty columns along the paved roads of Belgium thus prompting our entry into the First World War, from which catastrophe we have never recovered.'

And: 'People frequently ask the writer what he thinks of Geoff Boycott. Master batsman though he is, his selfishness and single-mindedness about Geoff Boycott's performance are legendary – and true. The fact of the matter, gentlemen, is that Boycott is an individualist playing a team game. He should have been a golfer where single-minded pursuit of your own performance means everything, but if he was a golfer and came to the Rotary club of Carlisle where could he sit? The right hand of God the father almighty and the seat opposite are booked!'

25 October 1982. Appleby books bought from EK Brown's catalogue – three pages worth of books, including *Scores & Biographies* vol. 8.

Meanwhile, recent obituaries of Badcock, Bakewell and JF Parker remind Appleby, then 51, that his age is 'rapidly decreasing between yourself and the subject of the obituary'.

### 1982/83 *The Borderer*

Appleby continued editing the Rotary Club magazine. He couldn't understand why the Club received letters of complaint about his writing. Current topics concerning Appleby:

'Turn down the central heating in the Magistrates Court. All public buildings are over-heated. If you are using someone else's money, who cares?'

'Discredited Home Office scientist Dr Clift. Suspended four years ago and hasn't worked since. Our courageous MP Mr [Willie] Whitelaw announced in the Commons last week that since his suspension he has received £49,736 salary and now he is 55 years of age is on an index-linked pension.' National Archive records on Clift are closed until 2074.

Appleby: 'There are many men in the private sector especially the manufacturing sector who have been made redundant through no fault of their own.'

He blames the 'world-wide recession', and says firms 'cannot obtain orders abroad because of crippling taxation', which is 'keeping people like Dr Clift in luxury for doing nothing and in increasing luxury as his undeserved pension goes up index-linked. Rob the poor to feed the rich and the undeserving.'

In a subsequent *Borderer*, he teases fellow Rotarians for their Scottishness, or dress sense, or interest in golf, or for their jobs. There's a piece on the Queen, 'who has access to the best food in the world but disciplines herself to keep her figure, which is beyond most of us, not only the Editor'.

Apologies Corner:

'In a journal of this kind, unless you confine yourself to non-stop platitudes or complete banalities you are bound to ruffle a few feathers now and again. This time, we have upset a member so badly, on three counts, that he will resign from the Club unless an immediate apology is forthcoming.

'Offence is always caused inadvertently and not wishing to diminish the Club membership, we are pleased to oblige.

'Firstly, we apologise for suggesting that members buy two nuclear submarines as Christmas presents. Although this was carefully explained to be a joke, apparently the mention of nuclear submarines at all was found to be offensive.

'Secondly, apologies are due, through the complainant, to the Greenham Peace Women. It was considered, apparently, that the writer was impugning their politics, which was not, of course, mentioned. What was mentioned was their lack of physical beauty and charm, which is only a matter of opinion. Beauty being in the eye of the beholder, we find that no doubt to some they must be extremely attractive.

'Thirdly, it is necessary to apologise, apparently, for making cheap jibes at the opposite sex. Although we are happy to do this, it must be stated that the complainant's wrath and disgust at the writer are as nought when compared with the displeasure of the writer's wife.

'A correction also from last month's *The Borderer.* A vigilant reader (yes there are some) has pointed out that the building that houses an aeroplane is a hangar, not a hanger. A most foolish oversight by the chief compositor.'

There's more:

'The president has received more complaints about the "wilder excesses" of *The Borderer*'s editor. The president proposes seeing a draft before going to press. "Disrepute or ridicule" is feared. Appleby says he has had "favourable" comments from district and national level. He reproduces a "fan letter" from the national magazine's editor "witty, lightly worn erudition, full of humorous care and reflections on the world around you". Appleby votes against "censorship". He says he is striving to not be "boring". He hopes the "fan letter" will "allay the worries of those fearing ridicule or scorn".'

The president writes of 'completely unrelated to Rotary' items such as indexed pensions. There is nothing wrong with good-natured repartee and gentle 'knife sticking' but it must not cause offence. There is a witch hunt to find out who complained. Fellowship must be increased, not decreased.

In the same issue, Appleby jokes about inviting Carlisle South Rotary to a hunger lunch, without 'letting on'. He says *The Borderer* has been declared a nuclear-free zone, so nobody will drop a bomb on it. Staff members are now an ethnic minority so are eligible for grants from the Arts Council, left-wing churches, GLC etc., and the publication has joined the anti-smoking lobby and will be awarded by David Owen and Tam Dalyell. In the quiz, 'nobody will begrudge Carlisle South their narrow victory'. Although Denis Compton never did play football for the full England team, and why was Huntingdonshire good enough as the birthplace for Cromwell, when Suffolk wasn't for Constable. These things do happen when 'quizzes are run in too amateur a manner'.

He carries on *The Borderer* in the same vein for two more years.

Chapter 21

# 1983 Panini

20 MAY 1983. EK Brown is recovering after over-working and has gone ex-directory and cut down his list and visitors to old friends/customers. He sent a lorryload to Phillips auctioneers with the help of collector Tony Winder, who came over to do the lifting. Winder's books would go to Phillips too, before long.

There's a letter from Geoffrey Copinger, the world's premier cricket book collector, to Appleby's Books, 13 May 1983.

Appleby has sent the *Indian Cricket* annual to Copinger, who bemoans counties not selling handbooks – he recently failed to get hold of Nottinghamshire 1978.

Copinger talks of Woodhouse's collection and says to come and see mine. He says he is not collecting as much because of high prices and wonders to whom to leave them. The space already taken by the collection does not please his wife.

Appleby tried to compete, collecting scorecards he thought would increase in value such as Surrey's 14 all out in 1982. Appleby wrote off for the scorecard, to be framed and hung in the hall. Then came Glenn Turner's triple hundred, Graeme Hick's quadruple, Turner's 141 out of 169, Richard Johnson's 10-45, Lara's 501 not out. At Lord's you could wait after the day's play while they printed a scorecard. Years later, in 2001, I picked up one when Mark Wagh scored a triple, interviewed him and got him to sign next to his 315. Appleby framed it.

In second-hand bookshops, on caravan holidays, Appleby would load up and fill the Thomson caravan toilet cubicle with stock to sell, not just cricket books, though there were always a few for himself. There would be piles of EV Lucas, HV Morton's *In Search of England*, Lake District interest such as *Herries Chronicles* and war books he liked. We'd spot bookshops out of the window, sometimes I'd point out bookmakers, half on purpose, and we'd screech to a halt, piles of books toppling over into the caravan bog, and pile into the shop. Then walk out when it turned out to be full of men smoking and watching greyhounds on wall-mounted tellies. If we actually found a real second-hand bookshop, I might get a football annual, as my parents filled their boots. 'Trade discount?' they'd ask, a standard 10% off.

Botham is aiming a drive through the off side on the cover of *Panini 83*. I'd joined the Ian Botham fan club, on the back of seeing him be a hero at Headingley in 1981 and was to see him on the A6 doing his leukaemia walk, with Brian Close, and the more unlikely Page 3 girl Linda Lusardi, in 1985. My Dad didn't know who Lusardi was, he said. In 2015, I was in the Hardy's wine box at the Lord's Ashes Test, Botham was 'coming up'. I didn't ask Botham about her, or Headingley. Instead I blurted: 'When's your next charity walk?' 'South Africa,' he replied curtly, and walked off. Earlier my host, my mate James had asked me to take a pic of him and Beefy. I'd fumbled. 'Not David Bailey,' I quipped. 'I know you're not,' replied Guy the Gorilla. Appleby would have got him going with a few stats and a few funny phrases, too eccentric to be seen to be competing with Botham's alpha maleness.

So my first trip into cricket collecting was *Panini 83*. I'd got *Panini 78* football, but only managed to collect a full set of Bristol City. That was like only doing a single side of a Rubik's cube.

*Panini Cricket 83* begins by featuring the Ashes (not contested that year), the County Championship Cup (actually called the Schweppes County Championship that year) and a Mike Brearley (no longer England's captain) foreword asking about the essence of cricket. For him it is a lifelong love; starting with persuading his parents or even a great aunt to bowl at him in the garden.

He continues on his early games on Bognor beach, to become lucky enough to play for Middlesex and England. He's a cricket fan as no other game compares for variety, speed, subtlety, brilliance and slow determination. When you begin to understand it you are too old to play. If he was a child again he would find collecting the stickers enormously exciting.

Wise words from cricket's psychotherapist and brainiest man, although he didn't realise that half the Panini collectors were adults, not kids.

Derbyshire are first in *Panini 83* (and not Cardiff Dragons or whatever team might precede them nowadays). Captain Barry Wood, toothless, resigned early doors to 'concentrate on his game'. Kim Barnett took over. He bowled a few leg breaks, which needed 'encouragement' (Cumberland gave him plenty in the NatWest Trophy round one at Kendal the next season – he took 6-24). Bernie Maher replaces Dallas Moir in the individual pics from the team photo, so there's two wicketkeepers in the 12 stickers. I couldn't say Moir's name properly and Appleby annoyedly corrected me – Moor? Myer? Moira? Mwahh? 'Bloody hell, it's Moy-er.' Then there was Maher. Mar-her? Ma-her? Mayer? Anthony Baer? Bayer? Bear? Let's call the whole thing off.

Essex look strong with two England captains (Fletcher and Gooch), plus lank-haired left-armer Lever, diamond-earringed music fan Derek Pringle and overseas pros Ken McEwan and Norbert Philip. Neil Foster is at the end of the book in the 'promising newcomers' spread, as is Paul Jarvis of Yorkshire. Six of the ten newbies played for England, but only 'Jack' Russell a whole lot. Cook (bearded Colin of Middlesex) never broke through. Chris Penn, Tony Wright and Nigel Felton had fair county careers. I can check their season-by-seasons on Cricket Archive now. I don't have to memorise *Wisdens*. Cook didn't play a first-class match in 1983. He became Bill Athey's brother-in-law. Cook went to Australia, online message boards tell me. Essex won the championship in 1983 losing one match fewer than Middlesex, the holders, who had a game abandoned at Lord's against Yorkshire, who lost 17 out of 23 games and won just one. YCCC somehow won the John Player Sunday League under 51-year-old Ray Illingworth, who was a year younger than my Dad and had made his debut in 1951, when Appleby was in the Navy in the Korean War.

Glamorgan lack stars, apart from Javed Miandad. Gloucestershire have four moustaches (Graveney's is best), plus three beards (and moustaches) – Zaheer's is best – and four clean-shaven.

Hampshire includes the awesome fast bowler Malcolm Marshall, sadly no longer with us, as my Dad would point out – amazing the number who have passed away. Marshall's neighbour (in the sticker book) Kevin Emery barely took another first-class wicket post-1982, when he took 83 in his first proper season. 'Marshall being at the other end helped,' Dad would advise.

Lancashire includes two future Cumberland players – Bumble 'start the car' Lloyd (who retired at the end of 1983 and then played for Cumberland, later coaching England), Steve O'Shaughnessy (who equalled PGH Fender's 35-minute century on the last day of the 1983 season, against joke bowling), plus Ian Folley who died during an operation to repair an eye after being hit by a ball during a match in west Cumbria in 1993.

Leicestershire has Chris Balderstone, his Carlisle United midfield stroller stardom days not mentioned. Also, Gordon Parsons – I have a Parsons benefit Bull head T-shirt, illustrated with a cartoon of a Parsons/Bull character.

Middlesex, the championship holders, boasts Simon Hughes, pre-'polo' monk hair baldness. Appleby was always quick to mock the 'eggshell blondes'. He had a full head of wire-like hair, getting whiter. I'd pencilled on hair to Panini's baldies, Stovold and Tunnicliffe and Kirsten, then rubbed it out. I can still see the marks now though.

Within the 1983 stickers, there are county grounds – eight including Cheltenham College and Chesterfield's spire with Worcester Cathedral as backing wallpaper. This page has come loose from the staples.

Northamptonshire has seven moustaches and one beard (plus beard and moustache Peter Willey). Cook and Larkins are openers. Cook wrote a foreword to a book by me about Durham CCC, 20 years later.

Nottinghamshire: Hadlee's not there. He was playing for New Zealand in England that year. Panini missed a trick there by not extending the annual beyond 17 counties to include the tourists, the away kits, the bronze, silver and gold stars, the legends, the umpires, maybe even the universities, or Harrow and Eton players, like *Wisden*.

Somerset had Roebuck and Denning – both gone now, differently remembered, Roebuck as tormented and Denning as bucolic carefree bumpkin. Roebuck, who seemed like a typical Oxbridge posh correct opener, turned out to be a very troubled character, jumping out of a hotel window as police sought to question him about a sexual assault. Dredge has a 'rather slinging action'.

Sussex: Wells brothers: Alan 'shows promise' but gets no sticker. Le Roux is 'fearsome'.

*Pitch invasion: Fans run on to Headingley to congratulate 1981 Test match winners Ian Botham and Bob Willis.*

*Maximum: Yorkshire beat Sussex at Scarborough in 1982 amid a plague of ladybirds, helped by a rare Boycott six.*

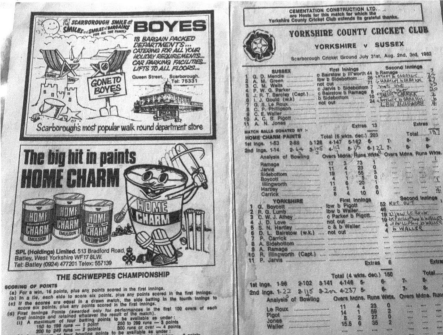

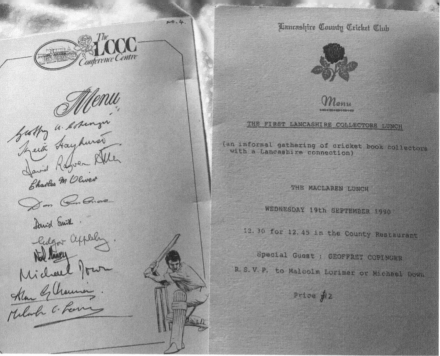

*Lunch: A 1992 get-together of leading collectors at Old Trafford featured a cricket-themed menu and a collective vast knowledge of the game and its artefacts.*

*Wisdens:* Wisden Cricketers' Almanack, *the Bible of cricket and the bellwether of the state of the cricket book market, and perhaps even cricket itself.*

*Captain: South Africa's Hansie Cronje at Lord's in 1998 wearing a cap that Appleby later won in an auction.*

*Library: Glass-fronted Minty bookcases preserve precious and eclectic items all with their own story, including Hansie Cronje's cap, an Indian Cricket annual, prized photos and autograph albums, files of letters from dealers and John Arlott's* Alletson's Innings.

*Nico: Cumbrian wicketkeeper Paul Nixon in 2007, the year when he made his debut for the England team aged 36.*

Benefit: MC Edgar Appleby and the author at cricketer Paul Nixon's benefit dinner in Keswick in 2007.

# THE CORRIDOR OF CERTAINTY

## Geoffrey Boycott

To. Edgar best wishes Geoff Boycott

SIMON & SCHUSTER

London · New York · Sydney · Toronto · New Delhi

Boycs: Geoffrey Boycott signed this autobiography for Appleby at Lord's during the 2014 Royal London Cup win by Durham CCC.

*Hero: Former England cricketer Geoff Boycott signs autographs for fans at Old Trafford in 1998 where he made his return to commentating for the BBC during the opening day's play of the third Cornhill Test between England and South Africa.*

both. Allin was released by Warwickshire in 2013, and returned to Devon, making one Minor Counties appearance in 2015. He played for North Devon in the Devon League, was involved in primary-school sports coaching in Barnstaple and Bideford, and was head of cricket at Shebbear College. "Such sad news to hear of Tom's passing," tweeted the England all-rounder Chris Woakes, a former team-mate at Edgbaston. "A great lad who always had a smile on his face."

**ANWAR ELAHI**, who died on October 19, aged 79, was a leg-spinner who played in the first Quaid-e-Azam Trophy match in Pakistan, for Sind against Bahawalpur (for whom Hanif Mohammad carried his bat) at Dacca in 1953-54. He played on for various teams until 1969-70, but never bettered his four for 64 on debut. His brother, Ikram Elahi, toured England in 1954 and West Indies in 1957-58 without winning a Test cap.

**APPLEBY, EDGAR**, who died on May 8, 2015, aged 84, was a bookseller in Keswick, in the Lake District, and president of the local cricket club. The shop's profits were not significantly harmed by his habit of discounting books – especially on cricket, where he specialised in overseas annuals – if the potential buyer could answer questions about the contents. Appleby was a sought-after speaker on a diverse range of subjects, including cricket, the sinking of the *Bismarck* and the *Titanic*, and the assassination of Archduke Franz Ferdinand. He recited his speeches without notes, having fine-tuned them on long walks with his otterhound, Hotspur.

**ARMISHAW, CHRISTOPHER JOHN**, died on March 12, aged 63. Seamer Christopher Armishaw played five one-day games for Derbyshire in 1973, taking the wicket of ... on debut, against Middlesex ...

*Obit: Edgar Appleby's obituary in* Wisden *2017, an accolade that would mean a lot to any cricket fan.*

*Claret, egg and bacon: Cricket fans having their lunch in the Harris Memorial Garden at Lord's.*

*Britain's loveliest: Fitz Park cricket ground, Keswick, where Appleby's ashes are scattered, showing Skiddaw in the background.*

Warwickshire: C. Old began 1982 as captain of Yorkshire and ended it needing a new county, having grown a beard.

Worcestershire were second to last, then Yorkshire.

Illingworth, the captain with the comb-over hair (inevitably drawn on then rubbed out by me). Boycs (in cap so no need for hair pencilling in) 'trimmed his scoring strokes to ones that serve him best'. Lumb – 'at one time', Athey – 'looks a better player now', Love 'finished the season with a hundred', Hartley (Neil) – they were still on about his fifty in a Roses match in 1979, similar to an amateur player's *Wisden* obituary waxing lyrical about a school game 70 years before. Moxon – 'supremely gifted', Kevin Sharp's knock for Young England of 260, even further back in 1977, is highlighted. Bairstow – 'pugnacious'. Stevenson 'last wicket stand', Sidebottom 'ex-Man United, 1983 could see him reap a personal-best harvest'. Whether it did or didn't, Yorkshire were by far the worst championship team that year, for the first time in their history. Boycs hit 1,941 Championship runs at 55.45 (next most was Bairstow with 1,102), including a slow 140 not out off 347 balls against Gloucestershire at Cheltenham, which caused the team to fail to win full bonus points. He ran out Sharp (Boycs used to run out his opening partner Richard Lumb so regularly trying to nick or avoid the strike that Lumb reckoned he was down 11-nil in that particular game). Athey scored 758 runs all season and then left to go to Gloucestershire, because of the dressing room strife, he later said.

Boycs was sacked at the end of the season, just as the miners' strike kicked off. When the miners went back, ground down, so did Yorkshire, caving in to give miner's son-turned Tory Boycs another chance to be a team man. That was when club president Norman Yardley resigned. The background to 1983's Yorkshire season was civil war. Appleby knew what was happening, through *Test Match Special*-commentating professional Yorkshireman Don Mosey, who Appleby supplied stats to for his books, one of which was a condemnation of Boycs' selfishness. The link had come through committee man Tony Woodhouse. Mosey was said to have had a big ego and a thin skin, maybe like Boycs, and maybe Appleby too.

### 3 July 1983 *The Borderer*

'A salutary tale. Quite recently, one of the junior Editorial Staff, weighed down by the burden of the rates, the criminal lunacy of the County Education Committee and the inability of county cricket teams to emerge from the pavilion because of the weather, decided to end it all by hurling himself off Eden Bridge into the swirling waters below. Shutting his eyes he felt a heavy thump and after a few moments opened his eyes on a sylvan setting so enchanting that he thought he was in the Elysian Fields.

'There were green trees in bud, their branches swaying gently in the breeze and delightful flowerbeds of azaleas and rhododendrons, surrounded by beautifully kept grass. With a growing sense of wonderment, he thought he detected the Giants of the Game coming across the green sward towards him, led by a large lumbering figure, who, despite his size, easily kept ahead of the others. Addressing himself to this figure, he asked in awed tones, 'Am I in heaven? Surely you are Mr Grace?' The figure replied: 'My name's not Grace and you're in Bitts Park. I'm a gardener on union rates and I'll thank you not to damage the flowers.'

'There are two morals to this story. Firstly, not all your rates go into keeping hundreds of overpaid, underworked people in the Civic Centre and building a needless sports centre [The Sands Centre – Carlisle's first proper concert venue] to keep them out of mischief, and secondly, if you want to do away with yourself, choose a high bridge. Also, the immortal doctor never played in Carlisle.'

## 11 September 1983 *The Borderer*

Appleby reports on a Rotary members' trip to North Norway: 'A journey that many members must wish to emulate. Time and money, lads, that's all we need.'

He goes on to how a talk on the Battle of the Somme stirred some of the older members into action. One has applied to enlist for the Kings Own Loyal North Lancashire Regiment and is taking pot-shots out of his bedroom window, while another is wondering if they will let him re-join the Pioneer Corps and is polishing his spade in readiness. A third has got his gas mask out of the loft and has put it on to inspect gardens in Longlands Road for incendiary devices. Meanwhile, a fourth got his khaki drill shorts out of the bottom drawer, ran a windsock up the flagpole in the back garden, saluted hopefully and wondered what time the canteen opened.

## 15 October 1983

EK Brown is sorry to hear the news about Appleby's work. He could expand his cricket book business that could help, but he would need a part-time job as well. Brown would not have been able to keep his wife going on cricket book profits alone and would have had to have sold general books or specialised in several other lines.

He understands Appleby won't be able to buy anything for a while.

R Lawson Engineers had gone bust. Blame Thatcher's Conservative government? The decline of manufacturing? The end of the North Sea oil boom? The recession? Appleby blamed the receivers. He still admired Prime Minister Mrs Thatcher. I didn't.

In *The Borderer*, 30 October 1983, Appleby has 'drunk several toasts to the memory of the immortal great man, WG Grace', who died on 23 October 1915.

A Rotarian has put on a portrait painting demo and was 'lucky in being able to obtain the services of such a handsome, young model'. The model is commiserating with a Scottish Rotarian 'whose bagpipes have had to be put down because they bit the postman'. Appleby can't get anyone to do the thumbnail sketch. He runs an obituary of a former member instead.

R Lawson (Engineers') hubris was a work-organised family weekend at the Langdale Chase Hotel in the Lakes, organised to show off the firm's success. I liked the Thomas Mawson-designed garden rooms and the luxury of having 'fruit juice' as a starter served by a proper white-jacketed waiter.

Maybe he wouldn't have felt so guilty, or angry about R Lawson (Engineers) going down the tubes if he'd accepted it was almost inevitable as a quarter of UK manufacturing output was shutting down, mostly thanks to the economic policies of Thatcher: a medium-term financial strategy aimed to restrict the growth of money supply in order to control inflation and the deficit that helped push the UK into a recession, led to a spike in unemployment and wrecked UK exports because exchange rates rose so much. The government said it was weeding out the inefficient. Sometimes you need a push to do something.

Chapter 22

# Hotspur the otterhound

## 3 February 1984

Brown tells Appleby his supply of the *New Zealand Cricket Annual* still hasn't come so he can't supply all orders. *The Cricketer* magazine review is wrong in price so he's losing 22p a copy. This is the last time he shall do New Zealand. Arthur Carman (1902–84) was the former publisher but it's harder now, as it is with the South African annual. Brown wants to concentrate on a better type of book.

Guess who took them on?

1 April 1984. Appleby in *The Borderer* informs us, among the usual list of members' heart attacks and hernia operations, that he has fallen down a manhole and has hurt his chest. This was at the local petrol station. He was walking Hotspur the otterhound in the dark and, preoccupied with talking to himself, didn't notice the gaping orifice.

## 6 May 1984 *The Borderer*

'Forced to endure Radio 1 last week, by irritating offspring, you could have knocked the Editor down with a sledgehammer when he suddenly heard the disc jockey [presumably Andy Peebles] give an articulate and knowledgeable run down on the current County Cricket scene. It just goes to show that you shouldn't have pre-conceived ideas and if he had listened earlier he may have learnt something.'

### 3 June 1984 *The Borderer*

'Did you read of the Police Inspector, aged 52, who took early retirement after an unwise remark about the coloured community? If, as was reported, he was getting in the teens of thousands a year, and was retiring on two-thirds pay, what are the chances that he made that remark deliberately? It must have been a strong temptation.

'The Editor regrets that due to a change of employ and difficulty in attending lunchtime meetings, he is unable to keep his not inconsiderable aural organ close to the ground, and a successor is needed to be found.'

He's been working as a foreman at the building of a milk factory near Dixon's Chimney in Carlisle. The factory is long since demolished. But now a new career is in the offing.

### 30 June 1984

Brown requests any souvenir issued for the Cumberland v Derbyshire NatWest Trophy game. There wasn't. But the game is one I'll never forget. Perennial strugglers Cumberland had qualified for the NatWest round one for the first time by coming high enough up the Minor Counties table.

## 17 June 1984

Brown hears from Appleby about a move to open a bookshop in Keswick in the Lake District. He sends a list of remainders from Booksmith Wholesale. This is the firm from which he bought the original Epworth collection.

Dad is back on his feet, having taken on the 'Gift Horse' shop in Keswick with my mother, selling books and gifts.

In the Cumberland–Derbyshire clash at Kendal in the NatWest Trophy first round, Bob Entwistle and Malcolm Woods walked inconspicuously to the wicket. The portly Enty had grey hair in an old-fashioned Brylcreem style, cotton whites and a bandaged bat. Teacher Mally Woods looked like a little bit like a Hawksdale club player to me, though he was a lot better than that. My Dad filled me in on who they all were. 'Enty's ex-Lancs', 'nearly made it'. Mally's from Carlisle, 'he's done well to get here, played against him'. Cumberland have no chance, I thought, there aren't any players from Carlisle in Panini cricket album 1983.

Actually there were county pros emerging from the Cumberland team, which won the Minor Counties Championship in 1986. Surrey's Monkhouse was from the Eden Valley farming village Langwathby, as was Paul Nixon, and Dean Hodgson from Carlisle played for Warwickshire and Gloucestershire. Deano was aged 18 when Cumberland qualified to play the Derbyshire match, too young to get picked. Nixon was 13, like me. They were both at the Derbyshire match. Everyone was. It was

like the Sex Pistols at Manchester Free Trade Hall or the
100 Club, or The Beatles at the Cavern, or The Smiths
at Carlisle's Sands Centre in 1986. You said you'd gone
even if you hadn't.

What I remember is Nixon, wearing casual Kenny
Dalglish gold trainers, a Nike jacket and a blonde-
highlighted wedge in the style of the day, meeting
Derbyshire and England wicketkeeper Bob Taylor
in front of the temporary stand. Taylor was cricket's
Gordon Banks. Both were from Stoke and dived to
catch the ball for a living. Both played in World Cup
finals. England's cricketers lost v West Indies in 1979,
with Boycott and Brearley methodically adding 129 in
38 overs and then Taylor getting a duck as eight batsmen
collapsed for 11 runs. Banks was England's goalie when
England won the 1966 football World Cup, so everyone
knows who he was.

I knew about Nixon from when I was at Trinity
School in Carlisle and Keswick School from when we
played Penrith Grammar School at rugby and cricket.
Nixon was bigger than most players, and better. He once
hit me for six to win a school match after I'd put myself
on to bowl when they needed one for victory. Earlier, he'd
got me lbw, which is not that remarkable, except he was
the wicketkeeper. He'd taken his gloves off to bowl for a
laugh as we weren't making much of a contest of it. We
lost by nine wickets. I was captain and ran out Nixon's
opening partner Jason Hale with a direct hit from cover.
He and Nixon looked amazed I could throw it that far. I
reckon I'd have missed 99 times out of 100. Maybe they

did it deliberately to give the next kid a bat. No one will remember now.

In Kendal, Nixon asked Taylor about keeping wicket, stepping to the front of a crowd of kids. Taylor, on the verge of retirement, must have advised fellow future England player Nixon well: keep down as long as you can, don't snatch it and concentrate on every ball.

Temporary marquees in front of the castle on the hill filled up. 'Our ground looks a picture,' they said in the bar as the players warmed up. But Cumberland lost the toss and got put in by Derbyshire captain Kim Barnett. Appleby said this was bad because if the boys didn't get many Derbyshire might win by 3pm.

They didn't get many. Enty got a duck, too slow to move his feet against left-arm inswinger Roger Finney. Their next guy was Qasim Umar, a current Pakistan Test player and Cumberland's big hope. He scored 6, out the same way as Enty.

The crowd stopped being expectant. Mally Woods squirted a few, and Bumble Lloyd was in with him. Lloyd was in the Panini sticker book and had once scored 214 not out for England. What was he doing playing for us? He was no media character then and was evidently right at the fag end of his playing days. Though before his England manager and Sky TV days, he'd gone down well with a recent after-dinner speech for Cumberland's annual do at the King's Head, a few miles south of Keswick (with Appleby as MC). The event was held at Thirlspot, beneath Helvellyn, because Brian Pattinson was landlord there, as well as being Keswick CC's groundsman. His ashes are scattered on Keswick's Fitz Park ground. There's a memorial stone in front of the pavilion.

Today's trip out to Kendal was a day skived from school by me, endorsed by Appleby. Mum was against, but Appleby thought it would do no harm to see such an important match rather than go to school.

Mally top-scored with 36 and Bumble got 28. Finney bowled 8 overs for 8. The 6ft 8in Scottish spinner called Dallas (Moy-er) Moir (1-19 off 12) got Bumble.

Appleby was uncharacteristically annoyed (for a cricket match) because it was going badly. Cumberland were 'nowhere near good enough'. Barnett took 6-24 – a part-timer rolling the part-timers. I didn't care because I liked the stat. *Playfair Cricket Annual* told me how good 6/24 was. Dad wanted to make contacts with local and Derbyshire cricket elite. We ate sandwiches and he met endless people he already knew. Mournful little chats. 'Not up to it. Have to get better players.' But then Cumberland president Harold Millican introduced Dad to Frank Peach, Derbyshire CC yearbook editor, and Dad perked up. A few pints helped. The smell of Jennings beer and special occasion Hamlets wafted around as the players signed autographs after ending the minnows' big day early. That distinctive aroma takes me back there even now.

Peach was impressed. In the archive, there's correspondence with Peach, who subsequently drops off dozens of county yearbooks in Carlisle, on the way to a holiday in the Hebrides. County yearbooks became one of Appleby's collecting manias. Seventeen counties and a century of publications meant a lot of gaps to fill.

## 10 September 1984

McKenzie sells Appleby *Talks with old Yorkshire Cricketers* for £26.

Appleby is finding it hard to let *The Borderer* go. He keeps issues edited by his successor that mention him, or to which he contributes. The new editor says it would be churlish to undertake the editorial chore without kowtowing to the previous incumbent, portly polymath the Great Edgar, who has resigned with all his prejudices intact and to travel daily to Keswick to follow the star of ex-fiancée. Appleby drags in his wake the three biblical urchins (we have names from the Bible) and monstrous heap of canine neurosis Hotspur, El Quadropedo.

One sunny Sunday morning, the new editor was guiding a rabble of Rotarians, including the ex-National Farmers' Union county chairman, up Cumbrian fell Causey Pike when the hound chased some sheep, who killed themselves with laughter as Hotspur floundered in their wake.

The new editor jibes Appleby in case he takes an index-linked pension and directorial freebies in his new job. He visited The Gift Horse and admired the pepper mills and scented drawer liners and talked to my mother before a great shaggy object appeared, slavering juicily. It was the Great Edgar himself, sniffing a free lunch. Appleby shows the new editor some books with rude or boring titles (*Self Abuse for Beginners*, *Scenes from a Welsh Pulpit*) then they go to eat together.

Chapter 23

# Driff

JOHN PLAYER cigarettes sponsored the Sunday League from 1969–84, televised on BBC2 from 1.55pm, anchored by Peter West or Tony Lewis. That meant Sunday afternoon was sorted, unless it rained.

14 February 1984, Brown adds to Appleby's collection FS Ashley-Cooper's *Gloucestershire Cricket* at £20 and *Dr WG Grace: King of Cricket* for £25.

We trained it to London on holiday that November.

It was cold, as the Christmas shoppers moved down Oxford Street. We joined them, going into Claude Gill's bookshop first. Gill was ex-Foyles bookshop, London's most arcane, where you had to queue for a chit from one counter to buy your book at another. Gill's was set up to sell ex-servicemen technical books – right up my Dad's street. Now Gill's was mostly remainders – independent bookshops were on their way out. The end of the Net Book Agreement in 1994 finished many (500 by 2009) new bookshops off as they were undercut by chains. Online sales killed off a lot more.

I browsed HMV, Virgin Megastore and a second-hand record place just off Oxford St on Rathbone Place. All are long gone now. We stayed in a hotel on Rathbone Place on a newspaper deal. It was like me and Dad did for the NatWest cricket final weekend, but this was on winter weekdays and all five of us were there. We tubed it to the Imperial War Museum, HMS *Belfast*, the National Gallery, National Portrait Gallery and a carvery. And we still managed to get to Lord's, for a guided tour of the empty ground. And we saw the legendary book dealer Driff on Charing Cross Road. My parents were fully immersed in books by then, having thrown their lot into The Gift Horse shop, after seeing the success of second-hand book market stalls in the Lake District, 32 miles from our house. They were commuting daily, dropping us off at Trinity School in Carlisle on the way (for a year). Buying books and selling them was like a holiday for my Dad. My Mum sold most of them. Appleby just talked to the interesting people.

We travelled up and down the road from Carlisle to Keswick and back in 1985, in limbo between childhood and adolescence. Driving 50 minutes each way in the gold Cortina estate, me airing my face as we hurried down Longlands Rd, Brampton Rd, Stanwix Bank, past Carlisle Castle, past Dixon's Chimney and Carrs' biscuits, through Raffles and past Margaret Forster's childhood house, rushing past the country villages of Thursby and Mealsgate, where the man with the bucket walked down the verge every day to feed his chickens. Then turn left at Bothel into the Lakes, past Bassenthwaite, below the flank of Skiddaw, past where we hit the deer, listening to Billy Idol's *White Wedding*, Billy Ocean's *Going Gets Tough* and Feargal Sharkey's *A Good Heart* on Radio One. Being allowed to hear that was the big concession from my parents. Arriving in Keswick at school, usually a few minutes late, I'd be told off, hating it in my green blazer. I'd go for lunch up the road at our shop if I could, then back there after school to the shop into the back room. I'd be doing my art homework, drawing everything in the store room, reading everything in the book room, not speaking much, then setting off back home at 5.30pm when they shut up. Once, my sister and I biked. Then you really got to know every bit of the route. It took three hours.

In Keswick, Appleby would nip out from the shop to buy his game pie from Michael's butchers. He didn't want to be a shopkeeper, but liked being an eccentric book dealer with his anniversary of the day notice in the window and sign on Lehmann J Oppenheimer's *The Heart of Lakeland* mountaineering book saying he 'was gassed in the war – on our side'. Oppenheimer died in 1916, aged 48, five months after a gas canister landed near him during action in the Battle of the Somme. Appleby got hold of a pile of remainder copies. The book was about the Edwardian golden age of Lake District climbing, which paralleled the golden age of cricket, both ended by the Great War, another of Appleby's specialist subjects that he would give talks on to local clubs and societies. These were always without notes and honed while walking the otterhound down to the lake. Hotspur the dog would come back with the odd otter, he'd say. Skinned, they taste like a cross between chicken and fish. The coats make sturdy gaiters, while any scraps of meat make a good curry – a 'chicken' tarka masala.

Appleby's inner sanctum office was where he'd invite these who were 'off rock bottom' to look at the 'good stuff'. My Mum, in her home knit hamster-like mohair jumper, ran the bit of the shop that made the money – the gifts, Ensor-like souvenirs, melamine table mats, Lakeland soap sheep, Moot Hall motif jugs, JMW Turner prints and pleather initial notebooks. The smell of pot pourri was overwhelming as I, bored, juggled Woods of Windsor or Crabtree and Evelyn soaps and potions waiting for locking up time.

Here's how it worked. Wisden Collectors' Club 2013 honorary chair Richard Lawrence gives insight in a book called *What Wisden Means to Me*, published by specialist online auction site Wisdenworld. He says 20 years before, when he was in his mid-twenties, he had collected the beginnings of a *Wisden* collection, lacking only 1971 of recent years. All were bought in second-hand bookshops. In 1992, in the Lake District for the late May Bank Holiday weekend with a church group, he found The Gift Horse, which he knew was Appleby's lair. Appleby was now advertising Indian, South African, New Zealand and other cricket annuals and books in *Wisden Cricket Monthly* to be ordered from The Gift Horse, 5 St John's St, Keswick, Cumbria, CA12 5WG.

Appleby had a filing cabinet drawer full of *Wisdens* including a softback 1971 at £22.50. Lawrence had left his wallet in his rucksack.

I can imagine Appleby's frustration at failing to make a sale having let this keen youngster into his office, which had taken the place of his old study room in Carlisle, where I'd once written to Hardstaff and Bowes.

Anyway, Lawrence rang Appleby ages later and Appleby sent a list of *Wisden Cricketer's Almanacks* available presently. Among them was a 1971 at £20. Inside was Appleby's pencilled £22-50 spidery writing. Lawrence wondered if this was the one that got away. It was, despite the uncharacteristic price cut.

Another insight into the book dealing world of that era comes from Driff, the undercover second-hand book star, mysterious acerbic, legendary and critical insider. Trade mags went on about him. He published a bookshop guide, which we used, more so after we'd come across his garishly decorated bike parked on Charing Cross Road on that last family trip to London in the mid-80s. A controversial figure, critical of book fairs and charity shops, which he said were taking over the trad scene. He was also scathing about booksellers he did not like. He appealed to me, riding around on his attention-seeking bike. His abbreviations here, used to describe customers and book terms, are from Driff's mag, bought second-hand by me much later and sold by parents on specialist website ABE for a tidy sum.

## ABBREVIATIONS
ABA: Antiquarian Bookdealers Association
AV: Average
Antorn: Antiquarian

AWYW: Asks What You Want
BGNS: Bargains
BKRM: Bookroom
BKST: Bookstall
BTR: Best to Ring
BTA: Better Than Average
D: Discussion
DIFF: Difficult
EC: Early Closing
EMPH: Emphasis
EPHEM: Ephemera
ETF: Easy to Find
ETGOW: Easy to Get On With
FARTS: Follows Around Recommending the Stock
IMP: Impossible
INT: Interesting
KUTI: Keeping Up the Image
MANFERRED: They Got a Man for This and
   A Man for That
MOG: Mogadon
NETGOW: Not Easy to Get On With
VETGOW: Very Easy To Get On With
WYLAH : Watches You Like a Hawk

Driff wrote guides to collecting authors and genres as well as grading which bookshops were any good. He also told tales about stuff like a trip to Ireland on his bike where urchins nicked his spare clothes while he was in a bookshop. In London, on that last holiday, I took a photo of his bike, coated in carriers. This was the glamorous end of book dealing, where the rogues and big money might lie.

The bicycling bookseller represented an age where charity shops and book fairs were threatening the expert knowledge of the book finders and specialist dealers.

When the internet came in, eBay would show that those very special items were not quite as scarce as everyone thought, and would make prices transparent, with the lowest priced selling first ('depending on condition', I can hear my Dad saying in a doomful voice).

Having the shop gave Appleby an excuse to allow his collecting to grow in fanaticism as he took every chance to buy stock books, plus whatever he fancied.

Little square parcels could be for selling now and didn't need hiding.

His collecting grew and grew, all as a result of war deprivations, years without possessions, his mother chucking away his cigarette cards, nostalgia, a love of game, and for investment, or whatever he wanted it to be.

Chapter 24

# Autograph album

ANOTHER AUTOGRAPHED thing is an unprepossessing worn brown leather album with gold embossed writing on the front and a stud clasp that opens to the title page 'LM Frances Jobson of Stoke Poges Feb 25th 1912'. There's another page of inscriptions you might skim by, then turn the page and there's 13 signatures of the 1912 Australian tourists, starting with Syd Gregory in a strong ink copperplate. That page is worth about £950.

Turn back and the second inscription is from 1935 and says the autographs of the cricketers were collected by John WHT Douglas, captain of England, the Gentlemen and Essex.

John WHT (Johnny Won't Hit Today) Douglas has asked the players at MCC v Australia at Lord's 20 May 1912 to sign, starting with CB Fry, also an international footballer, long jump world record holder and who tried to persuade Nazi German leaders that their nation should play international cricket.

Sir Pelham 'Plum' Warner has signed, as has Percy Perrin and Reggie Spooner.

Olympic boxing gold medallist Douglas was England captain. The book, taken round matches in 1912 by Douglas, was owned by master of Wellington College David Newsome, who had a house at Thornthwaite near Keswick. He wrote books about Victorians such as Cardinal Newman and AC Benson, who in 1901 wrote *Land of Hope and Glory*, about expanding the Empire 'wider still and wider shall thy bounds be set'. Newsome gave the unobtrusive album to my Dad at his bookstall one Saturday.

Turn the page of the book and it's the Indian prince Ranji, Jessop and England's fastest bowler Walter Brearley, which are worth £100 each maybe. Gilbert Jessop was the fastest run-scorer of his day, known for his match-winning, 75-minute century in the Oval Test against Australia in 1902. He was another to suffer in the war – from lumbago, which, in 1916, led to radiant heat treatment in an upended iron coffin. The lid got stuck and Jessop was trapped inside for a while, which damaged his heart. He took up writing and wrote his autobiography, *A Cricketer's Log*, in 1922, now worth about £80.

Next page is an Australian side v Rest of England 1911/12 with George Gunn, Tiger Smith and Phil Mead. Then Yorkshire, with Schofield Haigh, Major Booth, Alonzo Drake, George Hurst and Wilfred Rhodes. They wrote nicely then. Their names meant something, then as now. Appleby had inserted a sheet of foolscap, drawing attention to these player's unusual names, capital lettered and underlined. In later years he made piecemeal efforts to catalogue and price his collection. He was unable to master the internet, so that was difficult for him.

Next page is Kent with Frank Woolley and 'Charlie' Blythe, the shy spinner who died in World War One at Passchendaele, during the third battle of Ypres in 1917. A piece of shrapnel passed through his wallet, ripping through the face on a photo of his wife Janet, then piercing his heart. He's signed C Blythe (I wonder if he would have used his real name Colin if he'd spelt it out?). Most just used initials, apart from Ranji, who signs Ranjitsinhji of Nawanagar, which scores 47 at Scrabble. There's the odd Geo (Gunn) and Jas (Seymour) too. HJW 'Wally' Hardinge played one match for England and 623 for Kent. That would take 50 years now. England was only one match because Hobbs and Sutcliffe were regular openers. Those two have signed elsewhere in the album.

Hardinge's one Test was at Leeds against the all-conquering Australians of 1921 when he made 25 and 5. On retiring he briefly coached Leicestershire. Hardinge was a double international, capped at centre-forward for England against Scotland in 1910 (coincidently his match for England at cricket was also the only appearance for another double international, Andy Ducat). He also played for Newcastle United, Sheffield United and Arsenal. For a time, Hardinge worked as a sales rep for John Wisden & Co. This all adds up to make a dream number of links for a fan.

I handle the book with care. My Dad had left the worn tome near where he sat, alongside the fire in the front room in Keswick. Looking pretty valueless, the old softback lay unobtrusively on top of a row of run-of-the-mill cricket biographies, sitting at eye height in the middle of a whole wall of books. He wanted it near and easy to find. 'One day all these will be yours,' he'd repeat as a reassuring (to him) mantra.

The next page is really, really good, England v Australia third Test 1912, 19 August.

There's WG, Lord Harris, Hobbs, SF Barnes – a who's who of cricket. Hobbs scored 187. Barnes took eight wickets, including 5-105 in 46 overs in the second innings. Grace and Harris, then in their sixties, were retired from first-class matches, Harris just the year before, Grace in 1904. Douglas took three wickets in the match and scored 35, between collecting the signatures. England won by seven wickets.

Then a load of blank pages and you think that's it, then Sunningdale v Cambridge March 16th 1912, in childish letters, with a cutting. They are golfers.

More blanks then Stoke Poges v Cambs, again obscure golf.

More blanks, then a menu from the annual dinner of the Oil Industries Club at Mayfair Hotel 31 March 1933. Menu Barquettes de Caviar Frais, Grape Fruit Cocktail, Consomme Double au Suc de Tomates Brindilles Dorees, Crème Sultane, Aumon s'Ecosse Olga, Supreme de volaille Parisienne, Pate de Foie Gra a la Gelee au Clicquot, Salade Lorette, Poire Chatelaine Mignardises.

A pleasant snack for Appleby. He'd have the lot, then ask for 'an angel's kiss' more.

Then there was a toast list, starting with the King. Entertainment was popular comedienne Edith Price, Miss Jessie Wildon, Jack Crosbie – six feet of art and mystery – Rupert Hazell and Elsie Day in 'harmonylarity', and top of the bill, the celebrated Frankson with his cigarettes.

Then you turn over the page and see the land speed record racer Malcolm Campbell pencilled on the back, which is maybe worth £75. Campbell died of natural causes, which is unusual for speed record chasers.

Then my Dad's foolscap insert, listing the Australians of 1912.

'Missing WJ Whitty, W Carkeek – they are on a later page. Carkeek was a wicket keeper. Whitty was the oldest Australian Test player when he died, Northamptonshire's L Bulliver is the scorer, Claude Woolley was brother to Frank. The Dentons were twins. Yorkshire players Christian names. MAJOR Booth. ALONZO Drake. SCHOFIELD Haigh. AJ Evans played cricket for England once and wrote *The Escaping Club*.'

That book is a record of John Evans' World War One prisoner of war escapades. The pilot was awarded a Military Cross and bar. He escaped to Switzerland in 1917, but in 1918, he crashed his plane again and was imprisoned in Turkey, this time having to bribe a doctor to facilitate his freedom. Evans' book was often on our market stall, with a little blurb from Appleby about Evans' cricket career next to the slightly-higher-than-usual price.

The next page has Len Braund in flowing script, much neater than my Dad's hand.

There's a pencil insert card 'to Michael' from Tommy Farr, the boxer, worth another £75.

There's jockey Gordon Richards pasted in. Lastly, a totaliser signed by Michael Bearny. I don't know who he is, the internet's not helping, and I've got no one to tell me. He's maybe just a bookie.

JWHT drowned off Denmark, trying to save his father, after the ship he was on was rammed by another as they exchanged Christmas 1930 greetings in the fog, two months before Appleby's birth.

At the back of the album is a card from Newsome about how the autograph book is for you, of course with details of a date to meet Ian and Robin Dyer. Ian Dyer was a cricket book dealer, father of Warwickshire batsman Robin and someone Newsome knew my Dad would want to meet.

I took the album to the BBC's *Antiques Roadshow*. The expert said: 'It appears to be mainly cricket signatures. Have you heard of the dealer Christopher Saunders?'

# Chapter 25

# Lancashire collectors

19 JANUARY 1985 *Cumberland News* People in the News.

Edgar bowls out of the chair.

'Declaring after six years as chairman of the Carlisle and District Cricket League is Edgar Appleby. He and his wife, Susan, are moving to Keswick, where they have run a gift-cum-second-hand book shop since April. Edgar has been a committee member of the league for about 12 years. He has been a stalwart of the Hawksdale club since it was formed in 1971 and of its predecessor, Millhouse, near Caldbeck. Edgar played for Hawksdale until 1981 when a serious knee injury forced him to give up. He is now chairman.'

12 October 1985: EK Brown has had a rough time with illness and is pushing Appleby to take on his remaining overseas annuals UK dealerships.

There are just a few more chits and letters from EK Brown after that. In October 1985, he sells Appleby five Neville Weston WG Grace scrapbooks for £4–£7.50

each, including 'WG at Market Bosworth'. The invoice is for £70.82. There's New Zealand and South Africa annuals (invoice £53.27). By February 1988, Brown has to get a man to take heavy parcels to the post office. Appleby is now sending Brown New Zealand annuals, annually. Brown asks about trade in Keswick and longs for warmer climes.

This is the last letter in the file. Brown left the trade before the internet changed how it worked. He died in 1993. The EK Brown biography, written 20 years later by David Smith, has a section where Smith has interviewed Appleby, who was past it by then, but managed to say he first dealt with Brown in 1969 or 1970 and visited for the first time a decade later. He bought a lot of *Wisdens* from the 1880s from Ted at £17.50 each. The 1882 was £85 when Brown sold him it in 1979. Appleby remembers him as 'courteous, strict and not overly enthusiastic'. Smith writes: 'There was mutual respect because on retirement Ted handed on the distributorship of the overseas annuals to Appleby.'

Dad would send long notes with each copy of the overseas annual he posted, trying to match Brown's courtesy in his own way. To HW Warner, an ancient Kent collector, he'd go on about long-retired players PF Warner (no relation), Woolley, Hubble and Ames, usually citing anniversaries, records and odd memories such as the Hubble and Ames sports shop he once visited in Gillingham, or the Ames wartime service as a 'petrol pigeon'. He'd be in his office in the shop, 'counting books' as we called it, mainly looking up in books things that crossed his mind.

Appleby eventually handed the NZ and SA dealerships to book dealer Michael Down.

As I write this, there's a knock at the door. A 1980 *Wisden* (limp covers) arrives. Open it up and an advert for McKenzie is front and centre. I look up Procter's hat-trick of lbws at Cheltenham, decades ago.

There aren't any more letters in the file. The shop was a 'tie'. There were the market stalls to do too and three teenage kids are hard work. My sister Rachel left home in 1987, and me in 1989, with Daniel a year later, to the Marines rather than to be a student like his siblings. The dog died in 1990, so that was one less mouth to feed too. I'd long replaced Geoffrey Boycott with the Boycs of music, northern miserabilist monomaniac Morrissey, as my number one teen idol. I was more interested in fanzines featuring Moz's Wildean wisdom than Lilywhites listing Grace's greatest hits.

There are still a few curios in the archive though. The First Lancashire Collectors Lunch 19th September 1990 is one. Special guest was Geoffrey Copinger, the number one cricket book collector and *Wisden* stats collator. Cricket-loving Reverend Malcolm Lorimer (who once recovered an RG Barlow stained glass window from a skip) and Michael Down have organised the event – an informal gathering of cricket book collectors with a Lancashire connection. The guests have signed the luncheon menu. They include David Rayvern Allen and David Smith. Appleby's spidery script is in the middle. They ate: 'The McLaren Lunch' of Archie's Gastronomique opening of an excellent partnership of salmon and prawns laced with cognac, Copinger's rack of lamb captain-style with Walter Brearley roast potatoes, broccoli as Johnny Briggs would like it and cheese sauce Ernest (Tyldesley?). Then there was Hornby's cheeseboard and Barlow's coffee and mints.

When his children had gone, the collecting and being a fan picks up again. Appleby was enjoying being a dealer. He purchased on 16 June 1993 *Wisdens*, Yorkshire yearbooks and a 1932 signed photo of Yorkshire CCC team for £875 from a North Yorkshire rector.

And in the same spring, he bought Percy May's *With the MCC to New Zealand* for £125 from McKenzie after meeting him at a Swindon auction.

At Phillips West Two in Bayswater, London, there's £1,378.03 spent, in August 1992, on motoring and aircraft books, and *Wisdens* and other cricket. Lot 402 is 'the one I really wanted' – *Lillywhites* at £500.

At the same venue in August 1990, he bought a WG *Cricket* limited edition for £420, which is now 'in my possession'. There's a July 1989 auction catalogue at which he spent £2,332 on cricket, including £1,000 on 'S&B' – *Scores and Biographies'* first 14 volumes.

From Christopher Saunders, 30 March 2001 *Men in White* at £500, less £180 discount for *Wisdens* part-ex. This is the New Zealand cricket history book that's the size of a table. Saunders has thrown in the postage. I remember it sitting on top of a chest of drawers for years after, too big to fit on a shelf, its slipcase fading in the sun from the landing window.

There are invoices from Bodyline Books (Giles Lyon) and Boundary Books (Michael Down) including a 1967 hardback *Wisden* (ex-library) for £20 ('sold to Howard Allen for £25'). Allen was the cricket-loving headmaster of Keswick School, who once sent me home for wearing drainpipe jeans. I later bumped into him at Lord's and we talked like old friends. Most items are a lot more than £20, with plenty of signed old photos he had framed. *Lillywhites*, Ashley-Coopers, county yearbooks and collectors' limited editions, newly published.

Then there's invoices from Brook the bookbinder. He lived in the south Lakes at Lindale-in-Cartmel. Occasionally I joined my Dad on his evening drive there in the Ford Sierra. Once, in 1994, we had 25 *Wisdens* rebound at £10 each in 'good uniform binding', the sort Appleby loved but future collectors didn't. He also had the 1882 'furbished' along with 1915, 1934, 1909, 1912 and 1926. The Grace limited edition gets bound at £38 and 'on it goes', as my mother used to say.

A Larwood letter, sent from the Blackpool sweet shop he owned between 1946 and 1950, was rebound in 'rexine covered case' for £25, *Cricket Statistician* full bound in buckram £24, *12 Years of Ranji Trophy* quarter goat/cloth at £47, AJ Gaston's *Cricket in Sussex* quarter-binding in calf and suedel at £47 ('a luxury but very nice!'), *History of Yorkshire Cricket* cloth restoration £24 ('it hardly needed all that but it's better now it's done'), *Gloucestershire CC Scores 1870–79* quarter-calf with marbled sides. Label on front board and raised bands. Resew to release from stab sewing ('Beautiful extremely!'). Other books are 'v expensive but v nice!', 'expensive but beautiful'. *Cricketers Trip 1859* full Morocco £66 ('the only full leather binding I've had done.

At £66.00 it is expensive but for a book like this it is worth it – once in a while!'). WG letter encapsulated in 'secol' polyester, letter paper repaired, wallet fitted into rexine case £38 ('expensive but worth it').

There's another letter in the file from 16 January 1989 from David Frith, editor of *Wisden Cricket Monthly* saying the Indian and South African annuals are mentioned in the books section that issue. Appleby has sent Frith a cutting about Mrs Macaulay (the Yorkshire and England player who died in wartime Shetland, George Macaulay's widow?). Frith wonders if Australian cricketer Ted McDonald's Test cap, bought in a junk shop in Penrith 20 years ago, is from the Macaulay collection. Appleby has also passed on a contact for another ex-Yorkshire player, Jim Smurthwaite. Mentioned is Martin Wood, a dealer who advertised for lonely, incomplete *Wisdens* he could rebind, and sold from stalls at county matches. Wood had once sold a set of *Wisdens* to media magnate/fraudster Robert Maxwell, who fell to his death off a yacht in 1991. David Frith wrote two books about cricket suicides. Tony Winder was one. Incidentally, Wood had recently been asked to buy some *Wisdens* from another collector who later killed himself, Hugh Simmonds, who paid £5,500 for 1863 and 1864 copies at auction, leaving journeymen collectors and dealers wondering where they would ever afford what they craved. The cricket book market was over-heating.

Chapter 26

# NatWest Trophy 1989

THERE'S A signed scorecard presentation copy among the archive, from Cumberland v Lancashire NatWest Trophy tie on 28 June 1989 at Edenside in Carlisle. Edenside is next to the River Eden on the north side of the river where we lived, near the Chinese Gardens in Rickerby Park, where the river slid by on towards the Solway Firth.

I used to chew my home knit cricket jumper for luck and watch for the lucky Middlebrook Mushrooms lorry to go past from the M6 to Carlisle's supermarkets at Wednesday night cricket practice at Edenside. We did grip, stance and backlift x 100. The pitch had a dry ski slope with an old-fashioned worn-down, scrubbing brush-style base that we used to slide down on flattened crisp boxes scrounged from the cricket club bar.

We'd get home in time for *Blackadder*, then the next Wednesday night sing the *Blackadder* theme song while waiting for our turn to show off our batting stances to the coaches down the cricket club.

This pristine 1989 Cumberland–Lancashire scorecard maybe was a raffle prize or more likely bid for by my Dad in the fundraising auction held at the match. It is marked 'corporate hospitality marquee' so maybe they all got one for paying to get in there.

The menu began with morning coffee and homemade biscuits. Luncheon was Fresh Eden Salmon, Roast Cumberland Ham, Roast Local Chicken, Various Salads (presumably not from Cumbria), rolls and butter, selection of sweets, biscuits and cheese, coffee, red AND white wine. The hangover from state management of pubs, now gone for nearly 20 years, meant the city remained a culinary throwback.

Then there was afternoon tea: assorted sandwiches, scones with jam and cream, various cakes, pot of tea. My Dad would have been in his element with everyone he knew, with access to top players, like Wasim Akram and Phil DeFreitas. And Paul Allott.

But June 28's match didn't happen. Rain. Appleby wouldn't have minded an extra day. They played it the next day at Kendal, where we'd seen the 1984 NatWest Derbyshire game, Cumberland's first in the competition. DeFreitas and Allott quickly had Cumberland 9/5.

Appleby has a signed scorecard randomly placed a few pages on in the file. John Crawley's 281 not out in 1994 against Somerset at Southport. The best score since McLaren? No, my Dad would have told me. Eddie Paynter hit 322 in 1937 against Sussex. Neil Fairbrother scored 366 against Surrey in 1990. In Crawley's match Wasim Akram took 5-117 and 8-30.

The scorecard's opposite one for Nottinghamshire v Leicestershire 1960. He'd have been winding down his Navy career in 1960, soon to be working at Drax power station, volunteering for New Year's Day and Christmas Day duties and expecting everyone else to too, looking for that Navy camaraderie. For a lot more of the 1960s he led a peripatetic life. He taught me phrases such as 'bonnus notches' from working in Spain and he'd done Denmark, and of course the Korean War during his 14 years on the high seas in the Royal Navy. When we were born, he got offered a job in Saudi, tax-free. We stayed in Carlisle.

Back in 1960, Cyril Poole, c Watson b Pratt 72 was the 'highlight', judging by his notes on the scorecard. Leicestershire's Boshier opened the bowling about that time. Appleby often met with Boshier in later years after discovering the ex-fast bowler at his Dales café when he saw some Leicestershire memorabilia on the wall, an example of how he made friends with the ex-players, which is a classic fan's motif.

Boshier came out from the kitchen. 'Man wants to talk to you about cricket.' My Dad regaled him with tales of past deeds, learnt by heart from *Wisden*. They met every year after and had gin and tonics (Appleby would have had Cab Sav from New Zealand he had discovered on holiday there) on the patio of the Boshier house overlooking Wensleydale. Dad talked about Boshier being a bloody good bloke. It was more than a brush with his kind of star.

By the end of summer 1989, I was 18, about to go to art college, with long hair, drainpipe black jeans, Dennis the Menace jumper. Me and my lugubrious mate and near neighbour Craig had just been Interrailing, a rite of passage back then when you did a gap month rather than a year between school and university with a £300 Europe-wide under-25 train ticket and a tenner a day spending money. I missed things I'd taken for granted before – mainly the cricket scores. I found some in someone's *Daily Telegraph* on a 48-hour train crawl through Yugoslavia, and felt like I was reading EW Swanton's POW camp 1939 *Wisden*, the book that all those incarcerated by the Japanese in Burma wanted to read most.

A week after coming back from Europe, I completed my re-integration into UK society when me and my Dad went to the NatWest Trophy Final, as we had five times before.

Cumberland hadn't made the final, having been bowled out for 84 in the first round at Kendal by Lancashire, de Freitas ending up with 5-13.

We'd come down on the train as usual, on a weekend booked by my Dad, Hotel Russell in Russell Square, with its marble stairs, then walked down past French Franks for a coffee and bun to the tube and to the match at Lord's. 'Here at Lord's,' my Dad said regularly as a stock phrase. And we actually were. The expected murmur was really there as you stood on the escalator having got off the tube carriage on the Jubilee line ('the furthest one down because it was the last one to be built,' my Dad said, 'stand here and we'll be nearest the way out when we get off').

The NatWest Final was a big deal then. Crowds for the County Championship had fallen to about a million (1,046,194) by 1960, after the post-war boom epitomised by the Bradman 1948 tour. There were 76,000 fewer people at championship matches in 1961, the lowest since the war.

*Wisden* 1962 reported the recommendation that 'a Knock-Out Competition be introduced on the basis of one day matches as recommended in the Structure Sub-Committee's report'. The top minor counties were to be involved. There was a plan to alternate championship and one-day matches that didn't happen. The Gillette Cup came in for 1963 (65 overs) and John Player Sunday League in 1969 (40 overs). The Benson & Hedges (55 overs) started in 1972. The one-day World Cup started in 1975. The NatWest Final was more popular than many one-day internationals by 1989.

At Lord's, in 1989, John Carr and Desmond Haynes opened the batting. Middlesex crept to 210/5. Star batsman was Mike Gatting, one of several amusing characters in the classic dressing room tales cricket book, *A Lot of Hard Yakka* by Middlesex seamer Simon Hughes. Hughes' book turned me back on to cricket literature with tales of reserve spinner/wide boy Jamie Sykes telling 'Yozzer' his 'arsehole had fell out' when he backed away from fast bowling and Gatt's spotted dick lunches and subsequent rolling out to field. Gatt disappointed, only scoring 1 in the final.

Hughes had taken 4-20 in round one against then minor county, Durham. I'd found out all the scores because I'd asked my Dad to keep the papers when I made my one Interrail call home, reverse charges from Athens. Later, Hughes wrote *From Minor to Major* (compared to *Yakka*, a book more like the rest of the county cricket factual histories that Appleby preferred to fill his shelves). I read the Durham book on Christmas Day 1993. It was all about Durham going first-class. After an initial flurry of Durham books following the minor county's elevation, there wasn't another written on the subject until the *Daily Telegraph* county correspondent Tim Wellock's 2009 life of a sportswriter tome *A Summer with Durham*, apart from a slight pamphlet on Durham CCC's 100 greatest players, penned in 2004 by me.

My Dad liked Warwickshire's Newcastle-born all-rounder Paul Smith, despite his flailing locks mimicking his occasionally wild deliveries. Gladstone Small removed another Geordie, Mike Roseberry. Asif Din, who would go on to win man of the match four years later in the 1993 NatWest Final, caught the ex-Durham batsman. The Banks's bitter-drinking Brummies sang their version of the old Manfred Mann number *The Mighty Quinn*: 'C'mon without, c'mon within, ain't nobody like the mighty Din.'

Middlesex were winning, Warwickshire were going too slow on a dodgy wicket. Geoff Humpage, Andy Lloyd, Windies legend Alvin Kallicharran with a duck, all failed. Then the hairy pair Smith and Dermot Reeve got going.

England cricket was at a nadir. Gatting had been sacked as captain after having a go at 'cheating' umpire Shakoor Rana (I loved his apology note, written school rebel-like on a screwed-up scrap of paper), England had also just lost 4-0 v Australia. Gatt was about to captain a rebel tour to apartheid South Africa just weeks before Nelson Mandela was released. The anti-apartheid protesters at the Lord's final got sworn about by the MCC members, and Appleby.

We were neutrals, of which Appleby said there used to be loads at cricket. I didn't have much to talk about to my Dad, other than Interrailing, so it had to be a good match. And it was.

Middlesex hadn't seemed to be scoring slowly, though they were compared to today's rates. Warwickshire never seemed favourites, even though they only needed 3.5 an over, 211 in 60.

At the break 'you may perambulate' said the plummy tannoy wallah. We perambulated to the square to watch the groundsmen rolling the wicket, alongside lots of pointing men wearing faded beige or sky blue blousons and too-tight Daks slacks.

Reeve had figures of 12-4-27-1. He took 4-20 for Sussex in another NatWest final, in 1986 v Lancashire. I went to that too, three years younger but not much different. Sussex cruised that. If you batted first you generally lost at Lord's in September.

Paul Downton (one of a long run of England wicketkeepers I didn't favour because I wanted either Bairstow or later Paul Nixon to have the job) and spinner John Emburey managed a then racy 62 in the last ten overs for Middlesex.

The pacy Norman Cowans opened the bowling for Middlesex. Fraser and Hughes were lumbering in comparison. Warwickshire bumbled along, before strike rate stats had been invented, having all the time in the world.

Paul Smith came in and livened things up before being bowled by John Carr, son of DB Carr, a FEC– Former England Captain. Appleby was an SMM – Self-Made Man.

Asif and Reeve needed 89 with the score at 122/5 as the gloom set at Lord's, which they nibbled down to 39 required from seven overs.

Reeve was darting and busy. Asif was a slightly comedic figure to many of the Brummie fans. His bouffant hair, moustache and mammoth glasses singled him out for patronisation.

Four byes past Downton off Embers cheered me up. Reeve was run out, which didn't. Son of FEC Mike Smith, off-spinning all-rounder Neil Smith, came to the wicket. Another gogs wearer, not quite a Botham, or even a Reeve, in appearance.

Hughes bowled last with 10 needed, which was a lot in those days. Gatting said he'd have put his benefit money on winning.

Smith said he wasn't picking up Hughes' slower ball and that's what he expected him to bowl, so he decided to give it a go.

The result was to hit a six off a length ball. Hughes then bowled a wide and felt culpable. He soon felt worse when he slipped in his follow-through and a blocked ball got past him to seal victory for Warwickshire. Punters ran (not perambled) on to the pitch; Hughes had to get up quickly, or else he might have been trampled. We wandered on to stand in front of the pavilion for the prize-giving, the softness of the turf like carpet beneath our feet.

Neil Smith got picked for England (but not Geordie Paul, or Hughes, or Asif). This was when the NatWest Trophy cemented tour places, or produced bolters.

My Dad and I wandered towards the pavilion, tiptoeing down the Tavern Stand stairs behind the crowds, him watching his step, so as not to fall. People talked in the crowd and Appleby talked back loudly to no one in particular, about how he felt sorry for Hughes. Brave and bold Sir Tom (Graveney) announced Reeve as man of the match.

Appleby and I walked off down through the Grace Gates past the hotel on the corner where Middlesex were to celebrate, towards Baker Street, past the canal and the petrol station that became a flower stall, past the hookah café and the mosque and the Rudolf Steiner HQ (whatever that was) and the end of the road where former home secretary Leon Brittan once drove past and on beyond the Sherlock Holmes pub, that was too expensive, past Baker Street as the crowds of pastel-dressed, coolbox-carrying, sunhat-wearing middle-aged men thinned, over the road passing another pub that also wasn't any good, down into town, stalling at Rumbelows to watch a bit of the highlights, to a pub where it was 'two pints of bitter please', then we relived the match, couple more, then to a Greeko.

He'd say to me 'sit in the corner and look old', when he bought us pints of bitter. If we didn't get served, he said: 'It's because I look like a policeman.' Like they went on duty with a teenage boy.

He wanted kleftico; I could have Greek salad if they had nothing else vegetarian, or stuffed vine leaves – 'dolmades'. We drank.

A belly dancer came on in the Greeko. Things were looking up. Someone left a smoking cigar and I smoked the smoking cigar. He didn't say anything about that. But he did tell me he was reincarnated from a World War One soldier.

'It's a good thing to have the odd pint. Pa [Appleby's Dad, my grandad 1895–1987] wouldn't drink at all – not a thing apart from the odd whisky at Christmas – and no one ever died of the drink by having a few pints of bitter.'

I said: 'It's funny how I can sometimes predict what's going to happen in the match. I just kinda know something's going to happen.'

'Kind of, not kinda.'

'You can't force it cos you want it to happen, like Downton getting out or dropping a catch or Boycott hitting a four or something but y'know it sometimes happens.'

My Dad tried to empathise, not his forte: 'I always thought I knew what happened in the past.'

What did he mean?

'I believe I was reincarnated from a dead soldier from World War One. When I see the pictures of the trenches I feel like I was there … because … I know so well how they felt in the trenches. I just think that's what happened and that's what came about.'

The metal discs attached to the belly dancer's skirt jangled nearby – and saved us.

We went back to Hotel Russell. He said I should go out if I wanted. I drew a picture of the view out of the window while he slept.

Then I went to art college and forgot about cricket. He didn't, needless to say.

'Rambling with Edgar Appleby' by Allan King 20/11/93 *Cumberland and Westmorland Herald* (editor John Hurst). This was a kind of follow-up to the piece about the quest for the 1882 *Wisden* Hurst wrote a decade earlier in the same paper.

'Every Saturday morning on Keswick outdoor market there is a stall selling second-hand books.

'In many respects it looks like a typical stall, a place to buy entertaining and cheap paperbacks.

'But to cricket fans the man behind the stall is somebody special – Edgar Appleby, a lifelong cricket enthusiast and collector of cricketing books.

'In his Southey Street home at Keswick he has shelves full of books, some new, many old and most to be treasured.

'Although he recently retired from his second-hand bookshop, he still sells cricketing books and is still a regular personality on the market.

'"If you want a South African cricketing annual then the only bloke in the northern hemisphere you can get it from is me," he said. "The same is true of Indian annuals."'

King goes on about cigarette cards, with Navy ones highlighted: 'Explained by the fact that Edgar was in the Royal Navy for 14 years from 1947. Then he fitted boilers in rural Spain, Finland and Kuwait. In Denmark he was working on boilers for an oil refinery where the steam requirement had been so underestimated that three railway locomotives were needed to help out until the new boilers were commissioned.

'Edgar freely admits that his life changed in 1967 when he met his wife Susan and he gave up his globetrotting lifestyle.

'"At 36 I thought I had better try this settling down business," he joked.

'He spent 17 years with an engineering firm in Carlisle before his interest in books led him to launch his first market stall selling second-hand books. Ten years ago Edgar and his wife set up their gift shop and bookshop in Keswick.

'Throughout his life he has always pursued a passionate interest in cricket.

'"I played as much as I could in the services. But being on board a ship was not the ideal location for a cricketer. I was never in a position to practise, and I never got off square one. Mind you I would have only got to square two anyway," he added modestly.

'Edgar played for Hawksdale in the Eden Valley league, a team he is delighted to see is still going strong. Books on cricket are a major part of Edgar's home, filling the wall of one room and bookcases around the house.

'"I could talk about cricket books all day," he freely admits. "There's been a lot written about cricket. It ranks with politics and religion as the most written about subjects."

'Edgar has 2,500 to 3,000 cricket books which seems a huge number until he explains that the big collectors have far more. The books are handled with the greatest care and affection and kept in glass-fronted cabinets, protected from the dust.

'There is an 1891 copy of *Cricket* by WG Grace and a special edition of the same book signed by the author himself.

'It seems that, rather than produce hardback and paperback copies of a book, the Victorians produced hardbacks and "special editions" which have greater interest to the collector.

'Although prices for such books are not astronomical there is enough interest in the good ones to keep prices moving upward all the time.

'"The good stuff is recession-proof. In all subjects there is a lot of dross and people want to buy the good stuff. The latest offerings from Botham, Gower or Lamb will sell for £14.95 but in 10 years' time will be worth just £3.

'"At the other end of the scale are *John Wisden's* cricketers' almanacs which record all the cricketing results of the year and have done for 130 years.

'"The early ones are so rare that the first 15 have been reprinted. A complete set recently sold for an astonishing £20,000.

'"Most collectors opt to buy them one or two at a time.

'"Although 1916 saw little cricket because of the war that year's *Wisden* is one of the most collectable years because it contains WG Grace's obituary.

'"I noticed that many of the books, which originally had paper covers, have been rebound in hardback.

'"The paper covers of the early *Wisdens* did not last. They never anticipated that they would survive so long.

Nearly all have been rebound. The secret is to have them bound with the original covers inside the new binding otherwise values can be considerably reduced."'

King then falls back on what Appleby will do in his semi-retirement. Cathedrals and stately homes visits apparently. And watching more Yorkshire CCC and Durham CCC, as well as being a member of Cumberland CCC and the Association of Cricket Statisticians. And doing talks on the *Titanic*, *Bismarck*, and Gretna Green rail disaster.

King and Appleby talk about how 'local personalities' are chosen for the interview. Appleby pulls out Old Ebor's 1923 *Talks with Old Yorkshire Cricketers*. 'Like cricket, journalistic techniques endure through the ages.'

## Chapter 27

# 1995 Cronje cap

HANSIE CRONJE once won £50 for hitting two sixes into the River Greta in Keswick during a charity match for Leicestershire opener Tim Boon's benefit, which Leicestershire wicketkeeper and local lad Paul Nixon had helped arrange. Everyone liked Hansie that day. It was sunny down Fitz Park. Leicestershire's ex-Oxbridge opener Gregor Macmillan was fielding on the boundary of 'Britain's loveliest ground'. He got some friendly heckles from one or two drunken locals. 'Stick your Campari up your arse' being one. No one would have said that to Hansie. Cronje was a religious Afrikaner, a big name, and very polite.

At the benefit dinner at Borrowdale Hotel, Appleby sat next to the esteemed South Africa captain, and introduced the speakers, then bid high to win an auction for Cronje's cap.

The authorised *Hansie Cronje Story* by Garth King tells how Cronje was Afrikaner, Christian, Dutch Free Church. But he spent four years taking cash from bookies.

Hansie was a legend but he was flawed. Hansie's greatest battles were against himself. He was a 'fallen icon'.

The fan does not like revisionism, they don't want Hobbs to have hit two more centuries or Grace two fewer because some matches are now first-class, or not. But Cronje's record will be tainted forever.

'I must however acknowledge I was activated by a measure of self-interest. It was not initially my intention to throw any games or to fix results. I was driven by greed and stupidity and the lure of easy money.' He was banned from cricket for life. Two years later he died aged 32 when the plane he was in crashed into a mountain in the Western Cape.

## Chapter 28

# Membership cards

DURHAM 1990S, a day at the cricket with Appleby:

He would be impressed by the cost of a cup of tea if it was 20p. Or not, if it was £1. The cricket would be a pause between eating and drinking. Mainly eating sandwiches, ice cream, nutty (chocolate), fish and chips.

On entering the ground, first, buy a scorecard for 10p. Then you would identify players on the outfield as they warmed up. Then visit the shop. Then identify the players as they take their positions on the field. 'So it's Bairstow wicketkeeper, Phil Sharpe at slip,' etc.

Then start eating.

You would fill in the 10p scorecard with lots of landmarks noted such as 50 in the 23rd over (Boycott 14, Lumb 33, extras 3). Reading the *Daily Telegraph* between balls was also on the agenda in the morning – no good in the afternoon when the spinners Carrick and Cope came on, rattling through the overs.

At lunch, perambulate to look at and comment on the wicket. Then do a lap (walking) of the ground. Be sent looking for autographs of old players who were wandering about, or twelfth men and anyone else who might have played first-class cricket who was in attendance.

Comment on codes of behaviour/tidiness/haircuts of people in the crowd who were being too loud such as wags/chanters/drunks/streakers, or players who were fielding, batting or bowling well or badly. Talk to neighbour on bleachers with observations on play. Walk round ground again.

Look up impending records that might be broken, or where players are born/how old they are in *Playfair* (*Wisden* was too precious to bring). Quiz me on the records of players and other interesting facts, including anniversaries, which may be non-cricket.

Applaud landmarks such as half-centuries or century partnerships and generally be an educated audience member. Find out the other scores from someone with a 'wireless'.

Drinking could wait until later. Appleby didn't drink many beverages or any water but would have a few pints in the afternoon, depending on who he was with, and the price of the beer.

Call out 'run up' to lazy batsmen.

After watching Durham in 1995, Keswick CC stalwart and writer Keith Richardson wrote about Appleby for the *East Cumbrian Gazette*. He and Appleby had got into the Skipton Building Society marquee, probably thanks to Richard Ellwood, Cumberland spinner and Skipton Building Society manager in Keswick. At the table, among the dignitaries, was none other than Brian Bolus, until recently an England selector, whom Appleby could not resist reminding of an innings or shot he played at Headingley, The Oval or Lord's many summers ago. You see, Appleby had a computer brain which had the most extraordinary ability to record and remember facts. Mostly about his greatest passion, cricket, but also about things historical, like the *Titanic*, Gretna Green rail disaster, sinking of the *Bismarck* and the Battle of the Somme, all of which he will happily relate for a free nosebag.

Within minutes, Edgar had Bolus happily engaged in a chat about cricket history that included an impersonation by Bolus of Fred Trueman. Out in the middle was young New Zealand all-rounder Chris Cairns, who looked an awesome player, bowling fast and smashing the ball clean out of the ground.

But Appleby thought there was no substitute for the great players of the past. He's told his interviewer again how his love for the game started with a set of cigarette cards produced in 1938 to coincide with the visit of the Australian tourists. Appleby goes on about his passion as a seven-year-old for cigarette cards; again, their bright colours haven't faded.

He worshipped Wally Hammond, then Hutton. Anyone who reckons Boycott was more of a stylist should be shot. The aesthetics of Graveney and Lindwall are remembered too. After that they went for tea of sandwiches and chocolate eclairs. Wonderful nosebag, marvellous day.

There's a box of membership cards I have now from Cumberland, Yorkshire and Durham which shows his loyalty to the cause. They're hard to throw away as they are colourful but with no financial value.

My Dad was due for a third knee op. The fourth one (second replacement, different leg to first) was wonky so they redid it. The third (first replacement) had to be done after he knackered said joint batting for Hawksdale CC in 1981. That's when he retired from playing and filled the gap by supporting and collecting more.

Chapter 29

# 2001/02 *New Zealand*
# *Test Cricket Captains*

WHEN I was in New Zealand, I was fully immersed in cricket, visiting Walter Hadlee's Christchurch bungalow to research his archive. The 1949 NZ touring team captain wrote a foreword for my book on Kiwi Test skippers.

I even went as far as interviewing some of the Canterbury Cricket Club crowd at a provincial game against Otago. England were touring New Zealand. This was back in 2002, the heyday of the Barmy Army, the new mob of travelling England cricket fans that wore football colours and chanted ditties about the players throughout the day's play.

That was at QE2 Stadium 'Village Green' where Canterbury had started playing. Jade Stadium (the old Lancaster Park) was now too big. No one much came to watch so I asked those that did, why? Turns out most of them were English.

'The Barmy Army is yesterday's news. Meet the grey army represented by Steve Wright, 49, and Patrick Shaw,

what is the appeal of the game for Goodliffe?
he has had thousands of hours to ask himself
ion. Why am I here, particularly when I wait
in to stop? "It's partly aesthetic," he says. "It's
king game to watch. Some people say cricket's
mpared to rugby. My answer is that rugby is
cause there are a lot of stoppages, while cricket
that, while it may proceed slowly, is proceeding
ne. I think it's the best game in the world for
ating individual and team skill.'"

didn't I ask my Dad those questions? I did. And
up with the same answers.

ds have been in crisis since World War Two.
there was a boom caused by the novelty of the
ning back. That's when Appleby was young.
cricket' *Wisden* banged on about for the 1950s.
e was slow. One-day cricket picked it up. The
big viewing figures in 1981 when Botham won
s, for instance. John Player League coverage
day did well too. Sky has it all now on pay-
so not many watch. But there are big crowds
0s.

and Pat and Stephen were proper fans. Not too
equipped for the day out, studying the nuances.
those types of old school fans watch? Were
ng happy childhood memories at the cricket?
the aesthetics of batting, bowling and fielding?
grounds to get some order into their worlds?
work, women, families and the pressures of life
ing in leisure?

57. These slightly more mature fans are in New Zealand to follow the cricket.

'However, they are not too bothered about England's performance. Indeed, they have travelled halfway around the world to follow cricket but have yet to see the England team in action.

'"We're here watching Canterbury to avoid the one-dayers," says Steve, a retired railwayman, from Nottingham, as he sheltered from the cool easterly at Christchurch's Village Green. The odd couple would rather add to their list of first-class grounds visited and keep their lonely vigil on the cricket grounds of the world.

'After spending two weeks at Lincoln University for the under-19 World Cup, the eccentric duo continued their quest to wind their idiosyncratic way to some of the more outlying posts of the cricketing empire. Last week at Molyneaux Park, Alexandra, Steve and Pat were 100 per cent of the crowd.

'"They tried to say it was three but that was counting the sightscreen attendant," said an indignant Steve, the more laconic of the pair. Steve's aim is to watch 100 days of cricket before returning to England for the 2002 season in April. That's 50 in Australia and 50 in New Zealand.

'That's dedication.

'Unlike the Barmy Army, Pat and Steve take tea and sandwiches rather than beer and drums to the ground. Steve scores every game. Not that they don't like the Barmy Army's brand of soccer-style chanting and flag waving.

"I think they're great," says Pat, a retired chemical company manger from Huddersfield, West Yorkshire. But he does differentiate between the real Barmy Army, which started out in Australia in 1994/95 and the hangers-on, "only there for the beer".

'Both Pat and Steve are twice married and twice separated. Steve uses the home of a new lady friend as a base and his free rail pass to follow his beloved Nottinghamshire, home of Richard Hadlee and Derek Randall. The eastern line in England is more convenient for Steve to reach the grounds Notts play at.

'He knows the ins and outs if the rail system as well as he knows the finer points of cricket.

'Here, he and Pat perhaps differ from the noisier fringes of the Barmy Army through their discerning knowledge of the game. They reckon a couple of thousand of the fabled following will reach Christchurch for the Test next month, and 3,000–4,000 for the North Island international.

'And, with flask and scorebooks, the intrepid duo will be there too.'

I saw Pat at the Christchurch Test, later in the tour. New Zealand's Nathan Astle lashed 222 and nearly beat England by himself. The Barmy Army shut up for a while. I went off to report on club cricket before the end, perhaps to avoid seeing England lose. England won.

I found another follower in Christchurch, who epitomised the 'how to be a fan' philosophy even better: 'Dedication to cricket can be a lonely job. It can be lonely being a cricket fan. Players may come and go but there has been one constant during the past 25 years of Canterbury home games.

'Stephen Goodliffe, a 4( has been with the red and b bad, and continues to give he is the only crowd membe the game he loves.

'Remarkably, the Nottin missed just a single game sir Test match instead. He brir warm clothes to wine, sandw but, most importantly, he b

"That's the main thing' game unfold at its own pace skills without getting impa

'Over the years, the Canterbury colours have l pleasure to watch"), Richar and Canterbury run-scorin; ("always worth going to see of Nathan Astle, Chris Cai

'Conversely, Goodliffe the decline in people going lot of people will only go to Unless there are name playe Also, with New Zealand people tend to support a wi

"'Now it's not even wor class games. It would cost than what they would colle the days when Lancaster F not so many years ago.

'But
After all
the ques
for the r.
a nice-lo
boring c
boring b
is a game
all the ti
demonstr

Why
he came

Crow
Post-war
game co
'Brighter
The gam
BBC got
the Ashe
on a Sur
per-view
still at T

Steve
partisan,
Why dic
they reliv
Enjoying
Collectin
Avoiding
by wallov

Maybe there was some camaraderie with a fellow nut. Maybe they just didn't know what else to do. Academic tomes on being a sport fan will tell you these are the underlying reasons. But they mostly say it's the partisan nature of backing a team. I think in cricket, for the pre-internet fan, this is overplayed. They go for the love.

Cricketers become your heroes early in life through a shot, an innings, signing an autograph, or even sharing a birthplace. You enjoy their successes as if they are your own and find reasons to explain their failures.

As an adult, you would ask for an autograph to relive those childhood days, or to sell it. Now, it's much more likely you would take a selfie or use social media to criticise or praise your hero, with the connection becoming more remote.

In 2002, I was reporting ball-by-ball with someone I would describe a budding good ol' boy of sports journalism. He tried to liven up a dull passage by describing one player as having a 'wide-part' (i.e. bald) and another player as an expert in 'knocking up', both on the pitch and off it – his wife was pregnant at the time.

The reporter's boss came in: 'There's been a complaint from the team about the reporting.' I was relieved when the boss, a vastly experienced and generally friendly sports journalist, called the reporter out of the press box, which was virtually empty apart from us two.

The reporter came back a couple of minutes later and packed up his stuff. 'Sense of humour failure,' he muttered.

Out stomped the reporter and in came his (ex) boss. He explained the score, warned me about what language was appropriate to use and offered me the job. 'We need someone to report and do ball-by-ball until the end of the day.' Here was a dilemma. Should I show solidarity with the reporter, like Lech Walesa in Poland or Arthur Scargill's flying pickets? Or should I follow my dream and take my chance in proper sports journalism?

It took a second to decide. I said yes.

## Chapter 30

# Cricinfo T-shirt

I WAS at Lord's in 2002 when I found despair in Cherie Blair's gob (the glass oval of the media centre, which looks like CB's grin from the outside).

The old retainers rolled in one by one after I sat down 90 minutes before play and began pissing about with my pens, books, drink, biscuits, laptop, programme and phone. 'Who are you?' some old hack said.

'I'm writing for Cricinfo,' I replied. I even had the T-shirt (though I was in the correct Lord's uniform of a crumpled linen suit).

'What's your background?' my inquisitor enquired.

'I'm a teacher from New Zealand and I'm over for the summer. Stephen Lamb asked me to write about a few games.' I thought I'd show how eclectic I was by adding that I was a teacher as well as a writer and my cosmopolitan-ness by mentioning New Zealand and my connection by namedropping Lamb, the son of a Lord and brother of the old Northamptonshire bowler turned cricket administrator the Hon. Tim Lamb.

'He's a bloody teacher from New Zealand,' the bloke told the next person to come in, a former player, turned reporter. 'Taken my job, he has.' 'Too much of this sort of thing going on,' agreed the ex-cricketer. Another former player was next and the same conversation happened. 'I'm going to write to the Cricket Writers' Club.' 'So you should,' said one of the ex-pros.

I felt embattled and beleaguered. I talked shop to the other outsiders, freelancers from agencies. I keenly expressed my availability for work and my credentials. I wanted to be one of them.

Next day, the match programme included my report on the previous day's play. The editor, Ralph Dellor, once a John Player League TV commentator, had used it. I didn't know this was going to happen, but I was very proud anyway.

'Strauss conducts himself with aplomb,' I'd written. The future England captain had scored a ton in an early appearance. I'd talked him up as a future England player, even an FEC. Strauss was ex-Radley College, South African, played for Middlesex and had scored a century after all. I'd also used the word 'ironically' at one point.

My new enemy loudly read out the piece, laughing at the musical references and the word 'ironic'. 'Terrible,' he said. 'It shouldn't be allowed. Wait until the Cricket Writers' Club get my letter.' A few of the hacks in the press box expressed agreement. The rest got on with their work.

Next day, he had his reply. He read it out: 'I am appalled that you have had your livelihood stolen by a teacher from New Zealand. I will take this up with

Stephen Lamb. The Cricket Writers' Club must stand up against this cheapening of our trade.' Looking round, it seemed that everyone in the box agreed. No one was on my side. I rang my Dad, not something I'd usually do. Paranoia had overcome me. A couple of days in the box feeling that people were talking about how bad you were and how you shouldn't be there and how you'd nicked work from someone more deserving was getting to me.

Appleby was a last resort. I should have been boasting to him about my success in doing something he would have loved to have done. Anyway, he stood up for me, for the first time since I'd last asked him for help, back in 1983 when *Starstrider* came to school. The BBC quiz show auditioned for a team of pupils. What is myopia? Short-sightedness. Where will the 1984 Winter Olympics be held? Sarajevo. I qualified to take part.

But the age limit was 12 on 1 March. I was 12 a few days before. My Dad was a quiz expert, he'd won a Mini, he'd even won the Rotary quiz (when the question master was not too amateurish). Anyway, my Dad went in to school and complained, unsuccessfully.

Some 17 years later, in 2000, I called Appleby at home in Keswick. He said I should give Lamb a tinkle. I worried that rocking the boat would mean no more work, but I was so paranoid and anxious about everyone hating me that I had to do something. I rang Lamb.

He would explain that the job was fairly and squarely mine. It was all a rather unseemly business. The old reporter was behaving poorly. On the last day of the match, I entered the box, not wanting to catch anyone's eye. Later that morning Lamb rang the man. I saw him take the call. I could see what was happening. I could hear the reporter bluster. But would he listen?

The reporter backed down, more embarrassed about how he felt following Lamb's gentle chat than anything. He had no contract. The job was not rightfully his. The 'Kiwi' was a writer who had been a teacher and he knew his cricket. Later that day, the reporter, who is no longer with us, slid a Fox's glacier mint down the long, white smooth desk of row two of Cherie Blair's gob towards me. 'I'm afraid I've been rather a shit.' Even now, the taste of the mint in my mouth still brings a feeling of relief, joy and hope.

# Chapter 31

# 2003 *Durham CCC 100 Greats*

THIS IS my intro for cricket book three: *Durham Cricket 100 Greats*:

Cricket writer Matthew Appleby has been a fan of Durham, the nearest first-class team to his home county of Cumbria, for many years. His keen interest in the game was sparked by his father, Edgar, who is a well-known cricket expert, book collector, dealer and long-time Durham member. This is Matthew Appleby's third cricket book. He wrote the award-nominated history *New Zealand Test Cricket Captains* and the 125th anniversary history of Canterbury Cricket, both of which were published in 2002. For several seasons he has written for the website Cricinfo both in the UK and overseas. A journalist who works in London, Appleby has contributed on a range of subjects to dozens of publications worldwide.

*Durham Cricket 100 Greats* profiles household cricketing names who have played for the county such as Ian Botham and current England stars Paul Collingwood and Stephen Harmison. Appleby also delves into Durham's origins and its time as champion Minor County a century ago, discovering forgotten heroes for a new generation of cricket fans.

In years to come my Dad used to give the many leftover spares to cricket people who visited Keswick to see his books.

Meanwhile, Appleby was after-dinner speaking less often by now, after trotting out his *History of Cricket* (parts one and two), *Titanic, Quintinshill, The Origins of the First World War* and the unmissable *Rise and Fall of the Hapsburg Empire* talks to any club or society that asked for 20 years. He wouldn't (or couldn't) use illustrations, projections or computer presentations and grumbled those other speakers 'just showed slide shows of their holidays'. My mother said the punters at the local societies were beginning to expect picture-led talks. Appleby knew his speeches by heart, despite Hotspur the otterhound was now pushing up daisies in local optician Donald Cowen's field below Blencathra. They needed a JCB to bury him.

'Penrith Rotarians who met at the George Hotel on Monday enjoyed an elegant and humorous after-dinner talk on the history of cricket by well-known local raconteur Edgar Appleby, of Keswick,' reported the *Lake District Herald* on 26 April 2006. Long gone was editor

John Hurst, who had made Appleby's name locally when he interviewed the 'great collector' after the final *Wisden* was bought almost 30 years before. But Appleby batted on.

'Doubters stumped by the subtleties of square leg and silly mid-off were bowled over by the pace and variety of Edgar's delivery as he energetically reeled off centuries of the sport's history right back to its origins in medieval England.'

The article 'Rotarians Bowled Over By History of Cricket' added: '"If the game had spread across the Channel," Edgar mused, "it might have prevented the French Revolution."' Of course, Grace gets a good chunk, and *Wisden* did too when Appleby reached 1864 'when cricket came of age' and the great book began. In that year, Grace first played outside his native Gloucestershire 'at the start of his legendary career that would see his familiar bearded figure towering head and shoulders above his contemporaries for a full 50 years'.

Chapter 32

# MCC trolleys

CRICKET AND food Matthew Appleby June 2005.

Back in the UK for good, with Cricinfo having almost gone bust and having ditched most of its staff, I was writing about gardening. I tried to write about cricket again. An associate, who was working for *Waitrose Food Illustrated*, asked if I knew anyone who could write a piece on cricket teas. I decided he meant he wanted me to write it. I asked my Dad, who was once probably Cumbria's fattest cricketer, so he should know. He wore XXL MCC 'trolleys' gifted by my godfather Sibson after all, though the elite MCC with its 20-year membership waiting list, and Gamblesby, with its team featuring one-armed farmhands, are about as far removed in cricket terms as is possible in the UK. He eschewed the Rotary hunger lunches and the sportsmen's dinner gastronomy of 1980s Cumbrian hotels and suggested writing about a farming village in the Eden Valley called Gamblesby where they produced gargantuan cricket teas served on a farmhouse table.

This is what I sent:

When I started to play cricket there was much talked about a team called Gamblesby. It's a village team buried miles from anywhere in the Cumbrian countryside. People said their pitch was terrible, covered in cow muck and daisies. They said the changing room was little more than a byre and that the quality of the game was likely to be awful, particularly because the home umpire was the worst you could imagine.

But everyone still loved going there. It was because of the teas. They were piled high after an innings on a bumpy, dangerous wicket, played on long grass under a glaring sun. It was a sloping ground; long and narrow. And you could hit a cow if you tried hard.

Mr Sowerby, the local farmer, had given half the team out lbw for no good reason. Resentment burned. We trailed off to the Sowerbys' distant stone-flagged floor farmhouse for the mid-innings break. Usually the players, mainly single young men, had to provide tea for two – yourself and an opposition player. One bloke always brought two Jamaican ginger cakes. One always brought two bottles of cider, most of which he drank himself. Others brought a pile of Mother's Pride sandwiches their mums had made for sharing with the opposition. Battenberg, garibaldis and mothers' homemade cakes all went down well. Bringing just a Mars bar was not on.

At Gamblesby it was different. The players never minded the walk from the pitch to the farmhouse kitchen. There was pork pie cut in four, homemade sausage rolls, scones and Cumbrian ham sandwiches. Mrs Sowerby's speciality was a gooseberry plate cake, a quarter inch thickness of plate, an inch of pastry, an inch of gooseberry and then another inch of pastry, covered in sugar. Later in the season it would be the same thing but with apple and blackberry. There wasn't much else except fresh hard-boiled eggs and the Sowerbys' own crumbly cheese. Quantity mattered more than variety.

There was no sticky toffee pudding, bottled Lakeland spring water, damson gin, Grasmere gingerbread or Kendal mint cake. That was for the tourists. Cumberland sausage was for dinner, as was the other local speciality, lamb. Brian Sack and Frances Coulson had made the Sharrow Bay Hotel popular in the 1950s. Post-rationing, their use of butter and cream brought the fun back to eating. John Tovey, founder and consultant at nearby Miller Howe Hotel in Windermere later helped pioneer their trademark Cumbrian chintzy country house hotel afternoon tea.

These days Made in Cumbria (Foods), part of an economic development initiative from Cumbria County Council, seeks to raise the profile of butter and cheese makers, beef, lamb, pork butchers, home bakers and apiarists. Wasdale Water, Eden Ostrich World and Cranston's Cumbrian Food Hall at Penrith are now part of the 'Taste District's' campaign to attract foodie tourists.

Back in rural Gamblesby, it was more simple stuff. John Wesley, founder of Methodism, built a chapel there in 1784. Eighteenth-century red sandstone buildings surround the village's tiny green. I remember they had four blokes called Little in their team. None were related. In the Cumbrian vernacular they were called the La'als. The smallest, I think I remember, was a local auctioneer, Norman Little. He was the smallest of the Littles – La'al La'al. Gamblesby weren't a bad team. They were better after tea as their opponents grew fatter, having gorged at the table. The La'als knew better. Burping, full-of-stodge opponents paid all afternoon in the field for over-eating.

One summer's day my team had a big score to get after a particularly long tea. First in was our WG Grace-like opener Edgar. He was 18 stone, wore high-waisted trousers tied with a cord and had a mass of grey wiry hair. He had yellowing pads on and carried an ancient bat that he wrapped in yards of white sticky tape. Edgar had bad gout because of his love of red meat and rich food.

He was brought up during the war in times of rationing and had been taught to 'waste not want not'. If there was food on the table, Edgar thought it was rude not to finish it. At Gamblesby he gorged. He joyfully ate pies, sausages, sandwiches, scones, cakes and, just before he was due to bat, he scranned an exceptionally large piece of farmhouse cheese.

Known as a plodder, Edgar wasn't the best at running between the wickets. After his epic tea at Gamblesby, the ageing batsman became the world's worst runner. Quick singles were impossible. Twos became ones, threes were non-existent. He cleverly glided occasional boundaries down to third man and fine leg instead. Team-mates grew frustrated and when it was their turn to bat they slogged and were quickly out.

I was ten years old and keeping the score. Edgar crawled towards a half-century. These days he rarely scored more runs than his age. On 49 he prodded a delivery into a gap and set off. He thundered home, gasping as the day's gluttony caught up on him. He'd had it. Years of wear had caused his knee to pack up. Edgar needed a runner. For some reason, probably because the rest of the batsmen were so full, I got the job. Suddenly we could score quick singles. After looking like we would never win, we had a chance. From the last over, bowled by La'al La'al, we needed seven runs. Edgar and the last man were in. Edgar blocked and shouted for me to run. I scampered one, then another. Edgar missed a couple then had a rare slog. All his weight drove the ball to the boundary. Wobbling on his good leg, he needed one to win off the last ball. Edgar smacked it into his bad knee and fell. He somehow rose up and started running. So did I and so did our last man. Edgar wasn't meant to be running – I was there to do that. Everyone was shouting. In blind pain, Edgar stumbled down the wicket. He and our No.11 collided. I scraped home. La'al La'al took off the bails at the other end to run out our last man. The match ended up a tie. I cried. Edgar never played again. Edgar was my Dad.

Beer after the match involved my Dad telling me to sit in the corner and 'look old' while he got a round in, his knee bandaged with a pack of ice. We all talked about the game. I know Edgar still thinks about it. I tried to keep up with the slowest drinker, and not look like I was hating the foul-tasting bitter liquid. Food was bags of crisps. The proper eating had already been done. Then it was chips on the way home.

My associate didn't like it. He rang Yorkshire's caterers and wrote up a piece on what they did instead. In 2022, reports came in that cricket teas in the Eden Valley Cricket League were no longer required, because of concerns about being sued over allergens like nuts, celery, cereals containing gluten, prawns, eggs, fish, milk, molluscs, mustard and peanuts ('sounds like a pleasing snack' – Appleby.) 'It's just not cricket,' opined the *Daily Telegraph*: 'Cricket teas have always been just as much part of the game as WG Grace's beard.' Giles Coren wrote a piece saying 'I nearly choked on my pain aux raisins' in *The Times*. In the *Keswick Reminder* Keith Richardson had used Gamblesby as an example of what we were losing.

Chapter 33

# Ties

*Paul Nixon (Nico) 2007*

I'd interviewed Nico before, for *Wisden Cricket Monthly*:

MA: Why do you think you had to wait for so long to get a chance?

PN: England have had some world-class keepers. Alec Stewart and Jack Russell were world-class. Jack Russell was one of the best ever and Stewart was on the England team list for 10 or 15 years and was England captain. On the Pakistan and Sri Lanka tour [in 2000/01] I knew I'd only play if Stewart got injured. Then the selectors looked at one or two youngsters who never pushed on and came through. Now I'm in the right place at the right time. For Leicestershire I've got a few runs at the right time in big 20/20 games and I've been playing in a successful Championship and one-day side so you're going to be maintaining attention. The 20/20 really helped.

MA: Does coming from a cricketing backwater make it harder to get to the top?

PN: I think it does. There's so much more talent that doesn't get seen unless you get someone like my father who put the effort in ferrying me around the country for net sessions. There were other guys with more talent at school level who didn't have that opportunity. The answer is quality facilities and quality coaches and regular work with county coaches and county talent-spotters. At Durham and Lancashire and with us at Leicestershire we're trying to tap into that market.

MA: You have persevered with the double-handed sweep, after being criticised by cricket writers – why? You also stand in front of the stumps for fielders returns – how effective is that?

PN: I don't read the press much. My feeling is that you're never going to get a good press in Australia because they're so dedicated to their own teams, and they only give goodness to their own players. There's never any negativity in Australians as a race. That's something we could learn from in our country. I'm always trying to take the game to a new level – testing myself and getting away from the run of the mill. I'm trying to develop all the time on the cricket field or in life. The reverse sweep, whether down or up is a well-practised shot that hopefully puts the spinners' best ball to the boundary. If you hit their best ball to the boundary, you put doubt in their minds. It doesn't come off every time but in the last two years I've scored a couple of hundred Championship runs with it and got out once or twice and in one-dayers I've scored 400 or 500 in a couple of years and got out a couple of times. Duncan Fletcher is keen of practising new ideas and new mindsets and that's something I've been working on. If you take the ball in front and go backwards it's been proven it takes a shorter time. We work on it daily in practice. It's the usual thing now.

MA: You give bowlers such as Monty a lot of support and also the captain – what do you offer them, and do they listen?

PN: My role in the team is to look at the angles and point out where their batsmen are looking to hit and almost help set fields. Bowlers sometimes like key words at the end of overs. Just two or three words repeated like 'fourth stump' or 'fifth stump'. I just keep reminding them. Monty likes a bit more chat than most. He likes my idea of where the batsman's looking to hit him. We want the batsman to hit where we want him to hit rather than where he wants to. Monty wants to know what percentage of sliders or turning balls to bowl. It's just constant conversations trying to instil constant pressure.

And the badgering? First and foremost, you've got to back your ability and think what you bring to the party. But the drip-feeding of talk baiting the opposition is only a small percentage of what I want to offer the team and unit. The management's very keen I keep giving it to the opposition and my own players. The Steve Waugh method of disorientation works if you can create uncertainty in players. I've played with most of these guys for a long time. Little traits come out. It's impulsive sometimes. It certainly keeps my keeping more focussed and gives me a lift. I'm more aggressive catching the ball and more aggressive batting so it keeps me going. But if you're going to give it you'll receive it though I can't say I've had much back. The Aussies are a focused unit, and I haven't got many runs against them yet. I've just come in with a few overs left mostly.

MA: You're the senior wicketkeeper in the English game. What changes have you seen in the last 20 years?

PN: There's been massive changes, even in the last five years. Everyone is so much more positive. Everyone is more focussed on an elite level of performance and attention to detail. I've just come out of a 45-minute meeting looking at weaknesses in the opposition batting with an attention to detail on how to get out every individual player. Years ago people used to look after their own games. But people are more open now than they used to be.

MA: What are the team's chances in the World Cup – and yours?

PN: Getting picked for the World Cup team is about match-winning performances. But I'm a relaxed person. All I can do is my very best. If that's good enough, then so be it. If not then it's someone else's time. All I can do is give 100 per cent on and off the pitch. We have to individually peak at the right time and make sure our game is in order. We need good preparation and to work on our processes and do the basics better so everyone comes out on top. Beating Australia after underperforming in key areas of games showed a lot of character. Not many sides have beaten Australia in the last few years. To beat them you need to raise your standards constantly. We've suffered from injuries, but we'll hopefully get them back – Michael Vaughan and if we get to the final Kevin Pietersen is coming back. That's the goal. There's a strong chance of that so hopefully he will.

MA: What with Mal Loye's debut and talk of a call-up for Darren Gough, there's something of a Dad's Army look to England these days. What do you make of that?

PN: It's about a balance between youth and experience. The England 2003 Rugby World Cup winners got called a Dad's Army by the press. The Australian side is mature. You've got to have a balance now. Alec Stewart played to 40 and Jack Russell to over 40. As long as you're fit and strong and putting in match-winning performances that's what it's all about.

MA: You're getting on a bit. What about the future?

PN: I enjoy every day as a professional sportsman. It's a great life and I'm proud to do it. I know my career's coming to an end in the next few years but long may it last. I'm involved in a property project in Barbados. It's an eight-year development with nearly 2,000 homes, a casino, hotels and golf courses and a big marina. That's a huge thing and then there's my benefit year for Leicestershire this year launching on 22 February at the Walker's Stadium. A highlight will be a charity football and cricket match at Keswick on 13 May.

MA: How did it feel to get picked for the World Cup?

PN: It's nice that the energy and passion and work I do with the gloves and the bat paid dividends. It's great to be backed by the selectors to go and try and win the World Cup.

MA: How did that iconic picture of you in the crowd after beating Australia in the final come about?

PN: It was Freddie's idea. He wanted to say thanks to the Barmy Army for supporting us all winter. After the high of winning and beating Australia, I just thought it would be a nice picture to stand in front with the Barmy Army behind me, for my benefit as much as anything. It could have been my last moment as an England cricketer. I wanted to say thank you for the experience of a lifetime and then I got dragged into the crowd.

MA: What is your best sledge?

PN: I remember that when Andrew Symonds used to play for Kent, Jack Russell walked alongside and tried to get into his bubble. I said to Simmo: 'You just edge it and I'll send the scorecard every day for a whole year.' He didn't like that.

MA: What about your popularity in world cricket?

PN: It's been an amazing experience over the last couple of months – just going out to Australia in the first place and being around England's biggest players, Michael Vaughan, Andrew Flintoff, Kevin Pietersen. It's amazing to see how many people know the lads. We were getting stopped every couple of yards along the streets. It's amazing it's only been a couple of months. I just think people like my story. This old guy gets selected and England win. It shows if you work hard and do the right things it all comes around in the end.

I'd asked Dad what to say. He talked about the stats, beating Bobby Parks' wicketkeeping records and his own collection of cricket ties, with Leicestershire Championship-winning souvenirs prominent among them, in honour of Nico. He wasn't in Vic Lewis's league. The Middlesex CCC committee man, who described cricket as religion, even wrote a book about his 5,000 pieces of cricket neckwear.

## Chapter 34

# 2007 Nixon benefit

I'VE DRIVEN from the Malvern Spring Gardening Show to Keswick for Paul Nixon's benefit do. Nixon was on his way to Keswick from Derby, where Leicestershire had just lost to Derbyshire. He'd scored 42 and was second-last out but it wasn't enough to save his team. It's Saturday, 13 May 2007.

England Rugby World Cup-winning captain Martin Johnson is speaking at the Nico benefit evening do. Appleby is MC.

Nixon had opened Keswick CC's new £85,000 pavilion 13 years before, in 1994, shortly after returning from touring India with England A. John Hurst's *Lake District Herald* reported 'Keswick cricketing authority' Appleby saying Nixon was 'only 23' but it 'has taken him a long time to get recognition in the newspapers, so it is all the more creditable that he has got to the top'. The *Keswick Reminder* referred to Appleby as 'Keswick's cricket statistician'. It rained all day so the commemorative match was called off.

By 2007, Nico's playing career was well through. His Keswick benefit bash, part of a benefit season of fundraising dinners and golf days, was reward for ten years' service for Leicestershire. When I arrived home in Keswick, I was locked out. So I crossed Crosthwaite Road into Fitz Park, to the cricket club. First, I saw club chairman Richardson, who is co-organising the Nixon do.

'Alright Keith,' I say as he walked round the ground, watching his young charges in the seconds knock up a few against Appleby IIs.

'Ah, young Matthew.'

'How are they doing?'

'Not bad. Looking forward to Nixon's do?'

'Yeh, is that his Dad umpiring?'

He misunderstands. 'Your Dad's over there.'

He was, wandering round the ground collecting contributions 'to help with the upkeep of the club' from the straggle of punters standing or sitting in the park, situated below Skiddaw and alongside the River Greta.

'Good Lord, good journey?' Appleby says, after I catch up with him (not a difficult thing to do).

MA: 'OK, getting much cash?'

'Not bad.'

'Hello Edgar,' say the punters. He's the 'Iron Chancellor', the cricket club's tight-fisted treasurer.

'That Nixon's Dad out there umpiring?' I say as clearly as I can.

'Yes, that's Brian. Nico's on his way – Leicestershire lost badly. Johnson's here – in the pub watching Leicester rugby apparently.'

We wander round the rest of the ground. Appleby knows everyone. A few know me. Appleby's mate Knowles talks to me about Everest. I'd joined his trip to Base Camp the year before. Richardson was on it too.

A few locals had volunteered to run the Nixon fundraiser – Richardson, my Dad, Bryson the baker. At the night event 300 turned up, in their dinner jackets, with wives in party frocks. Local sports enthusiasts. I was on a family table. We settled down to dinner in the £4,000 rented marquee. My mother pointed out Carlisle United chairman Fred Story, who was paying for the tent. His then future wife Vivienne used to live behind us when we were little, my Mum told me. Vivienne and her sisters used to babysit for me and my brother and sister. My brother was two places round from me on our table, with his girlfriend and his best mate Morland, just back from the Marines in Afghanistan, either side. There was plenty of booze.

I had a goal for the night. I wanted to write Nixon's biography (in the future, not on that night – I could hardly hold a pen). He was the only player I could claim to even know slightly. I remembered how I'd first come across him in 1984, playing cricket and rugby and then at the NatWest Trophy between Cumberland and Derbyshire, when he'd asked Bob Taylor for advice. I remembered how he'd hit me for six in a school game. I envied his sportsman's poise (and his blonde highlights and gold flash trainers) then just as much as I respected his success and fame now. He'd worked at it – now it was my turn. He had a plan in 1984, aged 13. Now he was a gnarly old pro, playing for England in one-day matches, bald, known for his comic chirping of opposition batsmen from behind the stumps.

Nixon to Australia batsman Michael Clarke: 'You've changed your bat sticker. That's bad luck.' Clarke: 'Nixon, you're a club cricketer.' Nixon: 'How's it going to feel, Michael, to be caught by a club cricketer? How. Is. That. Going. To. Feel? You know what? You're going to make a club cricketer's day.'

He said it was playing Cumbrian village cricket as a teen that had toughened him up and made him start to put on a carapace of being as mad as a badger. The other apprentices when he started as a teen with the MCC at Lord's didn't get him. So he did the non-stop talking, cajoling and bouncing around act to fill the quiet times and to give added value. He made himself offer more than the rest of the wannabe pros.

Some Sussex-based comedian warmed up the crowd with sportsmen's fare.

Then it was my Dad's turn. I'd seen him through an ajar door practicing his speech, sitting on his bed in his trollies that evening. There was no dog anymore to walk round the block going through his speeches out loud. Canine-less and after three knee replacements, sitting on the bed had to do.

He did his speech.

Paul Nixon benefit match dinner Fitz Park, Keswick, Cumbria, June 2007.

Master of ceremonies: Edgar Appleby.

We're all true British patriots are we not?

And as such 21 October is an important date because on 21 October 1805 at the Battle of Trafalgar we wiped up the frogs, I'm pleased to say. Then we showed the Nelson spirit and someone here also born on that day certainly has the Nelson spirit.

Paul Nixon was born on 21 October 1970 at Fusehill St Hospital, Carlisle, brought up in Langwathby and schooled at Penrith.

Not everyone knows where that is – the popular press calls him the lad from Wordsworth country.

Nelson said engage the enemy more closely – that was Nelson's last signal. And Paul Nixon got stuck in. Do the best you can – that's the way you do it.

As a young player he was nurtured by his father Brian who has been his main supporter all his life. He became one of the best signings Leicestershire ever made. Taking someone from cold they could hardly have done better. And he's never looked back.

Paul had three years with Kent – the grass always appears greener but Leicestershire welcomed him back, which says a lot for him.

When a player leaves a county if he's unpopular they don't him want back at all.

So smiling or snarling, there's not much difference, 18 years later Paul is the senior wicket in county cricket with 788 catches and 66 stumpings as of today.

Chris Read is about 400 behind. But wicketkeepers these days have got to bat a bit as well and Paul certainly can. He's scored 11,249 first-class runs with 16 centuries and 52 fifties, as of today.

Now the media always says of Paul, 'At the age 35', which is a favourite hobby horse of mine.

Whenever you see his name it's 36-year-old Paul Nixon, as if it's a stigma being 36. What a load of rubbish. He's one of the fittest blokes around! You choose your best team, not necessarily your youngest team.

Our sportswriters are a very cosy bunch of self-satisfied kind of beggars, they hardly have an original thought between them.

Paul's highest score is 144 not out scored last season at Wantage Road, Northampton. Perhaps he was encouraged by the high standard of food at Wantage Road. I was there last year and it said on the today's specials board 'gravy and chips', which must count as haute cuisine in Northampton. Anyway, last season, at the age of 35, he was second to top of the batting averages.

All these writers say 'we should have a young team – youth. Look at the positives because in four or five years' time we'll have a good team'. I couldn't give a damn about five years – what we want is to win now!

Put your best team out, your best fella even if he is 36 years old, he should stay there.

Paul's a different sort of wicketkeeper with his chunter; he's a general nuisance to opposition batsmen who can't settle and then play a daft shot.

At the end of the innings there may be more byes which looks not as good on paper – but which one do you want? You want noise to buck your team up, 'get cracking, get stuck in'. Paul can do that, others can't.

Are you a man for crisis or collapse?

Geraint Jones was born in Papua New Guinea. I thought people from there had a bone through their nose.

Last year in that Test he wandered down the pitch and was run out for a duck. If that happened for Keswick seconds people would be saying 'what the bloody hell are you doing?'

You need a bloke who can raise your team.

At my age I only want for two more things in life.

I have a sexual passion for Nicole Kidman. I don't know if I'd be able to do much good now for Nicole but she could do me a lot of good!

And my other wish is to make Paul Nixon the full Test wicketkeeper.

There's only been one Test keeper born in Cumberland.

Monkhouse, you should know who that is.

'Nipper' Frank Nicholson moved with his family from Millom to South Africa aged two. You can't blame him for escaping Millom! And he played four Tests in 1935/36. I hope Paul Nixon can be the next one. I think he's done enough. He's the first Cumbrian to play 100 first-class matches.

It should have been you Monkhouse, if you'd started earlier and not spent years buggering around instead of playing.

Paul's played 299 first-class games and even you from Kirkoswald will be able to work out that next week his next game will be his 300th first-class game. You're sharp boys.

And that's good enough for me. He's far and away Cumberland's best first-class cricketer, a perfect example of the sportsman on and off the field. My favourite eggshell blonde. I sincerely hope he gets a Test cap but if he doesn't, he's still done enough for me. So get up on your hind legs – stand up for anyone who can't understand that.

There was applause. But mostly laughter, then Martin Johnson and Nico did their speeches, a bit 'follow that' in tone until they got into their after-dinner sportsmen's banter.

When Nico was on: 'Hard act to follow, Edgar.'

'Apparently, I've played 697 matches, scored almost 18,000 runs, taken 1,100 catches and 163 stumpings. Tomorrow morning I'll be sitting next to the radio at 9.30am, fingers crossed.

'Sadly, I'm not as organised as Edgar. I remember playing at Keswick CC as a 13-year-old. I wandered out on to a huge field and it was very daunting.

'Keith Richardson was the fastest left-armer I've ever seen. It served me well that day because I scored my first fifty.

'I'd like to thank one or two people. Keith. I hear he was sleeping here guarding the tent last night with his flask.

'And Edgar, he's going to be on *Mastermind*, what a genius.

'Neil Boustead's here. Bowie's one of my heroes.

'This is like *This is Your Life*!

'Dickie Spruce, my coach at under-10, 12 and 14 was absolutely brilliant.

'Mum and Dad. Their support and belief and trust every year was ridiculous. Dad took me everywhere, football, cricket, rugby, basketball. To Junior Blues training. They were special days. Mum has always been there. Her best advice was do your best and I've always done my best for her.

'I'm lucky making my living in professional sport.

'I've met legends – Steve Waugh over from Australia. In the heat of the battle professional sportsmen care about something – the respect professionals have for each other. Seven or eight years ago, Michael Jordan and Steve Waugh stood head and shoulders above other sportsmen. No one has a bad word to say in the world of sport about those two.'

The next day England's new coach (ex-Sussex coach) Peter Moores picked Sussex's wicketkeeper Matthew Prior for England. Nico's chance was gone.

After a game of celeb football (including some *Emmerdale* stars) in Fitz Park, Keswick, with Martin Johnson as opposition captain, I collared Nico.

The piece ran in the papers: 'Disappointed, not unexpected', etc. He'd already known during the dinner. The selectors had rung him during the county match. He kept up a brave face. He had played one-day internationals with some success, and a T20 I'd actually seen in Australia. But Nixon the England Test player – he would never be one.

## Chapter 35

# Nixon letter

IN EARLY 2008, I wrote Nico a letter. My Dad had got
the address from Nixon's Dad Brian, who often umpired
at Keswick matches.

Dear Paul,
I met you at Keswick Cricket Club in 2007
at your benefit dinner and spoke about the
possibility of a biography. Don't know if you
remember but my father Edgar Appleby was
MC.

My experience includes writing for Cricinfo
and Sky Sports and I have written three
cricket books.

I played against you as a teenager when I
was at school in Carlisle and Keswick and have
followed your career closely since then.

So I feel well placed to write a book about
you that would appeal to cricket fans nationwide
and internationally, from Cumbria to Kent and

of course Leicestershire, as well as those who saw your impact on the 2007 World Cup and the ICL.

Ideally, I'd like to talk to you about how to go ahead.

Hope you can help please,

Matthew Appleby.

Well, that maybe is what I should have written. Aware that cricket books Appleby had given me to read in my youth were quite same, with their chronological journey from cradle, via school cricket teams, getting in the county side, international call-ups, tours, then a chapter on thoughts on the game's future and one on 'my best XI', I decided that to win the William Hill Sports Book of the Year, I needed to shake the format up a bit. This was by including in the letter:

'My idea is to interweave your successful career with my experiences of cricket, contrasting the player and the fan's progress from similar starting points, and showing how their passion for the game can be equal. For instance, I remember you talking to Bob Taylor at Cumberland v Derbyshire during the NatWest Trophy first round match in 1984 at Kendal. I'd intertwine that with my day at that match. I remember playing against you at Penrith and getting bowled by you – a wicketkeeper! You also hit me for six to win the match. I hope this idea appeals and you think it will make an interesting perspective on your career.'

In 2012, Nixon's autobiography was written with Jon Colman, the Carlisle *News and Star* football writer. Nixon had starred in Leicestershire's T20 final win in 2011, his final match before retirement. Colman did a far better job than I would have. Nevertheless, I still had one cricket person I could maybe write a book about – Edgar Appleby himself.

## Chapter 36

# 2008 Lord's invitation

'THE PRESIDENT and Committee of the Marylebone Cricket Club request the pleasure of the company of Edgar Appleby at the Arts and Library Summer Party to celebrate the launch of the Museum's new exhibition "Going to the Cricket" and two new Library publications: *The Essential Denison* and *Captain of the Crowd* in the Long Room and Museum on Wednesday April 9th 2008. Drinks and Canapes 6.30–9.00pm. Lounge suit.'

I'd met book dealer Christopher Saunders a few times through my Dad. Appleby bought from Saunders' catalogues. Saunders had organised the Lord's event to launch a reprinted Victorian cricket book in the Lord's Long Room. He had invited his best buyers to the launch. My Dad and my mother came down to stay at mine in London for the event.

We got the tube from Tooting Bec to Lord's. Appleby was lame. There was lots to drink.

We looked round the museum and listened to Saunders' launch speech. What a kind man. He looked a bit like Bill Bryson, tweedy and beardy, round glasses. The collectors generally looked like the retired bank managers and accountants they were. They'd found their club. I was guiding the ageing Appleby about. By this stage, the internet had put a value on every cricket book and item of memorabilia, taking a bit of the fun out of collecting. But events like this brought it back.

I got chatting to two youngish women in front of a painting in the museum, trying hard not to sound drunk, egged on by my Dad. 'Presentable,' he said.

After a grand night out, I decided we'd get a taxi home. Even at £50, he didn't argue. He'd been 'ashore'.

## Chapter 37

## *Corridor of Uncertainty*

THIRTY-ODD YEARS after first meeting Geoffrey Boycott at Bradford Park Avenue and carrying his bags, I had *The Corridor of Uncertainty*, Boycs' latest autobiography, signed for my Dad at the Lord's one-day end-of-season final in 2014. This was no longer the Gillette Cup or NatWest Trophy as it had been known through the 1960s to the 1990s, when my Dad went most years, from his bachelor days to the attempted bonding weekends with the teenage me in the mid to late 1980s. Now the end-of-cricket-season climax was called the Royal London One-Day Cup. I went alone, for the first time.

At the match, the tannoy gent, still talking about 'perambulation', announced Boycs was signing his new autobiography during tea outside the shop, which we'd visited during every match Dad and I had ever been to at Lord's.

Boycs: 'Sign to?'

Me: 'My Dad, Edgar, a long-time fan of yours.'

GB: 'When did he first see me?'

Me: '1960s.'

GB: 'Where's he from? Bradford? I made a few good innings there.' [Actually 2,861 runs at 46.90 in first-class matches with ten centuries – Boycs' least successful home ground after Hull.]

Me: 'What do you think will happen in the match?'

GB: 'Durham need to pace themselves in and go carefully. They've not won yet. There's a long way to go.'

Boycs was right. Durham scraped home, thanks to Ben Stokes batting uncharacteristically defensively, maybe even Boycott-like. On the way back from Lord's the carrier bag that the book was in caught in my front bike wheel and I went over the handlebars. The book was a bit bashed and oily, as was I. There was no rubbing it clean.

A month later, I met writer, Nick Hoult, who assisted Boycs with the book, at former New Zealand all-rounder Chris Cairns' trial at Southwark Crown Court in London. We talked about how *The Corridor of Uncertainty* was something different from the ordinary cricket autobiography. Much was about Boycs' cancer and relationships. Not my Dad's thing.

When I gave my Dad the book I showed him the signature. I said I'd never seen that sort of Lord's crowd. It was half-full, they didn't seem to know what was going on, crowd catches, all that. Used to be a full house, the NatWest Final. If you did well, you went on the winter tour. Hoult said it had been like that for a while and it's all about Twenty20 now. I said the same to my Dad when I gave him the book, passing off Hoult's insight as my own. He didn't pass comment.

The Boycs book went on the shelf, next to where Dad sat. Months later, on another visit to Keswick, I opened the Boycott book's bashed covers. On the title page: 'To Edgar, best wishes Geoff Boycott.' The bookmark is left between pages 6 and 7.

Appleby was from Middlesbrough, of course. It just fitted better to say Bradford.

He hadn't mentioned the bruises or marks on the book. He had his own to worry about – skin cancer, half a lung, cataracts, plastic knees, diverticulosis, gout, loss of taste and smell and balance, and speech and mobility. There were fewer books now, after Keswick's River Greta flooded in 2009, when he reluctantly sold the *Scores and Biographies*, the county yearbooks, *Lillywhites* and more. There was too much to take upstairs when the river got high. His health was worsening and the books were becoming a lag.

## Chapter 38

# Collector wagon wheel

CLOSE TO the Boycott book on Appleby's closest shelf was *Cricket's Collectors* by David Frith, signed by Tom Graveney and Frith – number 45/150 copies. It was a 2012 publication.

The book starts with Anthony Baer, the properly eccentric fan collector, well outdoing Appleby. We'd seen him at the Winder auction sale back in 1986, the one where we drove down overnight and stayed in the car outside Phillips until they unlocked the doors. Baer, like Winder, was rich with inherited money to buy their collections.

Baer would be after cricket china and memorabilia generally. He shouted big bids at auctions. He was 'hopeless with names but good with telephone numbers'. Instead of using his name, he called Frith 'Guildford 32573'.

The collecting mania began with the Joe Goldman auction in 1966. A Phillips 1978 sale saw £34,000 come in for 121 cricket lots sold. Appleby would have read about this in an article written by Frith and decided to go next time. A WG Grace hankie made £850. Frith says he once got one for £2 in a junk shop.

The Cricket Memorabilia Society was founded in 1986 and important figures included Robert Brooke (and Michael Down). Brooke was the Association of Cricket Statisticians co-founder (with Dennis Lambert) and its book reviewer for many years. His segues into personal crusades reminded me of Appleby's *Borderer* writing. Brooke used to write critical reviews and even obituaries for society journals, saying what he thought, perhaps without thinking whether it might cause offence. If they were, in his view, inaccurate with their stats or interpretation of them, that could lead to criticism in the obit, which is traditionally seen as a eulogy, though increasingly in *Wisden*, following *The Guardian* journalist Matthew Engel's appointment as editor in 1993, as an entertaining piece of writing about late cricket characters.

Frith's *Cricket's Collectors* book recounts how EK Brown, in many ways, started the collecting mania off with the Epworth collection.

It tells of how Tim Bunting bought pioneer collector/statistician Geoffrey Copinger's huge collection via dealer Giles Lyon.

In an interview in 1992, art dealer Leslie Waddington warned that buying art for investment was a dangerous business and described the notion that people buy art primarily for investment reasons as 'Marxist nonsense'. They buy, he explained, either because they are interested in art or because they like to own what people richer and more famous than themselves like to own.

There's a fabled 1912 autograph book that belonged to John McLaren, an old Australian fast bowler, which was part of the Sheldon collection. Is it as good as my JWHT autograph book? McLaren includes 1911/12 England and 1912 Australia autographs, and all the teams they played against that summer. In the JWHT leather-bound book I have via Appleby from Newsome at Wellington College I only have Australia, Northamptonshire and Kent, but there is Fry, Ranji and Grace. There are also some seriously obscure items such as a 1939 Len Hutton wagon wheel of his 196 against the West Indies at Lord's, hit shortly before the war, during which the Yorkshireman injured his left arm so badly in an Army training accident it was left two inches shorter than the right. Appleby also broke his left arm in the forces, when he caught the limb in a bit of machinery in a frigate's engine room. His cricket remained at the same standard after a lengthy recovery, as Hutton's did.

Frith writes about the legendary RG Barlow stained-glass window found by Keith Hayhurst in a skip – a quasi-religious experience. The Lancastrian cricket historian Rev. Malcolm Lorimer collected cricketers' orders of service. Appleby had the sacred Hansie Cronje's cap. Frith compares Victor Trumper's blazer to the Turin shroud. Trumper's bat was on show at Lord's, the cathedral of cricket, when Yorkshire won the County Championship in 2015.

Frith says: 'The autographs obtained early in one's life surely remain the most sentimentally precious.' Maybe we're getting somewhere. My Dad collected cigarette cards of course, starting in 1938, and had a sentimental attachment to them. I've got a book of them signed, and also had them framed. I've got my autograph books and scorecards. When their Keswick house flooded in 2005, the autograph books, barely touched for 20-odd years, got damp. My Dad told me he was sorry. He never did that. He wasn't bothered about the computer that perished.

In FS Ashley-Cooper's *Cricket Highways and Byways* (1927) there's a chapter on collecting and why. There's an article on Tony Woodhouse in *Wisden Cricket Monthly* July 1983, written by Frith, which is part of a series on collectors. Woodhouse was my Dad's cricket-book collecting friend/associate. Frith reveals that Woodhouse was a tight Yorkshireman and never paid over £100 for anything. He goes on about how 'Woodlouse' (as Appleby called him habitually, because he thought childish rhymes were funny) never missed a day of Yorkshire playing, home and away, similar to Stephen Goodliffe, the Canterbury fan who diligently watches every game his local team plays often virtually alone.

Woodhouse had everything, even an 1893 Yorkshire yearbook – one of only 200 and the greatest want for many completist collectors. Frith relates how tape recorder-owning collector Don Rowan recorded 1,500 cricket voices. I once asked Walter Hadlee, the former New Zealand player and father of the great all-rounder Sir Richard, what the first New Zealand Test captain Tom Lowry sounded like. He might have been the last to know (Hadlee's first-class career started in 1933/34, the season after Lowry's ended). Hadlee said Lowry sounded 'posh English' and not like a New Zealander at all.

The book suggests collectors are fanatics, while investors are not fans. For instance, 'Arabs' might collect to invest, says one Australian collector.

The supply of these items is finite, and theoretically, diminishing as they get lost, or burnt, or water-damaged, or otherwise devalued. Auction site eBay showed there were more of many items than anyone thought, maybe even tucked away to keep values up. Condition, rather than content, is everything to the investor-collector. It's all about rarity and the state it's in. The market is driven by shrinking supply and demand, growing in areas such as unique high-end mint condition or signed items. No one really needs *Wisdens* as a statistical reference anymore with all the facts being online, so collecting them isn't really for the knowledge, but, thinking of Appleby and others, it could be as a relaxing pastime, to interact with fellow collectors, the appreciation of their aesthetic value and pride in owning them, for recognition by fellow collectors and for the challenge of completing the full run – the thrill of the chase.

You might want to donate your prizes, you might want to sell them after collecting as an investment. In *Wisden*'s case, much is about nostalgia, often reliving childhood – collectors sometimes begin with their birth year or the year they started loving the game. Then there's the desire to order, possess and control and the innate satisfaction of having that alongside you on the shelves. Maybe they have an emotional attachment to the subject matter, which represents simpler, happier days. The psychology is that there is a reservoir of good memories to fall back on, keeping the past to keep hold of a part of themselves they fear they will lose.

There's a fine line between ordered collecting and clutter and hoarding, which tends to be associated with living alone, mental health problems and having a deprived childhood. Buying things to make you happy, that might come in useful and mustn't be discarded.

PJ Mullins, another Australian collector, had an obsessive fear of fire. Dad sold a lot of books after Keswick's 2005 flood. More went after 2009's. There was another, final, flood in late 2015. Among the stuff that went was the Frith-edited full run of *Wisden Cricket Monthly*, including the series of articles on collectors Frith had in the series. Appleby was never featured.

Chapter 39

# Cumbrian cricket grounds

25 AUGUST 2013: Keswick v Furness, Cumberland
County Cup Final at Appleby.

It was a Sunday and we were visiting Keswick, me,
Bethan, William (four) and Ted (nearly two).

'I'll take him, it'll be fine,' I said.

'It's harder than you think. He can't walk, he'll need
help in the toilet and you won't want to do that,' said
my mother.

I said, 'It's not far – just down the A66. We'll come
back when he's had enough. I'll take the wheelchair.'
He'd stopped driving after a wobbly trip up the pass to
Whinlatter Forest. He'd just about stopped walking. And
drinking. And eating. And talking. And reading. But he
could still watch.

'Hold on to the back of me trousers,' he rasped. I
steadied him down the back garden to my car.

The garden didn't work for cricket now, it was my
mother's garden with cottage style, winding pebble paths
and no lawn to play on. Not like at Millcroft in Carlisle

when I was young, where I repaired the crease that I'd made under the willow and laburnum trees with soil and water.

Back to Keswick, well Appleby anyway. I'd never been before. Appleby is our surname, but the town has nothing to do with us. I parked as near as I could and pushed him to the virgin ground. It was scenic, next to the river. Near the entrance was Bryson, the Keswick baker. 'Dan's out already,' he exclaimed. Dan Gaskell had been run out. We moved on round the edge of the outfield, with me having to pull the wheelchair backwards over the rough bits. 'I'm alright here,' Appleby said. We watched, ate the sandwiches, not as greedily as he used to. I was worried about the toileting. 'Too hot,' he gasped out, so we moved to the pavilion in the shade. Ryder came along, a mate of Appleby, vice president to Appleby's Keswick CC president. He tried to chat to my Dad, who couldn't give much back. 'Good game, nice day, batting well, looking good,' Ryder battled on. 'Like a pint, Matthew?' he eventually tried. I said no, because my Dad wouldn't or shouldn't have one and because I was driving.

Paul Hindmarch was in the middle, with brother Steve. They were coached from a young age by Bryson and Paul had almost made it in the county game with Durham, his back injury too bad to play day-in day-out. He played a bit for the Unicorns, who were a county cricket aspirants' team. Steve Hindmarch had played football for Carlisle United. Progress was slow against Furness's splay-footed seamer Peter Lawson, an ex-Cumberland opening bowler. 'Furness think they're too good for us,' Ryder ventured. 'Taking it for granted, we'll show them.'

'Well played Steve,' my Dad managed as the opener walked past having got out for 35. Steve nodded. Gradually Paul accelerated, then he started hitting sixes off spinner Will Chapples into the churchyard, three in a row at one point. Geeth Kumara, Keswick's Sri Lankan pro, played lovely late cuts. I chatted away commenting on the play. Dad had wanted Geeth to stay on as pro when he was in bad form and his next year's contract was in question.

The committee met round our dining table. 'He's done just enough if you add in that he's very good with the young lads,' Appleby said, his 70 years of cricket fandom counting for something. Appleby wasn't the type to tell someone they weren't wanted. Geeth improved the next year and stayed for a decade.

Kes reached 213/5 off 40, Paul H holed out for 90. A proper John Player Sunday League BBC2 score. Lawson 0-24 off eight. Sri Lankan pro Ian Daniel 0-20 off eight, treated with caution, Chapples took 4/85 off eight. I suggested we leave, thinking my mother would be worried. He quite readily agreed.

We pushed on past Bryson; 'You leaving, Edgar? We'll let you know what happens, looking good.' He touched his hat, we drove home and he fell asleep.

'We won, we won!' Judith Bryson was on the phone. 'Tell your Dad we won.' I'll get him.

'It was amazing, when did you leave? Oh yes, well Paul bowled the final over, he shouldn't have really with his back but they only needed 15 and it was either him or Ben, and he's just a young lad, or Dan, so Paul bowled and he got their man out, it was amazing.'

This was a momentous final fitting act on that sunny afternoon. There were sixes, 20 of them, hit into the churchyard, the gardens of the vicarage and into the River Eden. There were only five runs in it at the end. Paul Hindmarch was man of the match.

Two years later, in December 2015, Appleby CC flooded, just as our Keswick house did again, after 2005 and 2009's damp interludes. A £6m glass-topped wall built alongside the River Greta did not help, but it did divert tonnes of silt and trees and other junk on to Fitz Park cricket ground. Keith Richardson got Fitz Park fixed. Appleby took a bit longer.

The year before the Appleby final we'd seen Keswick in another final at Threlkeld, which also subsequently flooded and got covered in silt and slate, leaving it useless for 18 months. A cricket calendar shot with players playing on the top of fells and in lakes raised cash to hire JCBs to clear the stones off the pitch. At the match, we left when it got cold. Keswick won.

## Chapter 40

# Missing dinners

RICHARDSON PRODUCED a Keswick CC annual magazine for the 2015 season. El Presidente: the one and only Edgar Appleby gets page 31, with a picture of him posing alongside Keswick's lake, Derwentwater, with Hotspur the otterhound, in about 1989. He sums it all up nicely. Appleby's bookstall, the navy, Middlesbrough, his love of anniversaries, Grace, his grandson WG, his speeches on rail disasters and sinkings and how he learnt them when walking the beast, which was the best-informed on the *Bismarck* and Grace in the world.

There was another sportsman's dinner on 22 October 2014, this time at the Skiddaw Hotel, Keswick. Guest speaker was former Lancashire and England seamer and Sky commentator Paul Allott.

This do followed a similar format to an earlier fundraising bash featuring Mike Watkinson, also of Lancashire and England, with the commemorative card titled 'Keswick Cricket Club Dinner (Introduction by the one and only Edgar Appleby) 21st November 2008, The

Greta Suite, The Skiddaw Hotel, Keswick. Proceeds to Junior Cricket Development at KCC.'

Menu then included Homemade Vegetable Broth, Chicken or Beef, Charlotte Potatoes, Sticky Toffee Pudding, Fresh Coffee and Mints. The evening began with a tribute to the late groundsman Brian Pattinson.

By the time of the Allott dinner six years on, the menus have grown longer (and the capital letters more random) and now included skillet of Cumberland sausage, Red wine and Bacon sauce with Herb bread and dark chocolate Torte, tomato Concasse and Brandy gravy. There's still Cream of veg soup and Fresh fruit salad, but this time with Honey, not syrup. The event is in aid of Great North Air Ambulance. And the MC is Richardson.

Written on the menu: 'To Edgar, missed you tonight!! Best wishes Paul Allott'.

Back in Keswick, I took him up to the first floor, which was more difficult than it sounds as he couldn't walk or talk (not that talking helps you climb). We sat in front of the *Wisdens* 1864–1928 and the other good stuff that 'has to be kept upstairs'.

I think he said 'Hammond?' Hammond what? I found a Hammond rebound book in a Minty bookcase, typed in the title on my phone and it was worth about £20. 'Rebound,' he said. Rebinding was worth doing to protect pamphlets, but not often worthwhile with *Wisdens* or most other books, I found out later. Collectors wanted the original bindings. The new shiny bindings reminded me of when I was working in the shop, the Gift Horse,

30 years before, covering books in protective plastic. The job was just to give me something to do. He worked out each plastic covering cost 30p a book, so doing it was not worth it in many cases either. It had probably cost more than £20 to rebind the Hammond book, but Appleby liked Hammond. And he liked nicely bound books that would last.

I wanted to ask him which books he wanted me to keep and look after. I'd told my wife that I wanted the collection, or at least the *Wisdens*, but that I felt uneasy about looking after them. I knew my mother wanted them sold. My brother has started saying that we hadn't gone on foreign holidays as kids because of the book buying. My mother increasingly talked about how untidy the deluges of books made the house.

I finally asked. What should we do with them? We'd just all been to the Keswick newsagents Youdales and optimistically ordered another annual subscription of the weekly *The Cricket Paper.* 'Are you sure you want it?' asked my mother. Of course he did. He also wanted an MOT on his mobility scooter. He couldn't read anymore or drive the scooter, but give up? No.

He couldn't answer about what to do with the books. He just gasped back at me. Not a sharp intake. He just struggled for breath, then my mother came up and the moment was lost and I would never know.

Next time I saw him he was lying in bed looking like a frightened rabbit. His eyes were the most alive part of him; the rest was hardly working at all. Motionless, he looked back at me.

On his bedside cabinet was a clock and his watch. There was a book about Garry Sobers' six sixes in an over in 1968 off Malcolm Nash, mostly about the ball. Someone has bought the ball at auction for £26,400, but author Graham Lloyd had found it was the wrong one and had written a book about the affair. 'Just journalism,' Appleby had told me. Maybe *Howzat? The Six Sixes Ball Mystery* was the last book he'd started reading. He hadn't really read for months as far as I could see. He was past that, health-wise, falling asleep all the time.

I looked for signs of him. The inky black skin cancers mark was coming back round his left nostril and towards his lip. Wordless, I glided out. Sleep is the great cure, my Mum always said. When you're ill, go to bed.

He had marks all over his hands, more marks than hands I thought. He looked like he'd been deflated. He boasted how much weight he'd lost, probably to combat the fear. Last time I knew, he'd lost seven stone. For a glutton, it was wrong he couldn't eat, because of his condition. He only had TV left, and dreams about old times.

I remembered tales of his trencherman behaviour, like his hair setting on fire from the overhead spotlight as he concentrated on loading up at the Swiss carvery.

Last time I saw him he had an almost rosy, sweaty face as my youngest Ted kissed him, held by me.

His square shoes were lined up near the door. Just outside are the cigarette cards of cricketers. Then there was the signed Hobbs framed picture. What would happen to that? Nothing would go before he died, and that would be a while. He had a strong heart.

## Chapter 41

# Funeral booklet

APPLEBY WAS in hospital. He couldn't swallow. An ambulance had taken him to Carlisle. Dan and my mother stayed with him. 'Good run ashore,' he was saying on the way up to Carlisle, according to Dan. That was one of his Navy sayings. Maybe he meant his life had been a good run ashore – a good experience.

I didn't expect it to happen now, at the start of the cricket season. Another call: he was not responsive – things had progressed.

On his bed was the lovat green hand-knitted cardigan, way too big at the end, folded on top of a faded tangerine blanket with shiny strips at the edge. Nothing else. On the bedside cabinet was a red glamour spanner (comb). He kept his hair to the end – wiry and white like his father's and mine.

I looked through the drawers – for what? Pill boxes, envelopes, nothing much. I was quick, so as not to be caught. Then I put my feet in his bat covers (shoes). Still too big.

Here's the obit we wrote by family committee:

Well-known Keswick bookseller Edgar
Appleby has died aged 84. He was current
President of Keswick Cricket Club and President
of Keswick Rotary Club in 1989/90. He ran The
Gift Horse shop in St John's Street with wife
Susan from 1985–94 and Appleby's second-hand
book stall on Keswick Market from 1981–2009.

Edgar was born in Gateshead in 1931 and
moved to Middlesbrough before being evacuated
to Bishop Auckland during the Second World
War. He joined the Royal Navy in 1946 and
served in the Korean War. He became a chief
petty officer before leaving the navy in 1960
to join engineering firm Foster Wheelers. He
worked in London and Spain before marrying
Susan Jackson in 1967 and becoming a director
with his cousin at R Lawson Engineers in Carlisle.

They had three children, Rachel, 46, who is a
teacher in Kenilworth, Matthew, 44, a journalist
in London, and Daniel, 43, who works on oil rigs
and is Keswick-based.

They moved to Keswick to run The Gift
Horse in the 1980s and lived on Southey St
then Crosthwaite Road. Those who knew
him best will remember him in champion
Rotary and Bank and Lake Road Tavern quiz
teams and at Fitz Park watching Keswick
CC, where he was also long-serving treasurer,

and was often seen collecting money from unwitting spectators.

At one time he had one of the largest cricket book collections in England, including a full set of *Wisden Cricketers' Almanacks*. He was a renowned expert on cricket history, as well as naval history and many other subjects, often giving talks to societies on topics such as the *Titanic* and Quintinshill rail disaster, which he always did without notes, often having learnt his speech while walking his otter hound Hotspur. Edgar was often behind the mic at Keswick exhibition cricket matches, where he would give impassioned and witty after-dinner speeches, often using amusing phrases he picked up during his navy career.

He and Susan's knowledge of the second-hand book market was vast.

He was a Rotarian for 38 years and treasurer for nine. Edgar leaves his beloved wife of 47 years Susan, his three children and seven grandchildren, who he doted on. He saw his large, imposing figure replicated in 11lb grandchild baby Ted, who he always called 'small angel'.

His memorial service will be at Crosthwaite Church moving into Lyzzick Hall on TBC, to which his many friends are invited, after a private crematorium service.

'Anybody died?' he used to say, meaning were there any obits in the paper or later on the internet, which he couldn't work.

The funeral food was margarita pizza slices – 'pitza' as he called it. Wedges, endless sandwiches, with loads left over. He wouldn't have liked that.

There was 'nothing behind the bar', i.e., no money. Buy your own. You look like you can afford it, he might have jibed.

Gorse was flowering, daffodils dying, roses blooming, lime green leaves bursting. Hawthorn was white. The cricket season had started.

Last time I'd been home I'd brought up some magazines published by Driff, the eccentric bookseller, pedalling against progress who we'd come across on that recession-led holiday to London back in November 1985.

I brought the magazines to Keswick to show my parents how I'd learnt my book onions from them, and to amuse Appleby with a memory of a time when he was fitter. My mother had sold the Driff mags, through the specialist bookselling site ABE, but they lay on the table unposted.

The holidays are what you remember. Seeing Driff then visiting Lord's the next day and then the Imperial War Museum. That was my Dad's idea of a holiday.

Before that, it was Cornwall in the caravan, watching the cricket at Weston Super Duper Mare and buying books from EK Brown in Liskeard on the way.

On the shelf near him on that trip to Keswick was another of the last books he had: *10 for 10*, about Yorkshire slow left-armer Hedley Verity's 1932 record first-class bowling analysis, in case you didn't know, which you bloody well should do.

The *10 for 10* book, by Chris Waters, talks about what Verity was like – the Yorkshireman was a serious character. But what was Appleby like? Did he like money, DIY, engineering, navy, books, Keswick? Maybe he should have had another career path rather than as a navy engineer. Until the bookshop, he did what he thought he should do.

Should he have been a politician? And who for? A writer? After all, he enjoyed writing the occasionally injudicious Rotary club editorials as *The Borderer*?

What did he do outside work? I remember he collected salvage – old papers for charity, until the price of paper went down and it wasn't worth doing anymore. He dug the back garden. He walked the otterhound. He went to the pub, the Near Boot. He played for Hawksdale CC. He collected cricket stuff.

Chapter 42

# New *Wisdens*

A MAN just came round with ten *Wisdens*, 2000–09.
Cost me £10.50, plus £3.30 postage on eBay.

The knock came as I watched the Davis Cup Final, on
a Friday afternoon. Ted was at nursery, William at school,
Bethan at work. I cursed and looked out of the window. I
saw a flash of yellow, like a glint of sunlight, or a banana
skin to slide on.

Him: 'Is Bethan in?'

Me: 'I'm her husband.'

Him: 'I'm here to deliver her *Wisdens*.'

Me: 'Great. I've got a bid in for the next lot as well.
They finish in 20 minutes. Do you live nearby?'

Him: 'I actually live in North London. I was in the area
anyway. I'd forgotten.' He was nervous. He'd rehearsed
the words. This was becoming like a conversation on
Keswick market, on our bookstall, where I'd stood from
1981, on and off until 2009.

He said he had a rare 1914 and 1899. God knows what
his story was. I said 1916 was the really rare one because

of Grace's obit. He said a whole set was worth £60k and he'd seen one at Lord's but he couldn't touch it because it was in a case. Depends if they're hardback or softback, I said. 'And condition,' he added. We were like two dogs in the park, sniffing each other.

I told him my sob story – 'My Dad died recently and my Mum sold them all, so I'm buying them back.'

Later Bethan said: 'You can't buy back what you've lost.'

Two days after he died on the Friday night I did a car boot sale on the Sunday, reliving that old Keswick market feeling. At the sale I talked and tidied and worked. A guy from the allotment said he was feeling dark. I said so was I. 'Black dog,' he said. 'Dead Dad,' I replied.

The Keswick house flooded for a third time the winter after he died. Maybe just as well Mum got shot of the books when she did.

# Chapter 43

# Funeral

FUNERAL SPEECH at Crosthwaite Church, Keswick, 18 May 2015.

I'm Matthew, eldest son. I'd like to pay tribute to my Dad through his great interest, cricket.

As my Dad would have said, he had not a bad innings.

He used to cycle from Middlesbrough to Headingley to watch matches when he was young, with a farthing in his pocket, just to watch Len Hutton. At least that's what he told me.

He'd become interested in the game through the cricket cigarette cards his Uncle Jack had given him. This began a lifelong love of collecting.

When he joined the Navy, on his first leave, he came home to find all the cards had been cleared out. I think this led to him collecting so keenly from then on.

Old England cricketer JG Dewes died a few days after my Dad. I'd have loved to have talked to him about that. Dewes' Test debut was at The Oval in 1948. Why is that match famous? My Dad loved quiz questions. It was Bradman's final Test. The greatest batsman needed just a boundary to average the perfect 100 in Tests. Hollies bowled him for a duck. Guess who was there? My Dad.

The first Test I saw was Headingley 1981, the Botham Test that England won against all the odds.

I often say how me and my Dad put a fiver on England to win at 500/1.

It's not true, but it makes a good story.

When we were young holidays would be in Cornwall. My Dad had an ulterior motive for going there. On the way we'd stop at Taunton or Wellingborough or Leamington Spa … because there was a cricket match on. My Dad would point out old players – Dennis Brookes or Bob Appleyard or Ted Lester and we'd get their autographs, and they'd be happy to be recognised. The rest of the family patiently put up with it.

Now's a good chance to thank my Mum for everything she did for my Dad throughout their time together. She ran the book business that made them both happy, as well as looking after him for half a century.

Talking of books, my Dad used to get 'little square parcels' regularly through the post. He'd love unwrapping them to find an 1882 *Wisden* or whatever inside.

That was another ulterior motive for going to Cornwall on holiday.

Cricket book dealer EK Brown lived there, and we'd visit him on our holidays.

My Dad took over some of EK Brown's book dealing. Posting out Indian, South African and New Zealand annuals to collectors. He'd take weeks doing it.

One year me and my brother did it because our parents were away. It took an hour to address, invoice, parcel and post 150 books. We wondered why it took my Dad so long. It was because he wrote a letter to every customer. They were the people he liked talking to. That was what he enjoyed.

When I was young, he'd get me writing to Bill Bowes or whichever old player asking for autographs and get me reading cricket books instead of Enid Blyton or whatever.

We used to go to matches together – with trips to Lord's for NatWest finals particularly formative experiences. He was so knowledgeable about the game, I'm still not very good at watching cricket with anybody else.

In later years we all loved his speeches, in particular for me, his cricket talks.

At Fitz Park just a few years ago he gave one
for local cricketer Paul Nixon. I'll do a bit, he was
a much better speaker than me.'
[I repeated part of his Nixon speech.]
It was not a bad innings.

At the funeral my brother Daniel told a couple of Navy
tales. One or two of my Dad's mates had had memoirs
published, full of acronyms and oceans of detail. My
Dad preferred to read about it rather than write it up
into a memoir, and to tell stories, preferably to a crowd of
paying guests.

Dan said he didn't actually write anything down; he
just went by memory after going through it a couple of
times. The stories have been told umpteen times and half
of Keswick knew them anyway: 'My Dad joined the Royal
Navy in 1947, completing his training at HMS *Rosyth*.
He left the Navy in 1961 at the rank of chief petty engine
room artificer. Those of you who remember him well
know that he used to like to tell stories of his time in the
Navy. I'm going to tell three of them.

'The first was when he was in England and was told
that one of the group of six petty officers would have to
remain behind on duty over Christmas while the other five
went home. They were left to decide who would remain
but were unable to do so. Eventually the best solution they
could come up with was for all of them to stay behind so
one man didn't have to remain on his own. This goes some
way to describe the quality of the men he served with and
my Dad himself.

'The second was again at Christmas when he was on another ship and was inspected by a commodore, who is a very senior naval officer and his wife, a very snooty lady who felt she had the same rank and status as her husband. There was also a competition being held for the best decorated mess deck. My Dad and his friends were all engineers and technicians so weren't very good at that sort of thing, so they decided to put a large tureen of rum punch at one end of the table which consisted of nothing but rum and a 14lb sledgehammer at the other end of the table. The mess decks were very cramped so the routine was just before the inspection you would put on your trousers and not sit down so as not to damage the crease. There wasn't room to do this all at the same time and as my Dad was the most junior man, he had to put his on last.

'Unfortunately, there wasn't time, so the commodore and his wife were greeted by an almost overwhelming smell of rum, a sledgehammer, and a young man from Gateshead with no trousers on. They didn't win the competition.

'Finally, in the early 1950s, my Dad was on a ship during the Korean War, off South Korea providing support to the troops on shore. Suddenly they started taking fire from the shore and shells were landing all around them. The captain ordered the engine room crew which included my Dad to get the ship out of there straight away. The engine room crew fired up the engine and sailed away as fast as they could. When they were safely out of range the captain, without realising exactly what he was saying, announced to the entire crew: "Well done to the crew for achieving the fastest speed the ship has ever done while retreating from the enemy."

'These tales showed the petty deprivations and humiliations and mate-ship of my Dad aged 15-30 which served him well from 30–84, which included a lot of relaxing at the cricket, when he could.'

My sister Rachel said at the funeral: 'Edgar Appleby my father was a larger than life character. He made a great impression on many people and his death has left a gap in all of our lives. Today all of us will be remembering Edgar – his patience and loyalty, his good humour, his expertise and amazing knowledge of cricket facts, his good nature and his love of good company.'

She then referenced his interests and related them to the characteristics of his grandchildren: 'He liked ice cream and so does Ted.'

One part referred to 'my father the great collector – many of you will have admired his *Wisden* collections. Following in his footsteps is young William, whose collection of Match Attax football cards is growing weekly.'

## Chapter 44

# Chris Cairns

ON 1 October 2015, I was reporting on former New Zealand cricketer Chris Cairns' perjury trial at Southwark Crown Court. The case was linked to a previous trial in 2012 where he successfully defended himself following a Twitter row about throwing a match in India. This time in 2014 I was at the start of the same trial, which was put off for 12 months because international cricketers weren't available as witnesses, because they were playing.

My Dad was also not available for me to talk to about the case. I'd covered Cairns' Twitter libel case at the Royal Court of Justice in 2012. I'd spoken to Dad then. 'Try your best' was his advice.

Cairns was a proto-Ben Stokes figures. Stokes was born in Christchurch in 1991 and I taught him cycle safety there a decade later, shortly before he moved to Cumbria, where his late father Ged was a rugby league coach for Workington, then Whitehaven. To my Dad, Stokes was the last in a line starting from Grace, through Hammond, Hutton, Milburn and Botham, to reach Nixon and the last local hero, Stokes. Stokes is a local hero to me. Fellow Christchurch all-rounder Cairns I'd met too, with his father Lance 15 years before, back when I was writing *Durham Cricket: 100 Greats*, at Lance's fudge factory in Ferrymead, Christchurch. The older Cairns had played for Durham after moving to the county to play club cricket (in 1980 for a £4,000 fee). The fudge business ended in late 2006 as the peripatetic pair moved on to other business interests.

While neither Cairns would know me from a bar of soap these days, Appleby managed to make friends with cricketers and cricket types and be remembered by them.

So, the history was that in March 2012, Cairns successfully sued former Indian Premier League commissioner Lalit Modi for libel after Modi posted on Twitter in 2010 that Cairns had been involved in match-fixing during 2008.

But Cairns and his former legal adviser Andrew Fitch-Holland were both subsequently charged by the Metropolitan Police with attempting to pervert the course of justice, for trying to get New Zealand player Lou Vincent to provide a false statement to the Twitter perjury hearing.

At the trial at Southwark Crown Court, Cairns, then 45, was facing a maximum sentence of seven years' jail. He denied the charge.

A jury panel of 16 was chosen. With about 50 witnesses, I was told the trial could continue until 20 November 'in a worst-case scenario'. It lasted until December and a great guy called Kevin Norquay came over from New Zealand to cover it as I couldn't commit to such as long trial.

Cairns was defended by Orlando Pownall QC. The prosecutor was Sasha Wass, who led the crown case against Australian entertainer Rolf Harris, 85, in the same courtroom the year before. Mr Justice Sweeney was judge. He had presided over the Harris case.

Cairns arrived at court alone at 8.45am every day wearing a dark blue suit, light blue shirt and dark blue tie. He stood in the dock alongside fellow accused Fitch-Holland and spoke only to confirm his name.

Described as a 'cricket groupie' in one report, Fitch-Holland was Cairns' legal adviser before the 2012 libel trial. They had become friends through the Lashings Cricket Club, a fundraising star-studded touring team based in the UK.

They were both found not guilty after an eight-week trial, both exonerated of all charges.

They walked from the court as free men, not out, bowled over by the verdict.

Chapter 45

# McCorkell

KESWICK, 31 October 2015:

A bit like fellwalking author Alfred Wainwright wanting his ashes to be the 'grit in the boot' on Haystacks on the Lake District fells, Appleby ended up on Keswick CC outfield in Fitz Park.

On scattering day, 31 October, it drizzled all day until clouds lifted to show a weak orange sunset over Causey Pike.

It's the day of the Rugby World Cup Final. New Zealand were winning. I found a card for his 75th. 'Happy birthday Edgar let's have 76th in New Zealand.' Boro won in the football. The cricket season was well over. The books were all going. Sky Sport, was gone. This was maybe the last family gathering here at How Keld before my mother downsizes. The ash scattering was in an hour from now.

Time to go. It was dark. We all headed to the park.

'Has someone got Dad?'

'He's in the ice cream box.'

'Strawberry chunk – he would have liked that.'

'That's not appropriate.'

'Trouble is they come in a really big pot.'

'You know the tubes whisky comes in, like that.'

'Which way?'

'No, on to the outfield.'

'On to the outfield?'

'Yes.'

'It's not Halloween, you know.'

The river slides by. Herd the cats.

'Is anyone going to say anything?'

Dan: 'Dad's final resting place is at the cricket ground he loved.'

I walk behind. It's 5.36pm.

'He'll always be playing cricket even in the night. He can field the ball in the outfield every game now.' Little William says: 'Except he won't because his legs are all chopped up.'

There's fat berries and apples and flattened grasses all around as we let off fireworks in the back garden.

Today, Sunday, eight days after the scatter, I bought two *Wisdens* off eBay. Maybe they were for research for this book, 1949 and 1963. More likely I bought them because the *Wisden* collection is being taken away next Tuesday.

I looked through 1949 that night, Bradman's duck first. In the averages I could think of a story about so many of the players featured from the 1948 season: McCorkell, who had died on Appleby's birthday two years earlier, aged 100, the 18th century of his career. And Dewes, Hutton, Compton, Yardley, Hollies, Aubrey Smith, Walter Hadlee and Tom Graveney, who died that autumn, a couple of days after the scattering, aged 88. He 'stood out among the grafters and accumulators as a throwback to cricket's golden age'.

Another of the last books Appleby bought – little square parcel – was *Touched by Greatness,* about Graveney, by Andy Murtagh. The book was an elegy for Graveney, who it turned out had Parkinson's, like my Dad.

This is the Professional Cricketers' Association obituary list from June 2015. Appleby, who always turned to the obits first in the *Daily Telegraph* and *Wisden,* fits in at the same date as Dewes:

Barrie Meyer, Brian Close, Philip Whitcombe, Clive Rice, Mike Turner, Bill Foord, Russell 'Rusty' Wood, Jim Brailsford, Bill Davidson, Neville Griffin, Ian Campbell, Lord Griffiths, David Blake, John Dewes, Jamie Bishop, David Fletcher, Maurice Fenner, Philip Hodgson, Ted Lester, Bob Appleyard, Kenneth Smales, Shirley Griffiths, Brian Reynolds, Harry Newton, Geoff Pullar, Peter Delisle, Dennis Marriott, Les Angell, Phillip Hughes, Michael Mills, Mervyn Winfield, Michael Frederick, Peter Sainsbury, Brian Roe, Damian D'Oliveira, Euros Lewis, John Bartlett, Don Bennett, David Allen, Michael Mence, Phil Sharpe, George Downton, Ray Flood, Peter Laker, Norman Whiting, John Mortimore, Michael Melluish, William Goodreds, Bernard Hedges, Alan Townsend, Graham Stevenson, Peter Jacques, Stuart Jakeman, Ted Williams, Ray Weeks, Reg Simpson, Cyril

Perkins, Jonathan Fellows-Smith, David Clark, Brian Furniss, Huw Jenkins, Keith Dollery, Paul Robinson, Dicky Mayes, Sir Colin Stansfield Smith, Fred Gibson, Ron Thresher, Mike Denness, Douglas Freeman, Ted James, Peter Hearn, David Mills, Neil McCorkell, Brian Langford, John Josephs, Tony Greig, Phillip Taylor, Michael Crawford, Eric Burgin, Ray Carter, George Chesterton, Jim Galley, Tony Pawson, Kevin Curran, John Turner, Lewis McGibbon, Harry Pilling, Ron Tindall, Geoffrey Lees, Barry Trapnell, Frank Forster, David Thomas, Don Wilson, Tom Maynard, David Gibson, Frank Parr, Martin Stovold, Louis Vorster, Jack Watson, Geoff Hill, Simon Massey, Doug Greasley, John Swinburne, Eddie Davis, Roy Tattersall, Basil D'Oliveira, Peter Roebuck, Graham Dilley, Elvis Reifer, Allan Watkins and Neal Abberley.

## Chapter 46

# The good stuff

THE BOOKS have been priced up and sold. The weak areas, reflecting today's market, are the rebound *Wisdens* and the books under £100. These days collectors want the books in original state where possible. But the pre-war original hardback *Wisdens* and the rarer books have gone up in value.

I did feel compelled to pounce on a few things, before it was too late, choosing in a hurry, slightly randomly. These included a signed Hutton benefit brochure; a picture signed by Mike Procter, Fred Trueman and Paul Allott that I planned to research the point of; a Jack Hobbs signed Churchman's cigarettes card; and G Neville Weston's copy of EM (Ted) Grace (WG's brother) biography by FS Ashley-Cooper. This is signed by Grace with a note on its importance by Appleby, which justified me saving the tome, which is probably a bit less rare than Appleby believed.

Best was the *Cricketer's Autograph Birthday Book*, a 1906 hardback with biographies of 1,000 players linked to a calendar of their birthdays and 130 facsimile signatures. The book, which I'm glad to document here so they are not wasted on me, was acquired from an unknown dealer or auction, and had a few proper signatures too so must be worth £500. One slightly wobbly one is Albert Trott, the only person to hit the ball over the pavilion at Lord's (in 1899), who died of the drink in 1914.

I've bought ten *Wisdens* off eBay for £10.50 (2000–2009) and have bid on 20 more in two lots of ten from 1980–2000. I could have 36 by next week, with one swap. I'll have a 1949, 1963, 1973, 1863 reprint (free with mag), a couple from the 1990s (one from Oxfam for £2) and these new ones, which will cost more to post than they cost to buy. 'You have to think why you're doing it,' said my wife.

Chapter 47

# Memorial event

APPLEBY'S OLD mates from Rotary and cricket organised a memorial dinner with speeches at the Skiddaw Hotel on February 13, 2016. I reprised his 2007 Nixon speech. I looked up 13 February for a suitable anniversary to talk about (he would have known one in his head). 13 February 1933. Australia v England Bodyline series fourth Test at Brisbane. Out strides Eddie Paynter, who has risen from his hospital bed and rushed in a taxi to the ground, and he bolsters the England innings before returning to hospital at the close. He scored 83. Perfect.

Anniversaries were often his conversation starter. 'One hundred years ago today, what happened?' He used to do a Quintinshill rail disaster talk to history societies, or any other group that asked. He died almost exactly 100 years after the troop train crash that killed 226, just over the border near Gretna. A signalling error caused the accident.

So, it's 13 February, Skiddaw Hotel: His old mates Ryder and Vic Wilson had organised a memorial night/

celebration. Sixty were coming. Bethan and I and the kids had driven up in the Mazda Bongo, staying in a holiday flat because Mum's house was far from fixed after the latest flood.

First up … in the back function room, off the market square, eight tables, eight on each, names on board on an easel in the entrance. This is where they held the weekly Rotary lunches, where he'd fine people for wearing pink shirts, or for having a suntan.

'Doug Lowther to start the proceedings.'

'Thank you, Vic.

'Good evening everybody, especially Susan, Dan and Matthew.

'I first met Edgar when I came to Keswick in 2001 and joined Rotary, and was made very welcome especially by one somewhat rotund gent called Edgar.

'When I told him I was from Yorkshire he at once raised that subject close to everyone's heart – Yorkshire CCC. I told Edgar I came from Robin Hood Bay and had gone to Scarborough cricket festival from being a boy and more recently Headingley. It immediately became apparent Edgar was passionate about cricket.

'I told him a former West Indies player is buried at Robin Hood Bay, Charles Ollivierre. Edgar astounded me with his encyclopaedic knowledge – he knew all about him.

'There were only seven black players on that tour. Ollivierre was top scorer with 883 runs and a top score of 159 v Leicestershire. Edgar knew all about that. Ollivierre started in England playing for Derbyshire from 1901–07 and was the first black county cricketer – a very good quiz question.

'I met Edgar a few days later and obviously he'd done a bit of reading up on Ollivierre. In 1904 he had his best season with 1,268 runs including 209 and 92 v Essex. This match was recorded that year in *Wisden* as remarkable because Essex scored 507 but were beaten by nine wickets! What Edgar couldn't understand was how Ollivierre came to be buried at Robin Hood Bay. The answer is simple, he came to Scarborough quite often. I was told I'd met him. I was only born in 1948 and he died in 1949. His dying wish was to be buried there.

'We all have our own memories and stories about his love of cricket. Edgar was passionate about many things. As sergeant at arms, he enjoyed fining people for things like wearing a checked shirt. He'd say it started life as a table cloth.

'Each week Edgar asked questions designed to show how thick we all were and fine us 20p, and if we were right being Edgar he'd fine us 40p. He'd fine Ian Raw when he was not even there!

'All the 20ps mounted up to a few hundred in the kitty for local charities. As president of Keswick CC we'd get a letter about how wonderful the team were and how skint they were, signed Appleby. We all knew Edgar was passionate about KCC, so the plea was nearly always answered.

'He was passionate about membership subs, and asked submarine questions expecting us to know which class they belonged to. Sam Hicks got us there in the end.

When he thought submarines, subs are now due. His talks didn't need notes. He had a rare ability to bring a story to life and always spoke with great passion.

'Ladies present recall Edgar with a glint in his eye, which is not surprising because Edgar was passionate about Joanna Lumley and Nicole Kidman.

'I'll always remember Edgar as a passionate man, everything he did he was passionate about especially Susan and his family.

'To Edgar, a passionate man.'

Mike Ryder, vice president of the cricket club, though probably president now as there's a vacancy:

'Happy cricket memories.

'Starting 12 years ago, Raw, Vic and myself every year go to one international in the north-east. They were fantastic fun days which Edgar thoroughly enjoyed. Edgar amused us with a selection of limericks at least to the A66 with a Navy or cricket theme not for repeating.

'There was plenty of refreshment. Edgar would make wicked comments and there was good-natured banter. We'd have a bar meal and most likely Edgar's choice would be a Barnsley chop – 'a very pleasing nosebag'. One year we arrived before opening time and had an impromptu game of cricket in the car park. Edgar was umpire. It was like *Last of the Summer Wine*.

'The car park near Old Trafford had a shortcut to the ground and Edgar got stuck on a gate. I was pulling, Raw was pushing, but we couldn't budge Edgar. A queue formed, and there was much good humour with Edgar getting more embarrassed at the situation. It helped when a loud cheer from the ground signalled a wicket had fallen.

'When international matches were getting too much, Edgar greatly enjoyed visiting Durham via Mainsgill Farm Shop near Scotch Corner.

'In the last year or two Edgar was in a wheelchair and was happy to support his favourite team Keswick CC. In the relaxed atmosphere he'd be chatting with friends and doze off and wake up for tea. He preferred backwaters in County Durham like Stanley, Pity Me, Bishop Auckland and in Barnard Castle The Haven where they served delicious fish and chips, and we'd take the scenic route through Teesdale and Weardale then on to home ground. It was an absolute pleasure to be in the company of one of Keswick's genuine characters.

'Cheers skipper!'

My brother Dan gets up.

'My parents sold second-hand books on the market from 1978 in Brampton to 1986 and in Keswick until 2009, at which point they were the longest-serving stallholders. And we've made special appearances since then for charity.

'He'd always comment on the weather, on wind or rain, to anyone listening and quite a few who weren't, saying the problem for books is not wind but wind and rain together!

'To that end we had a stall at the upper end of the market uphill from the Moot Hall, where it is much more sheltered, with several plots most sheltered. He was particularly fussy about the precise positioning of the stall with 1/16 of a degree angular misalignment making all the difference to save all the books being soaked.

'Initially Dad was quite useful on the stall, but as he got older, he did less and less. Mum took over and increasingly for both of them the stall was a social scene, where friends chatted, and they might even sell the odd book or two. Over the years stallholders and customers became friends, and some of them would travel long distances to come to Keswick just to be insulted.

'Books were all priced according to age and condition and popularity of the author but what Dad said was a good book he'd price up a bit. If it was not his subject, the price came down a bit. But one thing he was firm on was discount. He really disliked giving it if he felt a book was fairly priced and he gave anyone asking a hard time, typically saying it costs the same as a gin and tonic and you look like you drink enough of them!

'He knew an anniversary for every day of the year and as everyone knows, he liked asking and telling you them. One morning on the stall I had a humungous hangover. Dad was going on about batting averages etc, and I had a Eureka moment and asked Dad what was the anniversary today. Sinking of the *Titanic* or Hitler's birthday were his favourites. He said he'd think about it and wanders off.

'Nothing to do with cricket, Navy or World War One? He looks at me all confused – what else is there?! I don't know either but it kept you quiet for about an hour.'

Vic, a neighbour and Rotarian.

'Edgar was legendary at quizzes. He'd know the home grounds of Plymouth Argyle or Lincoln City, all 92 league clubs' home grounds. He knew all the answers. He'd learnt them all, so I asked how do you know that?

'He learnt lists. This was before Wikipedia and he'd know all the US state capitals, presidents, kings of England. His knowledge was phenomenal. Even at the end it was all in there but the problem was he couldn't get it out. Even when he couldn't go to the quiz I'd take him round the questions. He knew the answers but couldn't get it out.'

Now it's me. I stand up at my table, where Bethan is next to me and Mum is nearby.

'First of all thanks so much to everyone for coming tonight, wonderful to see you all. I think I'm definitely the youngest here.'

Richardson: 'No you're not, your wife is.'

MA: 'OK, I'm the youngest man here.

'My younger brother is younger than me but obviously he's a bit balder and greyer so he doesn't look it. As you've heard already my Dad was very into cricket and anniversaries so Richardson, what anniversary is it today? A cricket anniversary.'

KR: 'I never knew when Edgar asked me so why should I know now?'

MA: 'Appleby? Pridmore? No one knows. The 13th it is today, Feb 14th tomorrow in case you didn't know. Gents, what special day is that?'

Crowd: 'Would it be Valentine's Day?'

MA: 'It's quite hard to find good flowers in Keswick, just warning you Bethan! Now, 83 years ago today to give you a clue, 1933, oh you're an ignorant bunch. Who do I sound like now? It was the Bodyline series, 1933. Eddie Paynter rose from his sick bed. I knew this already, I didn't look it up.'

KR: 'Tim Sykes would know but he's gone to the toilet. Oh no he's coming back! Ask him again.'

MA: 'Tim Sykes, who rose from their sick bed in 1933 to play for England 83 years ago today?'

Sykes: 'A great man from Oswaldwistle.'

MA: 'Brilliant.'

TS: 'The great Eddie Paynter.'

MA: 'You're right. Ah Tim, glad you're here, the rest of you, you're a bunch of ignorant peasants.

'He beat the Aussies and won the Test at Brisbane.

'What else was I going to say? I'm not a very good public speaker like my Dad was.

'Oh yes, 2007 I remember Paul Nixon's benefit dinner saw one of my Dad's finest performances, Brian's here tonight. I was absolutely blown away. There's a picture of me and him there, you probably can't see it, but he was in his pomp then, still fat. I look just the same actually.'

Crowd: 'Modest!'

I narrated the Nixon speech again in true Appleby style – a good story never suffered for being told umpteen times, whether the audience wanted it or not.

This time, the crowd asked for more:

### Keith Richardson – Keswick CC chairman

'Edgar always spoke without notes.

'I've got one or two to remind me because I've had a couple of glasses of wine and a few beers.

'I was interested in the stories about the bookstall from Dan.

'Keswick, Saturday morning bookstall; Sue and Edgar were there and there gravitated Keswick personalities. Hank was there, a great character of Keswick as well. Edgar and Sue are special important bedrock people of this town. Humour, entertainment, an institution … this is the wine talking.

'There's too many stories, of his loves – cricket, books literature, art, war.

'Hotspur was named Hotspur of Northumberland fame. An otterhound. If ever a dog could have a greater character with a more hound of the Baskervilles presence it was Hotspur.

'I first came across him in Southey Street. I'd knock on the door and hear a woof from the bowels of the earth.

'This dog was remarkable. It had to put up with a lot.

'Edgar was dragged kicking and screaming along the shores of Derwentwater on walks, Hotspur heard resolutions on the sinking of the *Bismarck* word for word, the *Titanic*, great VCs, the assassination of Franz

Ferdinand, the Battle of Midway, the demise of the Hapsburg Empire. This dog was very confused. All it ever wanted was to hunt otters but it was dragged by a madman with a wide girth in a trilby hat being told information on historical events. No wonder this dog bayed for England.

'I've got two more stories.

'I was in New Zealand for five weeks on the South Island. Edgar and Susan were on the North Island. I didn't expect to bump into anybody. I was in the museum in Christchurch schlepping round the kiwis, and I saw this figure in front of me with a stick, with a cap with the words "Middlesbrough, Vienna of the North" on it. Can't be, only been one day in New Zealand, then I saw Susan, "bloody hell it is them". I came behind Edgar's right flank: "Are you frae round here?" He turned like a great ship. "Bloody hell, Richardson!"

'Chairman met president of KCC in a museum in Christchurch – what a coincidence!

'The other coincidence was food.

'Gateshead was the Paris of the north. We went to the cricket and Ryder was there. In Barnard Castle we stopped for food and entered an Indian, Cagneys, for a meal, a takeaway, to take back to Keswick. It was all a bit of a rush, raining, and we handed meals over and went to our houses and sat down and ate. I opened my takeaway: two veg rices.

'I rang Edgar, "I've got 2 veg rices" He said: "Oh, I've just eaten two chicken Madrases. They were both very nice."

'There's one cricket question Edgar asked Tim Sykes that Tim didn't know the answer. When was the only time WG Grace declared the innings on 98 not out and why? Because it was the only score he had not scored in first-class cricket.

'He cared, Edgar. He has left us but he's still here as far as I'm concerned. Still not out in cricketing terms for all time. What a fantastic character, Edgar Appleby.'

A week later I put all the books and other cricket stuff I'd inherited in the Minty glass-fronted bookcase in the front bedroom of my house in London. Apart from my 50 *Wisdens*, which are in the living room, middle shelf of the bookcase.

## Chapter 48

# Bodyline

A BOX arrived during kids' cricket practice in the school sports hall. I'd left to go to the shops after younger son Ted's practice, just as older son William got started.

Ted and I popped into home with milk I bought and there was a box there on the doorstep.

We opened it up, removing lots of paper and card to find another box inside. I pulled out 15 dusty, tatty cricket books and piled them on the stairs, then left to go back to cricket practice after putting the top three, two *Wisdens* and *Anti-Body-Line* by Alan Kippax, on a bookshelf.

Back at cricket practice, I told another Dad that a cricket book parcel had arrived with an 1898 and 1908 *Wisden*.

He asked: 'Are they in good condition? Are they worth much?'

'No. Maybe 50 quid each? The whole lot's worth 200, 300 quid maybe.'

The Dad said: 'My Dad's got some but when he moved we don't know what happened to them.'

'Ah, which ones?'

'Don't know, about 20 from the 1940s maybe. They disappeared anyway.'

'Probably worth a few quid.' I paused. 'In that box there's a Bodyline book as well written at the time by a whinging Aussie who played in the series.'

'That sounds interesting.'

We went back to watching the kids practising.

It wasn't until later that night that I looked inside the Kippax *Body-Line* book, a slim two shilling 1933 paperback, worn on the spine and musty as my Dad's old cricket bag, though not as musty as the box in that bag, which had seen service, judging by the stainage.

On the front is a cartoon of a batsman holding his head, based on wicketkeeper Bert Oldfield. During the third Test at Adelaide, Bodyline bowler Harold Larwood hit Oldfield with a bouncer, bowled to a leg side field as part of an intimidatory strategy, and broke his skull, much to the Aussies' dismay. The hit caused an international incident between Australia and England, perhaps the most famous cricket kick-off in history.

More than half the cover is covered in a quote: 'Mr PF Warner writing in the *Daily Telegraph* July 25th 1933 on Body-Line Bowling says: "I am and always have been definitely opposed to this style of attack. It may be within the law, but to my mind it is not in the best interest of the game. It savours of intimidation and certainly looks venomous."'

In pencil, inside, is signed 'PF Warner, Sept 13 1933'.

I flicked through the book, holding it gently.

Warner had underlined the points he agreed with.

I said to my son, William: 'Look at this. See this guy on the front. Look inside. It's the same name, isn't it?'

'Oh yeah.'

'It used to belong to him. It's about Bodyline where they used to bowl at people's heads in Australia.'

'That's not very nice.'

'No, they got stopped from doing it. The Aussies didn't like it. This guy was the manager.'

I didn't have anyone to tell. If I had I'd have gone on about how the grand old man of English cricket, founder of *The Cricketer*, former England and Middlesex captain Plum Warner's support of England outweighed his qualms over the fairness of their play. Warner even has a stand named after him at Lord's. His books used to fill half a shelf at our house when I was a kid.

My wife returned.

'Look at this. You know those books.'

'Those books I bid on for you?'

'Yeah. You heard of Bodyline? Aussies made TV serials about it. Well, England's manager was Warner, this is him on the front.'

'Can you not hold it like that?'

'I should be wearing gloves. Anyway, look inside. And he's underlined all the bits he agrees with.'

'Does that mean it should be in Bowral?'

'Warner could have stopped Bodyline but he was such a fan of England he couldn't criticise his own team.'

Plum Warner found Bodyline distasteful and against the spirit of cricket. The previous summer Warner had criticised Bill Bowes for bowling Bodyline, or leg theory as it was then called, for Yorkshire against Surrey. 'That is not bowling,' he wrote. 'Indeed, it is not cricket.' As early as 1920, he had written that such tactics were 'unsportsmanlike and quite contrary to the spirit and traditions of the game'. And that he 'would rather suffer a hundred defeats than put it into practice'.

After the first 1932/33 Test at Sydney Warner wrote to Billy Findlay, the MCC secretary, that Larwood 'kept more or less a length'. Larwood had taken ten wickets. England won. The Nawab of Pataudi scored a century but was dropped for the next match for refusing to field in the leg trap for Bodyline. The *Sydney Referee* dug up Warner's comment on Bowes and wrote 'what was abhorrent to him in English county cricket, [was] the very essence of sportsmanship in Australia' while the *Melbourne Truth* spoke of his 'gutless evasions'. Larwood also hit Australian captain Bill Woodfull at Adelaide. Warner went to the Australian dressing room to see how Woodfull was. Woodfull replied: 'I don't want to speak to you, Mr Warner. There are two teams out there; one is playing cricket, the other is not. It is too great a game to spoil. The matter is in your hands.'

Warner said Woodfull had apologised, which Woodfull denied. Warner later received a knighthood for services to cricket and served as president of the MCC.

Could Warner not reconcile his dislike of leg theory with his support for his captain and team? Was he too partisan to say anything, showing blind allegiance, as Australian opener Jack Fingleton said?

In *Cricket Between Two Wars*, he wrote that 'leg theory is a form of bowling which has been in use in this country for fifty years', Bodyline was 'absolutely and entirely different ... this type of bowling ... breeds anger, hatred and malice, with consequent reprisals. The courtesy of combat goes out of the game.'

The bits Warner underlined in the Kippax book are:

'Both Larwood and Voce bowled at the man ... with the object of intimidation'.

'Relies on intimidation.'

'He has to hit the batsman from time to time.'

'Brain would take second place to brawn if bowled regularly.'

He has underlined the line 'there are few cricketers among politicians' and that there was 'no evidence for the prosecution from Bodyline v MCC'.

'Because a certain method may now be ruled unsportsmanlike opposed to sport of game or prejudicial to the interests of cricket ... it does not follow that the person who employed that method is other than an excellent sportsman.'

Kippax said Warner 'would not deal with the whole crux of the matter which is the evil of intimidation generally.'

Warner underlined that too.

Meanwhile, Hugh Chevallier, co-editor, *Wisden Cricketers' Almanack*, tells me *Wisden* 2017 is at the printers. But he can tell me my father does appear in the obituary section. There is also a brief mention of his otterhound, who he recalls was named Hotspur.

I rang up John McKenzie to offer him the Warner/ Kippax book. I mention the recent Henry Blofeld auction sale of some of the BBC cricket commentator's cricket book collection. I had attended the sale two days earlier at Chiswick Auctions. McKenzie had bought a few things. I suggest the Kippax/Warner book is from the Warner auction sale in 1980. McKenzie remembered my Dad as a collector and overseas annual dealer in the 1980s and wondered what had happened to his collection. He says autograph sheets are sought after, as they are easier to display than, for instance, signed bats. Bodyline interest peaked in the early 1980s with the 50th anniversary of the 1932/33 tour.

We talk about EK Brown, the leader in the trade when McKenzie was starting out on his illustrious career as a dealer. Prices have ebbed and flowed since then.

I tell him about my Dad's obit in the new *Wisden*, which I found out about on that day.

Back in Keswick a few weeks later, I saw Richardson rolling the square as I ran by, coming off Walla Crag. I jogged over. 'You seen the obit?'

'When's the first match?'

'Next week … '

Chapter 49

# Gardening

I HAD a feature published in *Wisden* 2018 on cricket and gardening. There are pieces on cricket and the environment and cricket and sexism by Tanya Aldred, who is involved in the *Wisden* quarterly publication, *The Nightwatchman,* where I've now also had a few pieces printed, on Boycott, Cumberland, Derek Pringle, my sort of things.

Andy Zaltzman has written a piece in *Wisden* proper on James Anderson's 500 Test wickets. In 2022, I met the comedian-statistician at a match when our sons opened together. I told him the big deal that day was not England chasing down 299 to beat New Zealand in the second Test, but whether Shan Masood or Ben Compton had reached 1,000 first-class runs yet. George Dobell, who I met at Cricinfo, and Alan Gardner, who I met during the Cairns trial, have written *Wisden* features, as have Simon Wilde and Mike Selvey, who I came across 20 years before when I was trying to be a cricket hack. EM Wellings is long gone and the number of topical articles is much greater, so great that even the role of the Harris Garden at Lord's and a Chelsea Flower Show cricket-themed design are now deemed worthy of analysis.

Harry Pearson writes about 50 years of overseas players, featuring the Gavaskar and Sarfraz my Dad and I watched 30 years before. I read Pearson's *The Farthest Corner*, about north-east sport, while in hospital gasping with Covid-19 during Christmas 2020.

Matt Thacker writes about Eric Ravilious's *Wisden* wood engraving. Even more unlikely than my dream coming true of having had a piece published in *Wisden*, I've had a picture on the wall of the Royal Academy Summer Exhibition. It's about the pandemic and Dad is near the centre of a slate painting of *The Last Supper*. I play Jesus. A Dutch princess bought it. Life got surreal.

Hugh Chevallier edited my *Wisden* gardening and cricket piece, very sympathetically. It was a year since he'd told me about the next, and final, chapter.

Chapter 50

# *Wisden* 2017 Obituary

APPLEBY, EDGAR, who died on May 8, 2015, aged 84, was a bookseller in Keswick, in the Lake District, and president of the local cricket club. The shop's profits were not significantly harmed by his habit of discounting books – especially on cricket, where he specialised in overseas annuals – if the potential buyer could answer questions about the contents. Appleby was a sought-after speaker on a diverse range of subjects, including cricket, the sinking of the *Bismarck* and the *Titanic*, and the assassination of Archduke Franz Ferdinand. He recited speeches without notes, having fine-tuned them on long walks with his otterhound, Hotspur.

## Conclusion

A fan is generally viewed as an obsessed individual, says Garry Crawford in the academic tome *Consuming Sport*. Most become fans through family and peer, giving you an identity. They absorb the media through a syringe as passive dopes. This moves on to interpreting and criticising the message, which is now easier because of social media and the communities it encourages. Then the fan is starting to have power. This used to be by collecting the data and memorabilia deemed as important and therefore owning it. Influencing the game by writing or talking about it comes next, with a pseudo-sport competitive element of being keener than the like-minded (consuming, owning, watching idols at sport cathedrals or caring more) than the rest. So they move from interested consumer to engaged fan to enthusiast, to devoted cultist to professional. Running through it all, there's the simple escapist, vicarious thrill and beauty of the game.

What did I learn? Obsessive fandom is rewarding and comforting but can be damaging to families because of the time and money it takes. The appeal of the action, escape and aesthetic is the same for everyone. The geek need to collect is mostly male – the collectibles (mantiques) are male-based. The man cave is an example of male escape. Women may have had fewer opportunities to flee the family. This is mainly a story of Dads and sons that many will recognise.

The memorabilia needs saving, a good home, as an investment (always a good excuse even if it's only to stop someone else making money out of it), a memory and to enjoy. Things have changed since the internet arrived. Physical mementoes are less valuable as the information is online and prices are more easily comparable. Ephemeral interactions with stars on social media and through selfies and even non-fungible tokens and gaming can replace the books, photos, autographs and letters that linger on the shelves of children of the fanatics.

How has the obsessive cricket fan changed since Appleby's day?

Back then you would: Play (badly) or score, watch the BBC, like local players or players you have any connection with, read scores and fixate on the averages in the paper/ Ceefax, prefer the county championship, collect books (e.g. *Wisdens* through catalogues, shops and physical auctions) and memorabilia starting with cigarette cards and ending with Toby jugs of Brian Johnston, go to matches and collect autographs, get a season ticket, join committees, societies and contribute to their newsletters, go to cricket dinners, meet players at dinners, speak at cricket dinners, contribute stats to cricket biographies.

Now: Play digitally, join the Barmy Army, tweet players, fixate on Cricinfo and Cricket Archive, watch Sky or online, listen to podcasts, buy from eBay, send WhatsApp messages discussing cricket, make your own podcast, get selfies, join online tribe communities. Indulge yourself in this distraction from the real world, or better still, if you want to and can, try and make it a way of life.

# Acknowledgements

MY THANKS to Jane Camillin at Pitch Publishing for her encouragement and support; Bruce Talbot, who read the text and made some helpful suggestions and Paul Nixon, who was a favourite cricketer of Appleby's, for contributing the foreword. Thanks also to everyone quoted and who has helped or given permissions or contributions, including Bethan Norris, Clive Norris, James Bielby, Hugh Chevallier, Kevin Norquay, Jo Harman, Duncan Olner, Keith Richardson and Emily Atherton.

# Bibliography

*Wisden*
*Wisden Cricket Monthly*
*Cumberland News*
*Lake District Herald*
*Cumberland & Westmorland Herald*
*Daily Telegraph*
*Scores and Biographies*
*Barclays World of Cricket*
*Playfair*
*The Nightwatchman*


EW Padwick *Bibliography of Cricket* (Library
    Association 1991)
Garry Crawford, *Consuming Sport* (Routledge, London)
David Rayvern Allen, *With the Bookplate of AE
    Winder* (JW McKenzie 2008)
WG Grace, *Cricket* (J.W. Arrowsmith 1891)
DT Smith, *EK Brown Cricket Bookseller*
    (Boundary Books 2011)
Simon Rae, *WG A Life* (Allen & Unwin 1998)
Peter Wynne Thomas *Cricket's Historians* (ACS 2011)
Matthew Appleby *Durham Cricket: 100 Greats*
    (Tempus 2003)

Matthew Appleby *New Zealand Test Cricket Captains* (Reed 2002)

Garth King, *Hansie Cronje Story* (Lion Hudson 2007)

Chris Waters, *10 for 10* (Bloomsbury 2014)

FS Ashley-Cooper, *Highways and Byways* (George Allen & Unwin 1927)

FS Ashley-Cooper *Edward Mills Grace Cricketer* (Chatto & Windus 1916)

Irving Rosenwater, *Bradman the Biography*

PGH Fender, *Defending the Ashes* (Chapman & Hall 1921)

Gerald Howat, *Cricketer Militant* (North Moreton Press 1980)

Alan Kippax *Anti Body-Line* (Hurst & Blackett 1933)

Pelham Warner *Cricket Between Two Wars* (Chatto & Windus 1942)

Harry Thompson *Richard Ingrams Lord of the Gnomes* (Heinemann 1994)

TB Trowsdale *Cricketer's Autograph Birthday Book* (Walter Scott 1907)

David Frith *Cricket's Collectors*

Bill Furmedge *What Wisden Means to Me* (Wisdenworld 2013)

Bill Furmedge *The Wisdener Manual* (Wisden Collectors' Club 2014)

John Hurst *Cumberland County Cricket Club: A History* (Cumberland CCC 1982)

.